Marxism in Modern France

Marxism in Modern France

by George Lichtheim

Columbia University Press
New York and London

Second printing and Columbia Paperback edition 1968
Printed in the United States of America

For S. S.

The Research Institute on Communist Affairs

Marxism in Modern France appears in a series of studies sponsored by the Research Institute on Communist Affairs of Columbia University.
The Institute promotes studies on international Communism and on various aspects of Marxist theory and practice. While the Institute does not assume responsibility for the views of the authors, it feels that these studies contribute to a better understanding of the role of Communism in the world today.

Preface

The "end of ideology," so often proclaimed as a fact by contemporary writers, has never in practice signified anything but the end of socialist ideology. In the language of political analysis, as conducted under the conditions of advanced industrial society in the Western world, the term "ideology" denotes any critique transcending the official boundaries of those mental disciplines that have themselves grown up in response to the urgent practical and intellectual requirements of the new postbourgeois industrial order. The labor movement, as the traditional carrier of doctrines regarded as subversive by those in control, falls under the twofold suspicion of instinctive hostility to the status quo and of addiction to political myths stemming from the nineteenth century. In this perspective, Socialism and Syndicalism appear not as rational reactions to the social order of industrial capitalism, but as ideological survivals, due to be replaced by a pragmatic faith in piecemeal progress. As for Marxism, its latter-day association with the Russian Revolution and the Communist movement is taken as proof of its inherent irrelevance to the analysis of Western society. From the voluminous literature devoted to this topic one would hardly infer the existence of a Marxist tradition centered on Western Europe and quite indifferent to the issues later brought into prominence by the East European turmoil after the First World War.

It is a matter for regret that in harking back to the roots of the socialist faith in contemporary France one should be obliged to take account simultaneously of subsidiary topics stirred up by the political tension between East and West. The necessity of doing so arises from a political phenomenon peculiar in Western Europe to only two countries, France and Italy: the existence of a Communist mass movement. As will be shown in the following pages, the rise of this movement on Western European soil after 1914 was a response to certain structural weaknesses (now largely overcome) in a part of Western Europe which had not been fully industrialized, and where democracy had come to birth in the nineteenth century under conditions of open class war between bourgeoisie and proletariat. West European Communism—the latter term denoting a theory and practice stemming from the Russian Revolution and the rise of Soviet totalitarianism—was always anachronistic in relation to the real movement of contemporary society, but in France (and for different reasons in Italy) it was able to exploit the failures and weaknesses of liberal democracy, and to become for a time the main outlet for working-class hostility to the established order. In so doing, the Communist party inevitably fell heir to the theoretical and practical problems which had already confronted its Socialist and Syndicalist precursors and rivals: notably the problem of fashioning a mass movement held together by faith in the advent of a "total" revolution which in the end failed to materialize.

The consequent dissensions and debates are analyzed in the following pages. The analysis proceeds from a theoretical starting point shared with those revisionist Socialists, in France and elsewhere, for whom the critique of modern industrial society is to be distinguished from the dissection of the defunct market society of liberal capitalism. The latter having ceased to exist, at any rate in Western Europe, classical liberalism and classical Marxism have both come to wear a somewhat old-fashioned look. A fortiori it is scarcely possible at the present day to take seriously the claims made for the practical relevance, in a country like France, of Marxism-Leninism. There are signs that this fact is beginning to be perceived even by Communists, who on these grounds may well come to revise the traditional view of the proletariat as the class destined to make an end of capitalism. But in an analytical study such as the present one, it would have been illegitimate to pursue this theme beyond the point of theoretical criticism. The student in search of source material bearing upon the current internal strains and stresses of the French labor movement in its various branches—Catholic, Socialist, and Communist—will have to look elsewhere.

Work on this study has been made possible by a grant from the Research Institute on Communist Affairs at Columbia University. I take this opportunity of expressing my cordial thanks to the Institute and notably to its Director, Professor Zbigniew Brzezinski, not only for the help received, but for contriving to make my stay pleasant as well as useful. It would be agreeable to mention by name all those with whom I have come in contact during the months of working on this book, but the list is too long. I must, however, record the mental stimulus and technical help received from colleagues not directly associated with the work of the Institute, especially from Mr. Daniel Bell. My thanks are also due to personal friends and acquaintances in New York, Paris, and Strasbourg—notably Mr. Meyer Schapiro, Mr. Norbert Guterman, M. Maximilien Rubel, Mr. Norman Birnbaum, and the late Mr. Jacques Katel—for enabling me to procure information and literary sources not easily available. To Mrs. Christine Dodson, of the Institute, my gratitude for facilitating my preliminary travels in Europe, and for mysteriously solving all the technical problems connected with the preparation of the manuscript, is too profound to find conventional expression.

GEORGE LICHTHEIM

Columbia University
in the City of New York
February, 1966

Contents

1

The Origins

Roots of Revolution

The term "French Marxism" can stand for two things: the adaptation of Marxist theory to French conditions, or the growth and development in France of a socialist (later also a Communist) movement which after a century still relates itself to Marx. In what follows, no attempt is made to discriminate between these meanings, or to emphasize one at the expense of the other. It is taken for granted that the "subjective" and the "objective" aspects are conjoined in the phenomenon of a revolutionary movement which for a number of decades has interpreted its aims in Marxian terms. If the present study is mainly concerned with the theoretical side, and moreover centered upon a particular period—the decades preceding and following the Second World War—this artificial demarcation is to be understood as a deliberate abstraction from the totality in question: a totality which is not just the sum of its parts (whatever such a description may signify) but an interconnected whole grounded in the concrete experience of millions of people.

Even at the theoretical level, properly so called, the subject matter involves more than an analysis of concepts formulated by thinkers reflecting upon material conditions which they themselves did not share. Account must be taken of the propagandists who refracted, projected, and interpreted the new doctrine; of the political leaders and organizers who transformed it into an instrument of mass action;

and finally of the working-class movement as such. As if all this were not enough, the historical context—namely France itself: a country with an already ancient history and settled modes of thought—has to be kept in mind. At the very least, the phenomenon must be related to the transformation of French society under the impact of an industrial revolution starting in the 1830s, a few decades after the political upheaval of 1789-99 had disencumbered bourgeois society of its ancient trammels. This of course is equivalent to saying that no adequate account can be drawn up; nor need it be. The aim of a critical study of this kind is not to reproduce the texture of reality, but to lay bare the dialectic of "being" and "consciousness" which keeps a movement going until its impetus has exhausted itself. And if in what follows the material substratum is systematically neglected, this procedure is to be understood as a deliberate departure from the true business of the social historian. Ideally, every controversy ought to be examined in terms of its material background. It is only the impossibility of carrying through such a closely textured analysis that renders excusable the abstract concentration upon what is said and thought by the theorists of the movement: themselves involved in shifting political alignments, and in any event closely dependent upon forms of thought historically shaped by the culture to which they belong.

But while this degree of abstraction is inevitable, it does not dispense one from the obligation to clarify one's theme: in this case, the past and present role of Marxism in France. Every political philosophy implies an end to be attained. In the case of Marxism, its authors are deliberately trying to regulate the current of history, superimposing upon it the intellectual order of a unifying principle. Consciousness is seldom passive, and never so in the case of thinkers for whom theory and practice form a whole. Whatever may be dogmatically affirmed at a later stage of the movement about the status of theory, such thinking does not simply "reflect" an external world. Indeed, no critic of existing institutions ever supposed that his freedom was limited to contemplation. By its very nature the exercise of critical thought implies a discrimination between what is merely given and what ought to exist. The critique presupposes a vision of what is possible, as against what is merely actual. And by a natural extension, that which merely exists is declared to be not only undesirable but unreal.

If this holds in general, it applies a fortiori to Marxism, which came to birth under the twofold sign of Hegelian philosophy and the historic impulse given to European thought by the French Revolution. Marx was enough of a rationalist to believe that the actual world is a caricature of the real one: the world in which man's essential nature will have been liberated from the oppressive constraints imposed upon him by his past. Insight into the process whereby this liberation comes about is afforded by philosophy, though the later Marx (and even more so Engels) preferred to call it "science." Even in its vulgarized form, such an approach still differs from positivism in that it affirms the need to transcend the data of experience through an imaginative grasp of the historical totality in which they are embedded. Empirical thought cannot rise to this totality, because its categories are already so formed as to reaffirm the given environment. Dialectical thinking discloses a reality more profound than the circumstances of immediate experience. The statement, e.g., that bourgeois society will make room for a higher form of social organization, involves an understanding of history as a whole. It also implies a judgment as to what constitutes progress, for not everything that happens is progressive: only that which enables men to enlarge their freedom counts as historical progress.

Consciousness and progress are thus interrelated. Socialism assumes (as does liberalism) that there is a human essence which comes to fulfillment in history. Where Marx diverges from liberalism is in taking a different view of the process whereby this goal is ultimately attained: for Marxism, the historic agent of the transformation is the proletariat. History is kept going by class struggles, and the proletarian class interest is viewed as the form in which, under modern conditions, Reason affirms itself as the organizing principle of society. What appears to the empirical sociologist as the assertion of a sectional group interest is regarded by Marx as the (partly conscious) mechanism of a process whereby "prehistory" is overcome, and mankind is "brought to itself." The proletariat is the revolutionary class because it subverts the existing social order. It is compelled to do so by an urge which is both revolutionary and rational, in that it supplies a conscious direction to the whole of society. The ultimate objective of Reason requires a rational organization of the world, and this organization (socialism) is of such a kind as to provide an institutional arrangement which rules out inequality and class conflict. Meanwhile, however, the proletariat, by its existence, constitutes an indictment of the status quo. The prevailing irrationality—due in the last resort to the absence of conscious control—makes itself felt in economic crises which fall with special violence upon the class whose unpaid labor upholds the entire edifice. Thus the class interest of labor coincides with the general interest of mankind, while the growth of consciousness is represented by the socialist movement. The latter is not simply an "interest," but the embodiment of rationality as such. Hence the socialist revolution is, among other things, the triumph of reason over brute existence and the "leap from necessity to freedom."

When the Marxian "project" is described in these terms, it plainly appears as the intellectual counterpart of political stirrings which, since the days of the French Revolution, had promoted the gradual democratization of Western society. Marxism indeed was able to function as the theory of the labor movement because both were rooted in what Marx himself called the "bourgeois revolution." In the *Communist Manifesto* this link is made explicit: the proletariat is here described as the spearhead of a still incomplete social transformation, though at the same time it is viewed as the predestined gravedigger of the fully developed capitalist society. The fact that Engels, after the death of Marx, gave a determinist interpretation to this line of thought is of importance because of the problems it caused for later Marxists. But in relation to our theme what matters is that the mature Marx had himself become the theorist of a democratic labor movement. Such a movement presupposed the completion of the bourgeois revolution. Where the latter was still on the agenda—as in Eastern Europe—classical Marxism was not applicable. In these areas, socialists had to go back to the Marx of 1848, who was in effect the theorist of a bourgeois revolution.

The changing status of theory in the age of the First and Second Internationals was a function of this gradual shift from bourgeois-revolutionary to authentically socialist attitudes. In its youthful origins Marxism exemplified the union of critical thought with a praxis that subverted the existing order. Consciousness illuminated the status quo and thus rendered it unbearable to its victims.[1] The relation of critical theory to the inchoate mass movement was conceived on the analogy of the mind's relation to the body. The steering function was not, however, regarded as something external: theory does not impose utopian aims upon the movement, but clarifies its inherent purpose. It does not tell the workers what they are to do, but what they themselves want to do.

In the *Manifesto* of 1848 these assumptions are spelled out in relation to the Communist vanguard. The Communists "do not form a separate party opposed to other working-class parties." Their task is to represent "the common interest of the entire proletariat, independently of all nationality . . . they always and everywhere represent the interests of the movement as a whole." They are "the most advanced and resolute section" in all countries. "On the other hand, theoretically, they have over the great mass of the proletariat the advantage of clearly understanding the line of march, the conditions, and the ultimate general results of the proletarian movement." Thus the directing function is incarnate in a general staff whose relation to the revolutionary army is viewed in elitist terms.

In the development of the socialist movement between 1864 and 1914, and more particularly after 1889, this concept disappears to make room for the orthodox democratic attitude which denies to theory any function other than that of serving the practical needs of the movement. The latter determines both its short-range and its long-range aims through the instrumentality of elected representatives. There is no longer a self-appointed vanguard with directing functions: merely a loose assemblage of theorists (economists, sociologists, political scientists, etc.) who "specialize in generalization," without for that reason possessing the status of a "general staff." It needs no great

[1] Karl Marx, *Introduction to a Critique of Hegel's Philosophy of Right* (1844): "As philosophy finds its *material* weapons in the proletariat, so the proletariat discovers its *intellectual* weapons in philosophy." See also Karl Marx, *The Holy Family* (1845): "It is not a matter of knowing what this or that proletarian, or even the proletariat as a whole, *conceives* as its aim at any particular moment. It is a question of knowing *what* the proletariat *is,* and what it must historically accomplish in accordance with its *nature.*" See also Karl Marx, *Selected Writings in Sociology and Social Philosophy,* ed. by T. B. Bottomore and M. Rubel (London, 1956), pp. 232-33.

acuteness to perceive that this change has political implications. A movement steered by a self-conscious vanguard can transcend the goals of its putative mass following. It is thus ideally suited for revolutionary coups d'état. On the other hand, the tension between immediate interests and long-range aims here assumes a form that leads straight to authoritarian disregard of the real material interests of the class, which is precisely why, in the subsequent development of the European socialist movement, the authoritarian standpoint was quietly abandoned by Marx himself and by his followers.

From Blanqui to Marx

The problem was not thereby solved, but in the more advanced countries at any rate it was now possible for Marxism to shed its Jacobinical origins, and to transform itself from a doctrine conceived on the model of the bourgeois revolution into an instrument of labor's emancipation. In relation to France this change assumed an aspect of its own, by virtue of Marx's close personal contact with the French socialist movement. This is not the place to pursue the theme of his involvement with that movement. Suffice it to say that when the war of 1914 rang down the curtain upon an era in European history, the connection between Marxism and French socialism was already over half a century old: not only in the biographical sense, but in that the political model sketched out in the *Communist Manifesto* had been suggested to Marx by the impressions he derived from his stay in Paris in the years 1843-45, and from his assimilation of French revolutionary socialism on the eve of 1848. And although (as was remarked above), this particular model was destined to be replaced—from the formation of the First International in 1864 onward—by a different one, the original imprint remained sufficiently powerful to enable the bulk of the French workers movement to make the transition from Blanquism or Proudhonism to Marxism without any sense of having abandoned its ancient heritage. This is not contradicted by the fact that the conscious assimilation of Marxian concepts began only in the 1880s, for even at that late date the first self-styled French Marxists were either former Blanquists or quasi-anarchists, and in either case remote from the maturer and more democratic formulations which Marx's own thinking had in the meantime assumed under the impact of British conditions.[2]

The roots of this situation are traceable to the years 1848-52, when the fledgling Communist League, then dominated by Marx and Engels, was in close contact with the French revolutionary sects of the period, and Marx himself was inclined to regard Blanqui as the leader of the revolutionary movement in France. At one stage in 1850 indeed Marx was closely allied with the Blanquists and even agreed to set up an international organization with them.[3] Even then his notion of "proletarian dictatorship" differed markedly from that of Blanqui, who did not (as is often said) invent the term, though presumably he raised no objection to its inclusion in the joint document signed by Marx and the London Blanquists in April 1850. This refers to a "dictature des prolétaires" as a means of maintaining the revolution "en permanence"—thus giving currency to two later Communist key slogans at once. The Blanquists, who co-authored this document, may have felt that the stress on the industrial proletariat was an innovation, for Blanqui had talked often enough about dictatorship, but seldom about proletarian dictatorship. In any event he was quite clear that the actual power would be in the hands of a self-appointed elite drawn from the educated classes. This elite would represent "the proletariat," by which he meant quite simply everyone who performed physical labor. Apart from this, the only "dictatorship" he envisaged was that of Paris over the rest of France: a notion of

[2] Neil McInnes, "Les débuts du marxisme théorique en France et en Italie (1880-1897)," *Cahiers de l'Institut de Science Économique Appliquée,* No. 102 (Paris, June, 1960). See also Georges Lefranc, *Le mouvement socialiste sous la Troisième République* (Paris, 1963), pp. 32 ff.; Daniel Ligou, *Histoire du socialisme en France 1871-1961* (Paris, 1962), pp. 24 ff.; *Friedrich Engels-Paul et Laura Lafargue: Correspondance,* ed. by Émile Bottigelli (Paris, 1956-59). For the Anarchist tradition see Jean Maitron, *Histoire du mouvement anarchiste en France 1880-1914* (Paris, 1955).

[3] H. Draper, "Marx and the Dictatorship of the Proletariat," *Cahiers de l'Institut de Science Économique Appliquée,* No. 129 (Paris, September, 1962). The formulation occurs for the first time in his 1850 article series later published under the title *The Class Struggles in France.* But already in the *Manifesto* the elevation of the proletariat "to the position of the ruling class" is equated with winning "the battle for democracy," while "despotic inroads on the rights of property" are envisaged in the same passage. The whole concept is clearly Jacobinical, or rather Babouvist: democracy acts dictatorially, the assumption being that this is a *dictatorship of the majority,* its enemies naturally being the minority of privileged and propertied citizens, the bourgeoisie.

which Marx was already skeptical in 1850, and which after 1871 he rejected *in toto*. If one asks what was the significance of this particular episode for Marx, the answer is simple: it served him as a criterion for the elaboration of his own concept as against that of Blanqui. After 1871, when most of his French followers were Blanquist survivors of the Commune, this became evident, for those among them who did most to convert that generation of French socialists to Marxism abandoned the peculiar Blanquist elitism which went together with indifference to the actual labor movement and rejection of universal suffrage as a swindle designed to subordinate "the revolutionary minority" to "the distorted opinions of majorities subjected to all the influences of ignorance and privilege."[4]

The implantation of Marxism in France following the disaster of the Commune is the necessary and inevitable starting-point for any discussion of the subject. It is worth stressing, at the outset of the present study, that the Blanquist tradition was only overcome at the cost of incorporating some of its features into the doctrine of the French labor movement that was reborn after the Commune. No doubt Blanquism and Marxism reacted differently to the great débacle of 1871 which ended the brief but stormy history of French revolutionary socialism between 1830 and 1870. Indeed it has been said with truth that "the gulf between the Blanquist and the Marxist idea of revolutionary dictatorship was concretized around the Commune."[5] Marxism—heavily impregnated with quasi-Jacobinical no-

[4] Draper, "Marx and the Dictatorship of the Proletariat." See also A. B. Spitzer, *The Revolutionary Theories of Louis Auguste Blanqui* (New York, 1957). When asked by a court to define his occupation, Blanqui described himself as *"prolétaire,"* and explained that he meant "one of thirty million Frenchmen who live by their labor." In short, he thought in terms of "the toilers" versus "the exploiters." Despite their personal liking for him, Marx and Engels were quite clear about his theoretical insufficiency. In 1874 Engels commented in fairly scathing terms upon Blanqui's concept of minority dictatorship: "A dictatorship not of the entire revolutionary class, the proletariat, but of a small minority which has made the coup d'état and is itself organised in advance under the dictatorship of one man or a few individuals. As one can see, Blanqui is a revolutionary of the past generation." See Marx-Engels, *Werke* (Berlin, 1962), XVIII, 529.

[5] Draper, "Marx and the Dictatorship," p. 50. See also G. D. H. Cole, *A History of Socialist Thought* (London, 1957), II, 166: "The essence, then, of the Commune, as Marx saw it, lay in its unification and centralisation of the power of the majority, freed from class control, to govern through directly elected delegates to whom they could issue binding instructions. . . . Given such a basic political structure, the workers, organised as a class, would be in a

tions since before 1848, and given an additional Blanquist emphasis by Marx in 1850, when he briefly spelled out the "dictatorship" concept—had been reformulated in 1871 so as to absorb the gist of the Proudhonist-Bakuninist critique of the state.[6] But the resulting synthesis for a number of years served as a bridge from the old Blanquist to the new Marxist position. What passed for Marxism in the 1880s, when Jules Guesde, Paul Lafargue, Charles Longuet, and Gabriel Deville began to popularize the new doctrine, was at best an approximation and at worst a caricature. The theoretical level of these writers was considerably below that of the contemporary exponents of Social Democratic Marxism in Germany, and their Blanquist or Bakuninist inheritance was no help in the struggle to found a democratic mass movement (though from the later Communist viewpoint it was valuable in keeping alive a tradition upon which Leninism could be grafted with ease after 1917).

As regards the implantation of socialist theory, the 1880s indeed were a dead loss. What passed for Marxism before the 1890s—when the writings of Engels, Kautsky, Bernstein, and the Italian Marxist, Antonio Labriola, at last became known in France—was a mere parody, and this although Jules Guesde had been personally "converted" by Marx as early as 1880. The effective popularization of theoretical Marxism in France had to await the coming of Georges Sorel, whose knowledge of Italian enabled him to grasp the significance of what Croce and Labriola were doing in Italy between 1893 and 1898. (That Sorel, like Croce, subsequently helped to launch the revisionist movement is irrelevant in this context.)[7] If this background is kept in mind, the comparative ease with which Leninism was subsequently assimilated by revolutionaries drawn from a movement

---

position to impose their collective will. . . . The Blanquists saw the Paris Commune as a working model of the revolutionary *élite* in action, and blamed the Internationalists for having spoilt it by insisting on democratic notions quite inappropriate during a period of revolutionary dictatorship."

[6] Michel Collinet, *La tragédie du marxisme* (Paris, 1948), especially pp. 128 ff. See also *De Marx au marxisme (1848-1948),* ed. by Robert Aron (Paris, 1948).

[7] McInnes, "Les débuts du marxisme théorique en France et en Italie." For the orthodox view see A. Zévaès, *De l'introduction du marxisme en France* (Paris, 1947). The pre-1914 movement acquired a genuine understanding of Marxism only after it had shaken off the Blanquist heritage and adopted an outlook which went with indifference to "politics"—i.e., direction of the real workers movement by (reformist or revolutionary) intellectuals.

already radicalized by the upheaval of 1914-18, should occasion no surprise. France, unlike Central Europe, had experienced neither defeat nor civil war, and even the antiwar opposition within the Socialist Party had at no time seriously thought of adopting "revolutionary defeatism."[8] But patriotism was one thing, reformism another. The Blanquist tradition might permit those two veteran survivors of the Commune, Jules Guesde and Édouard Vaillant, to adopt a patriotic attitude in 1914: had not Blanqui in 1870-71 done the same? But that same tradition was the counterpart of those antidemocratic elements in Lenin's political and personal make-up which in 1917-18 enabled the Bolshevik leader to make short work of the nascent Russian democracy. To say this, after all, is to say no more than that Marxism—as it was understood by Russian socialists, though not by Germans—incorporated the heritage of the French Revolution at its most dictatorial. These traditions might indeed conflict. By 1920, when the Socialist party split at Tours, Vaillant and Guesde had become symbols of "social patriotism," as much as the revisionist and reformist Jaurès, whose assassination at the outbreak of war in 1914 had removed him from the arena of this particular combat. Socialists could, with a clear conscience, adopt either course. The republican tradition was still alive, and to be a Jacobin was to be a patriot.

These circumstances are recalled here only because in what follows they will perforce have to be taken for granted. Every other procedure would exceed the limits of what is, after all, only intended as a critical study of French Marxism since the close of the First World War. It was necessary to begin in this fashion because it is too often forgotten that Marxism has been the major link between the French and the Russian Revolutions. This does not exhaust its significance, even on the political side, but since we are dealing with France it is worth bearing in mind that the terminology of what after 1920 came to be known as Communism did not have to be imported from abroad, any more than did the Marxist socialism of the 1880s. In both cases an authentically French movement adopted a doctrine which had indeed grown on foreign soil, yet under the impulsion of ideas orig-

[8] For this and the following see Annie Kriegel, *Aux origines du communisme français 1914-1920* (Paris, 1964), I, 12 ff., 31 ff., 52 ff. See also Kriegel, *Les Internationales ouvrières* (Paris, 1964), and *Le Congrès de Tours. Naissance du parti communiste français* (Paris, 1964).

inally developed in France. The difference lay in the fact that, whereas the Marxism of the 1880s and 1890s represented a break with the elitist and utopian tradition which had suffered shipwreck in the Commune, the Leninism of the 1920s was a reversion to precisely this predemocratic tradition. The split of 1920, which set Socialists off from Communists (both claiming to be followers of Marx), did more than wreck the political structure laboriously erected before 1914: it disclosed the ambiguities inherent in Marxism and, ultimately, in the thinking of Marx himself. A study of the subject must begin by confronting the fact that rival interpretations of the doctrine have coexisted from the start. More than that: the Blanquist source of Leninism, which is the secret of the French Communist party's "national" appeal, has also been responsible for the sectarian character of both the movement and the doctrine that now goes under the name of Communism.

In conclusion it may be worth stressing a circumstance sometimes overlooked by historians of the Second International (1889-1914) who tend to treat the European Socialist movement of the time as a fabric held together by an overriding commitment to Marxian doctrines more or less clearly understood. While it is a fact of importance that Marxism did during this quarter century provide the intellectual integration, at any rate on the Continent (for the British development was somewhat different, the Labour party not yet committed even to Fabian socialism, and Marxist Social Democracy a mere sect), one must not lose sight of the profound divergence between the French and the German situation. Marx and Engels had originally come out of the German democratic movement which climaxed (and failed) in 1848. It was natural for them, and for their followers, to identify the new "scientific" socialism with Germany, and Engels at any rate went pretty far in stressing this identification. German Social Democracy from about 1890 onward took pride in being "Marxist." At the same time the peculiar development of Germany had the effect of turning the Social Democratic movement into a political expression of residual bourgeois-democratic sentiments, as well as into an organization of the industrial workers. Both trends went together quite effectively, though there was also a latent tension which came to the surface in 1918. Imperial Germany being the kind of country it was, political tendencies which in France found their outlet in ordinary republicanism had to be channeled into the Social Democratic party. The latter, in consequence, evolved something like a double personality: while its official terminology was socialist and even Marxist, the driving force behind it came largely from unsatisfied democratic yearnings which only needed a bourgeois framework, as the post–1945 development was to show.

Quite different was the situation in France. Here the Republic had been established in 1871 on the ruins of the Commune, and socialism was identified with an attempt, however shortlived and utopian, to set up a proletarian dictatorship; added to which were the memories of the *semaine sanglante* and its twenty thousand victims. It took a generation before socialists and bourgeois republicans (though the latter had for the most part stood aloof from the massacre, and had eventually passed an amnesty for the surviving Communards when circumstances permitted) were able to find common ground. The entire political spectrum was much further leftward than in Germany, and in consequence French Marxism was from the start the doctrine of a revolutionary workers movement: a movement nonexistent beyond the Rhine. Unless this is grasped, much of the subsequent story becomes incomprehensible. Class lines were sharper in France, and so were mutual hatreds. In this respect 1914-18 marked a watershed, for it inaugurated the reintegration of the working class within the national community: patriotism forming a bridge which enabled Socialists to join the *Union Sacrée*. The subsequent antiwar movement, which provided the main impulse behind the formation of the Communist party in 1920, was a revolt against the endless bloodletting rather than a principled rejection of patriotism. It sprang from weariness, not from acceptance of anarcho-syndicalist tenets which before 1914 naively counterposed a supposedly homogeneous proletarian class interest to the patriotism of the bourgeoisie and "its" state. Insofar as such notions remained in being after 1914-18, they had to be reformulated along Marxist lines under the inspiration of the Russian Revolution. And in the end the Communist party managed to get on without them.[9]

[9] Paul Louis, *Histoire du socialisme en France* (Paris, 1950). Maitron's great history of Anarchism significantly ends in 1914, and the author closes on a note of resignation: the nineteenth century—i.e., the era between the Revolution of

From Proudhon to Sorel

In a letter to Péguy of November 17, 1901, Jaurès—then engaged in the revisionist controversy whose echoes had reached France from Germany—distinguished two different and contradictory aspects of the *Communist Manifesto:* an evolutionary theory of capitalism and its transformation, and a political strategy designed to transform the "bourgeois revolution" imminent in 1848 into a "proletarian" one. He might have added that the *Manifesto* likewise embodied two different, and indeed contradictory, visions of the working class: as a downtrodden proletariat (successor to the slaves of antiquity and the serfs of feudalism), and as a rising class destined one day to take the place of the industrial bourgeoisie. This unresolved contradiction—already inherent in the earliest formulation of Marx's doctrine—prefigured the dissension between "reformists" and "catastrophists" which from 1918 onward was to range Social Democrats and Communists on different sides. But even prior to the great divide of the Russian Revolution, the doctrine of 1848 had been transformed into a body of thought at once more gradualist and more in tune with the actual requirements of the workers movement. If there is a consistent line of thought running from the Babouvists and Blanqui, via the Marx of 1847-50, to Lenin, there is also a parallel movement linking the author of *Capital* with contemporary socialist thinking properly so called.[10]

So far as France is concerned, the historical roots of all subsequent splits and divergences go back once more to the Commune, whose moderate wing can in retrospect be seen to have constituted the original nucleus of the later Socialist movement. For paradoxically it was not the Blanquist majority, but the Proudhonist minority of the Commune whose political outlook anticipated what from the 1890s onward came to be known as Marxism. This minority had joined the

1789 and the war of 1914—in his view had on the whole been a libertarian age, whereas the twentieth century seemed doomed to authoritarianism. "L'époque est aux plans, à l'organisation, à la discipline," Maitron, p. 450. This of course was more or less what Marx had affirmed against Bakunin after 1871, but the "libertarians" were not listening.

[10] Collinet, *La tragédie du marxisme,* p. 93.

insurrection without sharing the Blanquist illusions, and had taken part in the defense of Paris while opposing the terrorist tactics of the dominant wing. Its outlook was substantially similar to that of Marx—a circumstance veiled by his impassioned defense of the Commune, albeit the catastrophe of May 1871 had confirmed his earlier warnings against an armed rising. In later years these dissensions were tacitly overlooked, and it became common for adherents of both groups to invoke the authority of Marx, who was thought to have synthesized the basic elements of Proudhonist and Blanquist teaching—as, indeed, in a sense he had. The fact remains that the synthesis was attained only at the price of a certain veiled ambiguity; a circumstance which down to the present day has made it possible for both Socialists and Communists in France to describe themselves as followers of Marx.[11]

The complex process which between 1870 and 1905 led to the formation of a more or less unified Socialist movement cannot be described here.[12] A point that needs stressing, because it is so often overlooked, is that the movement arose from a fusion of rival factions which could find common ground only after the historic disputes between Proudhonists and Blanquists—and subsequently between Marx and Bakunin—had begun to fade. The outlook of the growing labor movement around 1900 (including both its Socialist and its Syndicalist wing) was necessarily eclectic, embodying as it did elements of all these traditions. There had been from the beginning a strong libertarian tradition lacking in the contemporary German movement. Proudhon was never forgotten, and the desire to incorporate some

[11] Collinet, *La tragédie du marxisme*. See also Lefranc, *Le mouvement socialiste,* p. 16, and Conrady's preface to the German Social Democratic edition of Marx's pamphlet on the Commune, *Der Bürgerkrieg in Frankreich* (Berlin, 1920). It is notorious that by 1881 Marx had virtually gone back on his earlier judgment and condemned the 1871 rising as a utopian venture which, with a little commonsense, might have been avoided. This was also the attitude of the moderate minority in 1871 which, in addition to the Proudhonists, included the "Internationalist" Eugène Varlin and the solitary "Marxist" Leo Frankel.

[12] For details see Ligou, pp. 24 ff.; Lefranc, *Le mouvement socialiste,* 32 ff.; Edouard Dolléans, *Histoire du mouvement ouvrier 1871-1936* (Paris, 1946), pp. 18 ff. For the relationship of Marx to Proudhon, and of both to their common ancestor, Saint-Simon, see Georges Gurvitch, *Les Fondateurs français de la sociologie contemporaine.* I. (*Saint-Simon sociologue*) (Paris, 1955 and 1963), and the same author's *Cours public 1963-64* on the anniversary of Proudhon's death, with the subtitle *Proudhon et Marx: Une confrontation* (Paris, 1964).

part of his heritage has been *the* distinguishing trait of French Socialism (as distinct from Communism) down to the present day. From Paul Brousse and the leaders of the moderate minority wing of the Commune, to Jaurès; and—in neighboring Belgium—from Caesar de Paepe to Vandervelde, the effort was obstinately pursued. Men like Brousse and Malon, who tried to find a middle ground between Marxist centralism and Proudhonist pluralism, were no less important than Guesde and Lafargue on the other wing. They have not received their due. To present-day Communists they are suspect as "reformists." To academic historians they are a puzzle, notably outside France, where the filiation of ideas from Saint-Simon via Proudhon to Marx is seldom understood. In consequence, the formative period between 1880 and 1905, when the French labor movement—by way of innumerable splits, dissensions, and doctrinal quarrels—worked out its characteristic attitude to the major issues of state and society, tends to be treated as a mere propaedeutic to the political upheavals that followed. Yet for anyone concerned with the manner in which basic attitudes (as distinct from mere ideological notions) determine the character of political movements, these years are crucial, for it was then that French socialism received the stamp it has never lost.[13]

On the theoretical side, what obviously mattered most after 1870 was the gradual fusion of Marx's analysis of capitalism with the indigenous doctrines of the movement. This took time, if only because Marx's French followers were weak in economics. Beyond this there loomed the wider problem of making the transition from the traditional idealist moralism of the French to the new scientific materialism of the Germans. The first few authentic Marxists in the France of the 1890s had to steer their vessel between the sentimental idealism of Benoît Malon's *Revue Socialiste* and the caricature of Marxism offered to the public by Guesdists like Lafargue. If they were not shipwrecked, this was largely due to the intervention of Georges Sorel, who between 1894 and 1898 made his major contribution to the

[13] McInnes, "Les débuts du marxisme théorique en France et en Italie," pp. 30 f.; Dolléans, pp. 89 ff., 117 ff. See, "Karl Marx et les socialistes français," in Robert Aron, p. 55, for the relationship of Marx to Proudhon, and of Sorel to both.

diffusion of the new doctrine. The theoretical journals he and they founded—mainly the *Ère Nouvelle* and its successor, the *Devenir Social*—did not reach the standard of Kautsky's *Neue Zeit* and were heavily dependent on foreign contributors; but the decisive step had been taken. By the time Sorel, toward the end of the 1890s, had broken with orthodox Marxism, it had become possible to be a revisionist, just because there now existed an orthodox school, however weak compared with the German. The same was true in Italy, where Benedetto Croce's secession in 1898-99 preceded, and to some degree provoked, that of Sorel. The subsequent emergence of a distinctively Sorelian viewpoint (in part formulated under the influence of Bergson's philosophy) showed what could be done by a gifted though unsystematic thinker who had grafted Marx upon the Proudhonist stem. Ultimately Sorel made himself available both to the followers of Lenin and to those of Mussolini, but until 1914 his synthesis of socialism and syndicalism was guided by a desire to see the workers movement free itself from the patronage of the politicians, whether parliamentarians or Jacobins. A Proudhonist at heart, Sorel belongs to the libertarian tradition, and for all his many faults he managed to evolve an interpretation of Marx that was freedom-loving and—in the best sense—utopian. Syndicalists who followed him had at least been inoculated against the totalitarian heresy, and those among them who after 1919 joined the Communist International did so with reservations which turned out to be crucial when the true character of Leninism began to assert itself. The tradition they had inherited from Sorel was both revolutionary and libertarian.[14]

[14] In *La décomposition du marxisme* (Paris, 1907), *passim,* G. Sorel makes it clear that it was disgust with the reformist adaptation of Marxism to parliamentary politics which had driven him back upon the revolutionary syndicalism of Fernand Pelloutier, and in a measure upon the ancient doctrines of Proudhon and Bakunin. For the rest, his animosity was reserved for the Jacobins and their Blanquist successors. He makes the important point that Marx substituted the concept of *class* for the Blanquist one of *party*. This hostility to Blanquism naturally made it impossible for Leninists after 1917 to make use of Sorel, notwithstanding his openly proclaimed sympathies for the October Revolution: witness his *plaidoyer* "Pour Lénine," penned in September 1919 as an annex to his *Réflexions sur la violence* (Paris, 1908). See also the Sorelian text reproduced in the *Cahiers de l'Institut de Science Économique Appliquée,* No. 121 (Jan., 1962).

Guesde and Jaurès

The reverse side of the medal was the enduring strength of traditional republican patriotism in its Blanquist and Guesdist forms. Here the irony of the post-1920 situation becomes evident, for the newly founded Communist party inherited the Blanquist heritage en bloc (minus the vision of France as the chosen revolutionary nation). Yet in 1914 it was precisely this heritage which fed the fires of anti-German feeling. A veteran of the Commune like Vaillant represented the ancient revolutionary patriotism of 1870, as did so many *militants* whose political philosophy had remained Jacobinical. For these former Blanquists—all of them by 1914 self-styled Marxists, and some of them destined to become Communists in 1920—France was still in some sense the living incarnation of the Revolution. Hence the almost total absence of resistance to the official patriotic line—quite unlike the situation in Germany, where antiwar sentiment was active from the start on the left wing of the Social Democrats. In France it took many months before a minority could be got together on a pacifist platform, and their opponents never lacked the good conscience that went with memories of the Commune. War to the bitter end had been a revolutionary slogan in 1870-71, and a surviving Communard like Vaillant, or a veteran Marxist like Guesde, could say with perfect sincerity that in working for national defense in 1914 (Guesde even joined the government) they were simply following tradition.[15]

It becomes necessary then to ask what exactly Marxism signified in the four decades between the aftermath of the Commune and the upheaval of 1914. For practical purposes it meant Jules Guesde and his disciples. But the Guesdists (who took their line straight from Marx) could not have imposed themselves upon the reviving workers

[15] Ligou, pp. 238 ff. The handful of antiwar syndicalists—men like Merrheim, Monatte, and Rosmer—were quite aware that the entire working class had been carried away in August 1914 by a wave of nationalism. Indeed, Merrheim plainly said that the workers would have lynched their leaders had they tried in any way to interfere with the war effort. As for those Marxists who had come out of the Blanquist tradition, they never hesitated for a moment to support the national cause. See M. Dommanget, *Édouard Vaillant* (Paris, 1956), pp. 236 and 248; A. Rosmer, *Le mouvement ouvrier pendant la guerre* (Paris, 1936-59), I, 13, 159, 221.

movement of the 1880s had they not been able to form a tactical alliance with the Blanquist survivors of the Commune.[16] The latter indeed took their time—something like two decades—before they accepted the new Marxist principles: internationalism and the class struggle. Blanqui had been opposed to both, and the more nationalist Blanquists quite consistently ended up as Boulangists in 1889, while Vaillant and his friends moved in the opposite direction. The Jacobin chauvinism of the Commune was solemnly renounced and, at least in principle, replaced by the new internationalist faith which proclaimed the solidarity of the workers across national frontiers. But the crisis of 1914 was to show that the conversion had not gone very deep. For the rest, the class struggle in its Marxist interpretation —with the stress on the industrial proletariat, rather than on "the toilers" in general—was accepted by all concerned, thus terminating both the Blanquist tradition of revolutionary populism and the Proudhonist dream of a nonpolitical labor movement concerned only with the workers' immediate sectional aims. Guesde and his associates took considerable, and not wholly unjustified, pride in thus having left sectarian quarrels behind and placed the movement on a "scientific" basis. This did not prevent Guesde from relapsing on occasion into the old catastrophist manner, as when in 1885 he envisioned the dawn for a very near future: indeed for the coming general election, which would sweep the bourgeois Radicals away and open the floodgates of revolution—a revolution which would certainly not be parliamentary, though its leaders would presumably be chosen from the deputies of the new Mountain.[17]

These were passing follies. More serious was Guesde's failure to prevent the rise of a Syndicalist labor movement which repudiated his

[16] Dommanget, pp. 60, 202; also Ligou, pp. 86 ff. The transition was achieved by way of the Blanquist manifesto of 1874, *Aux communeux,* wherein the memory of the Commune becomes a bridge to the new understanding of "communism" in the sense of "collectivism."

[17] "Ce sont les dernières réserves de la bourgeoisie qui entrent en ligne. Battues, elles ne laissent place, dans quatre ans au plus tard, qu'au passé monarchiste ou à la révolution prolétarienne. C'est la dernière carte de leur classe qu'ils sont appelés à jouer." Cited by Lefranc, *Le mouvement socialiste,* p. 136. This was quite in accordance with the 1874 manifesto issued by Vaillant and his fellow Blanquists, wherein the left-wing Republicans were described as the "derniers défenseurs du monde bourgeois mourant. . . . La fin des radicaux sera la fin de la bourgeoisie. . . ." Ligou, p. 90.

formulas.[18] The myth of the General Strike made a deeper appeal to the workers than did the Guesdist version of Marxism, which rested upon the monotonous exposition of a single theme: the coming "expropriation of the expropriators," i.e., the more or less forcible dispossession of the capitalist class. In the Guesdist scheme—which in essentials has remained that of the French Communist party to this day—the antagonism of capital and labor is seen as leading inevitably to a dramatic confrontation which transfers the means of production to the collectivity. This revolution dislodges the bourgeoisie from the citadel of political power, henceforth occupied by the working class: a class whose constant numerical growth transforms it into a majority of the population, thus enabling the political changeover to take place in democratic forms (save for the limiting case of armed resistance on the part of the former owning class). But for the stress on the probability of violence, this was more or less what Marxist socialism between 1880 and 1914 signified in general, and Guesde had every reason to regard his interpretation as orthodox (in the sense understood by Engels and Kautsky). The self-appointed revolutionary elite dear to the Blanquists had indeed dropped out of the picture; but then it had been, tacitly or explicitly, abandoned by most European Marxists. It took the Russian Revolution and Leninism to place it at the center of the whole conception.

If this drastically foreshortened and simplified version of Marxism made rapid headway in France between 1880 and 1914, the prime cause must be sought in the country's social transformation. It was during these decades that Frenchmen for the first time became acquainted with the full meaning of the industrial revolution. In 1870 large-scale industry had still been the exception even in Paris, whence the persistence of Proudhonist illusions about cooperation and "mutualism." From the 1880s onward these dreams faded. The new Marxist faith corresponded to actual circumstances in which a numerous, but badly organized, industrial proletariat confronted a bourgeoisie in possession of almost unlimited political and social power. Slogans such as "class against class" were a perfectly suitable response to this situation; so was Guesde's ambiguity about democracy. Universal suffrage was indeed affirmed as the democratic method

[18] Lefranc, *Le mouvement socialiste,* p. 138; Dolléans, pp. 35 ff.

of conquering political power, but the threat of violence was held in reserve. As for cooperatives and other forms of self-help, these were dismissed as a distraction from the real aim, now defined as the socialization of the means of production. All this was fairly orthodox; it also fitted the situation, for Marx's socio-economic analysis had actually run ahead of the French (though not of the British) development, so that after 1880 France might be said to be simply catching up with the Marxian prospectus.[19]

Against this background it is not surprising that the rather eclectic doctrine of Jaurès presented itself from the 1890s onward not as a *revision* of Marxism, but as an *adaptation* of Marx's doctrines to the traditions of French socialism, and indeed of French republicanism.[20] For Jaurès, as for his disciples down to Léon Blum, the question was how Marxism could be incorporated into this body of thought without doing fatal damage to the basic assumptions of eighteenth century rationalism and moralism. Philosophically, the issue presented itself in terms of moral idealism versus scientific determinism: Lafargue having acquainted French readers with the notion that Marxism was to be understood as a further refinement of the positivist scientism they knew so well. Politically, the question turned on the vision of democracy as a community embracing all social classes, even the proletariat—though the latter was for the moment effectively excluded. The moral fervor of Jaurès drew its special tone not only from

[19] Ligou, pp. 49 ff.; Lefranc, *Le mouvement socialiste,* pp. 32 ff. For details of the political alignments, see Engels-Lafargue, *Correspondance,* Vols. II and III. For Marx's own contribution, see his *Enquête Ouvrière* of 1880: the detailed questionnaire he drew up for Malon's *Revue Socialiste,* shortly before Guesde's visit to London, which resulted in the formal drafting (in collaboration with Engels and Lafargue) of a socialist platform for the coming elections; see Karl Marx, *Selected Writings,* pp. 203 ff. The platform and the questionnaire of 1880 represent, as it were, the inauguration of reformist socialism in France—though in fact Marx was simply reverting to the tradition of the First International (1864-76), as laid down in its *Inaugural Address* of 1864 which he had drafted.

[20] Jean Jaurès, *Les Origines du socialisme allemand* (new edition with preface by Lucien Goldmann, Paris, 1959). Originally published in Malon's *Revue Socialiste* in 1892, this was an attempt to graft post-Kantian German idealist philosophy upon the stem of traditional French socialist and democratic thought. Or should it rather be described as an effort to dilute French moralism with Marxist materialism? At any rate, Jaurès—by profession a philosopher before he entered public life—made it clear in this learned tract that he preferred Kant to Hegel, and Lassalle to Marx.

the implied rejection of violence—for even the Guesdists gradually relegated such notions to the attic—but positively from the belief in a peaceful transformation of society through the democratic process (which he more or less identified with the electoral process). Some of this went back to the reformist labor movements of the 1880s, but the intellectual formulation was achieved with the aid of scholars like Lucien Herr and Charles Andler who were steeped in German philosophy and acquainted with the original Marxian texts. By 1905, when the Socialist party was formally unified, the Jaurèsist wing had come into possession of a doctrine which could hold its own, and which after the Socialist-Communist split of 1920 was to serve Blum's party as its intellectual and moral foundation.[21]

The doctrine was couched in evolutionary terms. Politically, Jaurès (after breaking with bourgeois republicanism) entered Socialist politics in 1893 as a lieutenant of Millerand: later destined to give prominence to the issue of Socialist participation in bourgeois governments. Theoretically, he accepted Herr's and Andler's friendly yet critical interpretation of Marxism. This amounted to a conviction that it was possible to conceive the coming transformation along lines different from both the narrow Guesdist dogmatism and the antiquated Blanquist catastrophism of Vaillant and his friends. With Jaurès, the synthesis of socialism and democracy ceased to be an aspiration and became a way of life. The new doctrine was grafted upon the democratic tradition stemming from 1793—minus the Babouvist element to which both Guesde and Vaillant remained faithful, and which was to be revived by the Communists after 1917. If the Dreyfus affair around 1900 served as a catalyst, it did so because it gave Jaurès an opportu-

[21] Charles Andler, *La Vie de Lucien Herr* (Paris, 1932). For Jaurès' large and varied literary legacy, see the bibliographical note attached to Louis Lévy's *Anthologie de Jean Jaurès* (Paris, 1946). For the filiation from the reformist labor socialism of Paul Brousse, via Benoît Malon and *possibilisme,* to Jaurès, see Lefranc, *Le mouvement socialiste,* pp. 65 ff. It is perhaps worth noting that Malon and Allemane were unique among the founders of the post-1870 socialist movement in being authentic workingmen. Allemane indeed was the central figure of the group which around 1890 attracted youthful intellectuals of bourgeois origin like Herr and Andler. His *Parti ouvrier socialiste révolutionnaire* stood for the general strike—one reason why Andler and Herr (both critical of Guesde and contemptuous of Lafargue) favored it. For the rest, both men were skeptical of Marx's German followers, and inclined to believe that France would continue to make an important contribution.

nity to come forward as the spokesman of a cause which was also that of the intellectual Left—not only of the workers movement. From 1905 onward, when a unified Socialist party came into being, all these elements entered into an unstable synthesis.

It is impossible here to enter into a discussion of the political and theoretical disputes whereby this synthesis was achieved. At some point between 1895 and 1905 the memory of the *semaine sanglante* had faded sufficiently for socialists to become reconciled to democracy: to the point of being willing to defend the Republic against its enemies on the Right. What needs stressing is that this evolution closed a gap between the workers movement and the democratic intelligentsia, and thus made it possible for socialism (in its idealist Jaurèsian form) to compete with radicalism as the dominant ideology in the educational establishment—the *Université*. The process whereby a majority of the teaching profession (starting at the bottom, with the elementary school teachers, but also at the very top, among some leading *universitaires*) was gradually converted to reformist socialism, took several decades. It began with the Dreyfus upheaval, was spurred by the war of 1914-18 (when socialism became syonymous first with patriotism and later —after the country had become war-weary—with pacifism), and finally affirmed itself with the anti-Fascist struggle of the 1930s and the war-time Resistance. The literary intelligentsia, save for its right-wing nationalist component, underwent a similar evolution. All of this was quite unlike the parallel development in Germany, where during these decades the educated stratum became increasingly conservative, reactionary, and hostile to the Enlightenment tradition, so that in the end it was possible for "National Socialism" to sweep the country on a wave of far from artificial fervor. In the last resort this momentous difference goes back to the impact of the French Revolution. But here the point is rather that the existence of a democratic tradition within the middle class made it possible for the Socialist party—once it had come to terms with democracy—to transcend the specific narrowness imposed upon it by the sectional outlook of the workers movement. Not that this movement had ever rejected individuals who "came over to the side of the proletariat." But for the Socialist party to embrace both the working class and a sizeable stratum of the intelligentsia it was necessary that the intellectuals as a group, and the workers as a class, should agree on fundamentals. This fusion was achieved, from the Dreyfus upheaval onward, under the leadership of Jaurès and his friends, who thus made it possible for Socialism to take its place within the political and intellectual spectrum traditionally known as "the Left." In this sense the unified Socialist party of 1905, the S.F.I.O. (*Section Française de l'Internationale Ouvrière*), for all its professed Marxism, had by 1914 become a democratic party.[22]

The significance of this evolution for the future Communist party will be considered later. Here it may be said that, while this fusion of the democratic and the socialist tradition made it possible for the working class and the left-wing intelligentsia to find a common language, it also reinforced the ingrained habit of viewing social and industrial conflicts in revolutionary terms. This was the reverse side of a situation which enabled democratic intellectuals to bridge the class issue. For intellectuals and workers to speak the same language, both had to fall back on a terminology stemming from the French Revolution. The problem subsequently affected Socialists and Communists alike, though in different ways. Some Socialists even before 1917 were not quite comfortable with the Jacobin-Blanquist heritage, while the Communists thereafter gloried in it. One has only to study the documents of the 1920 split to see how important it was for both sides to remain in tune with the revolutionary tradition.[23]

For the time being, i.e., until the great schism provoked by the October Revolution, these latent tensions did not matter. The Socialism of 1914 rested upon a disciplined political organization, though numerically far weaker than in Germany, and the unified party led jointly by Guesde and Jaurès seemed to have attained the necessary balance between its democratic and its revolutionary components. It took the 1914-18 war, and the Russian Revolution, to

[22] Ligou, pp. 179 ff. In strict accuracy one has to note that the compromise formula of 1905, which held the S.F.I.O. together until 1920, was too Marxist for the taste of some "independent socialists" who broke away and formed their own groups: most of their leaders eventually becoming ministers in various left-center coalition governments. But this does not affect the argument that socialism had become respectable.

[23] Kriegel, *Le Congrès de Tours,* particularly Léon Blum's speech, pp. 101 ff., which raised the debate to the level of political principle. Blum, who had come to socialism through Lucien Herr and Jaurès, felt no doubt that Leninism represented a revival of the Blanquist heresy, which it had taken the movement half a century to outgrow.

bring this apparently solid structure to the ground. But even before the great debacle, there was the awkward phenomenon of revolutionary Syndicalism to remind all concerned that the fusion of democratic reformism with Marxism, or quasi-Marxism, had not quite solved the problem of unifying the French workers movement.

Syndicalism

Syndicalism is too complex a subject for a brief sketch, the more so since it involves a consideration of the issues dividing "authoritarian" and "libertarian" collectivists (in later terminology: Socialists and Anarchists) from the 1870s onward.[24] But if a formula is permissible, one may say that the French syndicalist movement between 1890 and 1914 saw itself, and was seen by others, as the dialectical union of Anarchism and Marxism. That at any rate was how Sorel envisaged it, and Sorel is the only important theorist the movement has produced.[25] Having won his spurs in the 1890s as an interpreter of Marx, he could later claim to have brought about a synthesis of Proudhonism and Marxism, and indeed his first coherent attempt to state the new doctrine occurred at a time when he still regarded himself as a follower of Marx.[26]

What Sorel got from Marx—at any rate in 1898, when he had not yet begun his descent into myth-fabrication and the advocacy of violence for its own sake—was the notion that socialism was the

[24] Maitron, pp. 34 ff. This gives the Anarchist version of the story, but in a scholarly fashion, and with due emphasis on the role of Proudhon in fathering the whole tradition, at any rate so far as France is concerned.

[25] Though its real animator was Fernand Pelloutier. See Maitron, pp. 253 ff.

[26] Georges Sorel, "Avenir socialiste des syndicats," in *Matériaux d'une théorie du prolétariat* (Paris, 1919), pp. 55 ff. The essay was first published in March-April 1898 in the revue *Humanité nouvelle* and later reprinted as a pamphlet. The new Preface of 1905—composed while Sorel was already working on the draft of his *Réflexions sur la violence*—differs considerably in tone from the original text. In particular it contains a savage assault on Jaurès, who is accused of having betrayed the syndicalist utopia for the sake of gaining the friendship of wealthy bourgeois supporters, notably the "Dreyfusards de la Bourse." The tone of this Preface is a distant prefiguration of Mussolini's subsequent invectives against liberalism and socialism, and it explains how Italian Fascists in the 1920s could see themselves as disciples of Sorel. More immediately, it met a current coming from the Maurrasist Right in France itself, where the notion of fusing nationalism with socialism was beginning to take shape in some minds. A degree of antisemitism was part of the mixture.

conscious expression of the proletarian class movement. From this it appeared to follow that the mechanism of the coming social transformation was to be found solely in the class struggle, and more particularly in the strike movements led by the *syndicats:* movements destined to culminate in the revolutionary General Strike which would sound the knell of bourgeois society. The trouble, as Sorel saw it, was that the official Socialists—mostly intellectuals of bourgeois origin—would have none of this: their socialism, which they decked out with citations from Marx and Engels, was political and parliamentary, hence reformist. This perversion, in his opinion, was rooted in their class outlook, since they were in fact bourgeois intellectuals in search of a proletarian clientele. In this way Sorel's critique rejoined that of Proudhon, though by a circumlocution made necessary by the growing prestige of Marx and the impossibility of ignoring him. It is amusing to find that in 1898 Kautsky was Sorel's particular bête noire because of his readiness to welcome intellectuals into the labor movement,[27] whereas Lenin a few years later cited Kautsky by way of reinforcing his own thesis that the workers movement, left to itself, could not develop a proper socialist consciousness. Yet in 1918 Sorel was to hail the Bolshevik regime because it had, as he thought, destroyed the intellectuals along with bourgeois democracy: the form of government best suited to their interest.[28]

If the question be raised why the nascent French Communist party nonetheless proved able in the 1920s to employ the syndicalist platform as a launching pad for its own journey into political space, the answer must be that revolutionary syndicalism as such had suffered shipwreck in 1914: not so much because most of its leaders adopted a patriotic position, but because the myth of a revolutionary proletariat was no longer tenable after the *Union Sacrée* of August 1914 had shown that the overwhelming bulk of the working class responded to national sentiments. Syndicalism had indeed always rested upon a

[27] Sorel, *Matériaux d'une théorie,* pp. 93 ff.

[28] *Ibid.,* p. 53 (post-scriptum of 1918 to the unpublished Preface of July 1914): "La sanglante leçon de choses qui se produira en Russie fera sentir à tous les ouvriers qu'il y a une contradiction entre la démocratie et la mission du prolétariat; l'idée de constituer un gouvernement de producteurs ne périra pas; le cri 'Mort aux Intellectuels,' si souvent reproché aux *bolsheviks,* finira peut-être par s'imposer aux travailleurs du monde entier. Il faut être aveugle pour ne pas voir que la révolution russe est l'aurore d'une ère nouvelle."

minority of active *militants* (craftsmen for the most part rather than ordinary factory workers); but the elite possessed a self-confidence fed on the belief that in a crisis the masses would follow it. This vision was shattered at the outbreak of war, when it became overwhelmingly evident that the revolutionary credo was merely that of a tiny minority.[29]

If Sorel's writings between 1898 and 1918 are examined in this light, they seem to point in several directions at once, so that it has been possible to claim him for Bolshevism and Fascism, as well as for the Syndicalist tradition. The paradox is lessened when one reflects that these movements shared a common hostility to liberal democracy as the political form of an apparently decrepit and corrupt (at any rate in France and Italy: the two countries with which Sorel was personally concerned) bourgeois society. But there was more to it: in his confused and confusing fashion, Sorel had stumbled upon a genuine problem. Setting aside his venomous polemics against Jaurès, and against the reformist intellectuals in general, the core of his argument had some bearing upon what was to become the central issue of the labor movement in the twentieth century: its relation to the state. Immediately this took the form of disputations over the nature of political power and the proper means of capturing (or liquidating) it. But in the long run something else was involved: given that socialism

[29] Kriegel, *Aux origines,* I, 53 ff. See Collinet, *La tragédie du Marxisme,* p. 64: "L'ouvrier actif de 1906, qu'il fût socialiste et à plus forte raison anarcho-syndicaliste, était un militant jaloux de son indépendance intellectuelle. . . . Au contraire, la discipline de la grande industrie moderne pousse le manoeuvre spécialisé dans les rangs d'un parti hiérarchisé et totalitaire." The masses were, however, already indifferent to anarcho-syndicalism in 1914, when the test came, and this depressing realization sounded the knell of the whole Proudhonian-Sorelian tradition. Many of its adherents then bowed to the evidence and made peace with democracy—which under the circumstances meant renouncing the idea of a revolutionary general strike. This débacle later provided a *leitmotiv* of Communist writing, even among the anti-Stalinist sects that split off from the main stem. For a typical assessment, see the obituary article on the veteran Alfred Rosmer in the July-September 1964 number of the Bordigist, i.e., left-wing Communist Paris quarterly, *Programme Communiste.* "Le syndicalisme révolutionnaire est bel et bien mort en 1914, mais non pas toutes les conceptions qu'il a inspirées et qui nient la dictature du prolétariat. . . ." p. 62. For the followers of Lenin—down to the present-day Trotskyists and the Italian pupils of Antonio Gramsci—the prime lesson of 1914 was and is that "the class" cannot be relied upon to follow the true revolutionary line unless it is guided by "the party."

aimed at the establishment of a planned and centralized economy, who was to manage it, and what was to be the role of the workers? Was the functional separation of physical and mental toil to be perpetuated? In that case, would not the intellectuals constitute themselves as a new ruling class? These issues were already inherent in the original dispute between Marx and Bakunin (most of whose followers had been erstwhile Proudhonists). But they took practical shape only in the new century, and this for the best of reasons: large-scale industry and modern scientific technology underwent a drastic change *after* the Marxian version of socialism had been more or less formulated. Marx had indeed anticipated a good many features of the fully developed industrial society, but—adamant in his refusal to "write recipes for the cookshops of the future"—he had not provided his followers with a blueprint of the new order. His magnum opus was a critique of capitalism, not a sociology of industrialism. He left it to the future to disentangle these aspects of social reality. This attitude was scientifically sound, but it made things awkward for his disciples, unless, like Kautsky and the German-Austrian Marxists generally, they were content to play variations on a single theme: the coming crisis of capitalism. If they tried to look beyond this to the actual management of a socialist economy, they were bound to enter terra incognita.

Hence the disturbing influence of Syndicalism which—in the actual practice of the movement rather than in the writings of Sorel or Lagardelle—transcended the horizon of parliamentary reform. But Sorel spoiled his case by muddling up two quite distinct matters: the role of Socialist politicians in helping to keep bourgeois democracy going, and the hypothetical function of a new managerial caste drawn from the ranks of the middle class. Now and then he caught a glimpse of the future.[30] More often he confused matters by making it appear that the hungry office seekers, whose opportunism he stigmatized, were the forerunners of a new exploiting class. When he blamed them for

[30] See his perceptive comment, in *Matériaux d'une theorie,* p. 90n, on the Saint-Simonian tendencies current among Socialist *universitaires* like Jaurès, who in 1897 had urged the employment of impecunious young men of talent as government functionaries concerned with industry. Characteristically, Sorel coupled this with some nonsense of his own about the parasitical growth of science: this in a country which was suffering from backwardness and neglect precisely in this field!

trying to infiltrate the workers movement, he was echoing Proudhon.[31] When he commented on the functional division of labor in modern industry between (intellectual) overseers and (manual) executants, he was anticipating the key issue of the future.[32] The distinction never became clear to him; in other words, he never grasped that the future technocracy, whose coming he foresaw and detested, was not in the least dependent on the lawyers and journalists who got elected to the Chamber of Deputies on the Socialist ticket. It was typical of his muddled perception that Bolshevism appeared to him as the triumph of the workers over the hated intellectuals: had not Lenin dissolved the Constituent Assembly and instituted the rule of workers councils? In fairness to Sorel, such sentiments were widely shared at the time among the remnants of revolutionary Syndicalism. It took years of growing disillusionment to dispel the notion that the October Revolution had given birth to a workers state.

The Sorel of 1898 stood closest to Marx in his insistence that only an autonomous labor movement could bring about that "emancipation of the working class" in which both men believed. He differed from Marx in exalting the trade union movement, the *syndicats,* above the political party: on the grounds that the political wing of the movement was hopelessly corrupted by the intelligentsia, and compromised by its involvement with bourgeois parliamentarianism. The time was to come when Communism would draw the appropriate moral: to remain incorruptible, the party too had to be proletarian, or at any rate led by true sons of the working class. Moreover, its center of gravity must lie outside parliament. Sorel would have approved these conclusions, though with an important reservation: he would have scented in the Communist authoritarianism the germ of a new hierarchy subordinating the toilers once more to a directing stratum. Moreover, he would have been right, though the new bureaucratic masters differed from the old ones (e.g., in rejecting individual liberty and the rule of

[31] "Ces Intellectuels, mal payés, mécontents ou peu occupés, on eu l'idée vraiment géniale d'imposer l'emploi du terme impropre de *prolétariat intellectuel:* ils peuvent ainsi facilement se faufiler dans les rangs du prolétariat industriel. . . . La véritable vocation des Intellectuels est l'exploitation de la politique." *Ibid.,* pp. 97-98.

[32] "La hiérarchie contemporaine a pour base principale la division des travailleurs en intellectuels et en manuels." *Ibid.,* p. 89.

law). In the face of this phenomenon, though, it might have been difficult for him to retain his optimistic assurance that Syndicalism pointed toward a future when the working class would at last stand on its own feet.[33]

If the reformist version of Marxism emphasized the lessening of class tensions and the unique importance of liberal democracy (at any rate for Western Europe), the Sorelian critique may be said to have fastened upon those aspects of the Marxian synthesis which obscured the latent rift between the autonomous workers movement and the future directing stratum of the socialist order. Marx had envisaged a transformation stemming from the working class itself, and in this respect every Syndicalist could feel himself his heir. The democratic and libertarian character of Marx's doctrine was not really in question, for all the Anarchist complaints against him. Tensions and uncertainties arose rather from the growth of doubt concerning the ability of the working class to bring forth new institutions which could take the place of the old political and social hierarchies. The Sorelian "wager" on the General Strike was already a piece of romanticism, and on the eve of 1914 it had come close to being an act of desperation. On the other wing of the movement, reformist labor bureaucrats like Jouhaux after 1914 came increasingly to expect social emancipation from the influence of the public authorities, thereby establishing a link between the parliamentary Socialists and the union movement. The war itself destroyed revolutionary Syndicalism by showing up its pretensions. The disappointment caused by the "degeneration" of the Soviet regime was the finishing touch, and helped to drive some former Syndicalists into the Fascist camp.

These issues were inherent in Sorel's critique of Marx, and this must be the excuse for giving them a brief and inadequate airing. It can never be stressed sufficiently that for Sorel the class struggle was "the alpha and omega of socialism," and the emphasis upon it "that which is really true in Marxism."[34] What separated him from the

[33] *Ibid.*, pp. 131-33.

[34] *Ibid.*, p. 67, where he also insists that "le syndicat est l'instrument de la guerre sociale." This follows for him from the general notion that "la lutte de classe . . . n'est pas un concept sociologique . . . mais l'aspect idéologique d'une guerre sociale poursuivie par le prolétariat contre l'ensemble des chefs d'industrie."

orthodox Marxists was their seeming reluctance to draw the appropriate conclusions from their own premises. As for the Jaurèsian synthesis of reformism and republicanism (not to mention its technocratic overtones) he abhorred it all the more because its leading representatives had entered into a parliamentary alliance with the bourgeois Radicals. This came natural to them, since as former pupils of the *École normale* they were basically committed to what by 1900 had become the official ideology of the Third Republic. Behind Jaurès stood Durkheim and the whole corps of academic sociologists and quasi-official moralists who were busy inculcating the new *laiciste* ideology of Science and Progress. In certain respects reformist socialism around 1900 appeared as a variant of bourgeois progressivism. On this point at least Sorel was at one with the Marxists, who from the start had distrusted Jaurès precisely because he was a product of the *École normale*.[35]

Integral Socialism

At our present distance from the scene it is plain enough that the Jaurèsian version of socialism—like its Fabian counterpart in Britain—had an unconscious social function. It satisfied the needs of the new professional and managerial class, or at any rate of its intellectual elite which was veering towards socialism. In a fully developed industrial society the importance of this stratum was bound to grow, until in the end it would lay claim to leadership of society (and of the socialist movement). In the 1890s the issue still appeared in ideological terms, as a quarrel over the proper interpretation of socialist doctrine. Instinctively, both Engels and Sorel scented danger, but Engels' French disciples—with Lafargue and Guesde in the lead—refused to take the matter seriously. Secure in their newly acquired Marxist creed, and confident that the industrial proletariat was the class of the future, they dismissed Jaurès as a muddled purveyor of antiquated prescientific concepts. They saw mere retrogression where Sorel perceived a threat to the autonomy of the workers movement.

[35] Cf. Engels to Laura Lafargue in 1893: "As to what you say of Jaurès, that fills me with terror. Normalien et ami, sinon protégé, de Malon—which of the two is worse?" *Correspondance,* III, 270.

One may say that both the Marxists and the Sorelians, in their different ways, were concerned to preserve the proletarian character of the movement against the subtle corruptions stemming from the bourgeois intelligentsia, with its natural hankering after an evolutionary doctrine of progress. What they failed to grasp was that the intelligentsia was ceasing to be bourgeois. Before long it would be necessary to find a suitable place for it within the socialist movement. Then it would become evident that the movement was in fact made up of two different strata: workers and intellectuals, and that the latter—by virtue of their social function—would claim the directing role both within the political party of their choice, and within the social order they hoped to establish.

It would be a mistake to suppose that the participants to the pre-1914 debate saw the matter in this light. Men are not moved by sociological considerations. What mattered to Guesde, Sorel, and Jaurès was the truth of their respective doctrines. Jaurès in particular was so fervent a moralist as to define his position almost exclusively in ethical terms. Just as he had plunged into the Dreyfus Affair at a moment when most Socialists hung back (or refused to intervene in a quarrel between "two bourgeois clans"), so he had earlier become a convert to socialism when he felt able to interpret it as something more than the predestined outcome of economic change, or the reflex of the class struggle.[36] This is not to say that he neglected the theoretical aspect. He could hardly have done so without falling afoul of his teachers.[37] But his "integral socialism" (a heritage from Malon and the pre-Marxists) was integral precisely in that it encompassed a moral appeal to timeless values. This was the link between Jaurès and his rebellious pupil Charles Péguy (who subsequently broke with him on quite a different issue). One approaches the heart of the French situation—so different from the German, where moral issues were never allowed to interfere with *Realpolitik*—when one bears in mind that Péguy (later a convert to Catholicism and nationalism) had begun

[36] Lefranc, *Le mouvement socialiste,* pp. 94-95. "Herr a convaincu Jaurès de la possibilité d'un socialisme autre que le guesdisme ou le blanquisme."

[37] Andler and Herr, both Alsatians and steeped in German philosophy, were in some respects the theoretical equals of Marx's German disciples, and far superior to Lafargue and the other Guesdists.

as a passionate *Dreyfusard,* and indeed never regretted his early enrollment in that campaign. For those who participated in it, the fight for "justice" ("abstract justice," in the rather absurd phrase of the Guesdists) was part of the struggle for the moral regeneration of France and the Republic: a struggle which gave universal meaning to what they called socialism. Jaurès was as clear as Péguy that the movement (there was as yet no unified party) could not stand aloof from the Dreyfus Affair. To have done so would have meant condemning it to political and moral impotence.[38]

The point of recalling these distant controversies is to bring out the filiation linking the "integral socialism" of Jaurès and his friends with the theory and practice of the men and women who in 1920 refused to join the Third International. There is a distinct line which runs from the minority faction of the 1871 Commune, via Brousse and Malon, to Herr and Jaurès, and finally to Léon Blum and the later S.F.I.O. Those who adhered to this tradition were democrats, though most of them also regarded themselves as Marxists. What separated them from the radical wing was their attachment to certain values they shared with other democrats, who might not be socialists or collectivists, but who were concerned to maintain the spiritual health of the Republic. Ultimately the moral community of the French nation meant more to them than mere working-class solidarity—though in their fashion they tried to be loyal to both. In 1914 they had the satisfaction of seeing the followers of Guesde and Vaillant coming around to their viewpoint. But even before the watershed of the First World War, "integral socialism" had outgrown its dim reformist origins and become a principled position to which both Marxists and non-Marxists could adhere. Its doctrine might be eclectic, but it possessed a hard distinctive core. At bottom it rested upon a refusal to separate social-

[38] Andler, pp. 116 ff. "L'éternel honneur de Jaurès, celui par lequel il restera grand dans l'histoire, sera de s'être rangé derrière Lucien Herr, d'avoir compris qu'un innocent envoyé au bagne, fût-il millionnaire d'origine, éprouve la destinée même du prolétariat, qui est précisement d'être exclu de la justice. . . ." For Péguy's role in the *Affaire,* and his subsequent break with Jaurès on the issue of Franco-German enmity and the approach of war, see Paul Thibaud, "L'anti-Jaurès," *Esprit* (August-September, 1964). Also Jacques Virard, *Esprit,* p. 225: "L'heure de Péguy commençait à sonner en 1932, quand Andler raconta la vie de celui qui fonda la S.F.I.O. avec Jaurès, et de nouveau, en 1920, avec Léon Blum."

ism from humanism. The appeal was not to history but to a distant goal which, in principle at least, all men could share. This was the socialism of Jaurès, and in a measure it remained that of the party he helped to found.

What saved that party from becoming a mere assemblage of middle-class reformers was the fusion with the Guesdists. In this manner the intellectuals encountered the proletariat and had to come to terms with it. The resultant tension makes up the greater part of Socialist history. In what follows we shall have few occasions to revert to these distant origins, which were decisive in shaping the character of the movement. What needs to be retained is just this—that the movement was already born with the internal contradictions which subsequently propelled it along: the tension between patriotism and internationalism, between reform and revolution, between working-class solidarity and the claims of the national community. The lines criss-crossed,[39] and there was constant straining after a synthesis which would somehow embrace Michelet, Proudhon, Marx, the Commune, Guesde, Jaurès, and their respective followers. This eclecticism was a source of both strength and weakness. Unlike the rival Communist party, which after 1920 constituted itself on Leninist foundations, French Socialism never moved very far away from the national mainstream. It may have been this attachment to traditions and values largely shared with the rest of the community that enabled the movement to survive a succession of catastrophic defeats and disappointments. Here we simply register the existence, and the continuing importance, of a Socialist tradition older than the Russian Revolution: one which had already absorbed and transformed Marx before encountering the challenge of Lenin.

[39] On the issue of antiparliamentarianism, for example, the nationalist Péguy was closer to Sorel than to Guesde, not to mention Jaurès. Indeed nothing enraged that fervent spirit more than Jaurès' parliamentary maneuvres, and in general his reliance on parliamentary government as a vehicle of moral and political regeneration. Under French conditions, such an attitude was quite compatible with faith in democracy, though Péguy's present disciples on the left wing of Catholicism have had to come to terms with ordinary democratic politics.

2

The Great Divide

Dissension and Reconstruction

Between 1920 and 1945 the French labor movement underwent a transformation which resulted in the Communist party becoming the principal organized force on the Left, while its Socialist rival was pushed towards the political center and deprived of much of its former influence over the industrial working class, notably in heavy industry. At the same time the traditional understanding of the movement's long-term aims received a new interpretation, so far as the Communists were concerned, through the manner in which the new Leninist faith was grafted upon the older Guesdist and Blanquist stems. Rather paradoxically, this was accompanied by a more systematic indoctrination with Marxian concepts, so that something like a coherent philosophy became available to intellectuals who joined the postwar movement. Most of them during these years came to Marx by way of Lenin, with the inevitable result that whatever was incompatible with Leninism did not enter their mental universe. For an adequate presentation of the full and unabridged corpus of Marxist doctrine, France had to wait until the 1950s. The older pre-Leninist tradition was, it is true, carried on by the Socialists; but for a variety of reasons they did not, during these years, succeed in transforming their heritage into a comprehensive world view capable of meeting the new challenge. The failure was especially pronounced where it mattered most urgently: in the domain of political theory, notably in relation to the complex "imperialism-war-revolution." No one will ever know what Jaurès' attitude would have been in August 1914, but his prewar synthesis of republican patriotism and democratic socialism did not meet the new situation, though the Communists never explicitly repudiated the Jaurèsist tradition, and indeed went on employing his vocabulary whenever possible.[1]

As noted before, the unified Socialist party of 1905 had arisen through the fusion of several quite distinct trends. As late as 1902 there were two separate parties: the Jaurèsian *Parti socialiste français,* which descended from the reformist group of Brousse and Malon, and its rival, the *Parti socialiste de France* of Guesde and Vaillant: the latter itself a fusion of the Guesdist *Parti Ouvrier* and the Blanquist rump. The S.F.I.O., as formally constituted by the Paris congress of April 23-25, 1905, was a repository of all these warring traditions. Not surprisingly its unity was strained beyond endurance by the 1914-18 war and the Russian Revolution. The 1905 program had defined it as a "parti de classe qui a pour but de transformer la société capitaliste en société collectiviste ou communiste." This struck the requisite balance between the reformist and the anarcho-syndicalist trends, though in practice reformism became the unspoken creed of the parliamentary party, while anarcho-syndicalism was left to the *Confédération Générale du Travail,* where the more radical elements entrenched themselves. The unification formula, in fact, represented a compromise which lasted while the peaceful attainment of socialism within the democratic framework was more or less generally accepted. When the Bolshevik seizure of power revived the notion of a revolutionary and dictatorial shortcut, the prewar integration collapsed: not because Marxists and non-Marxists separated, but because the Marxists themselves were now divided over the legitimacy of the "Soviet experiment." In 1905 democracy had not really been an issue, for by then not even the erstwhile Blanquists denied that it *might* lead to socialism. After 1917 the Communists denied just that: as they saw it, bourgeois democracy was a trap from which the movement must free itself.

[1] Annie Kriegel, *Aux origines du communisme français 1914-1920* (Paris, 1964), I, 32 ff., II, 791 ff., 863 ff. For Jaurès' attempt to pour the new socialist wine into the ancient republican container see his *L'Armée nouvelle* (Paris, 1910, 2d ed., 1915).

The split of December 1920—when the Communist majority at Tours formally separated from the Socialist minority on the issue of joining the Third International—thus superimposed new antagonisms upon old ones. It did not correspond to the prewar dividing lines, and needless to say it had nothing to do with a social cleavage between the "labor aristocracy" and the rest. In fact, Communism at first was strongest in rural areas, among peasant smallholders who thus gave vent to their antimilitarism, and weakest in the industrial centers and among the miners.[2] It took the Communist party more than a decade to reverse this situation, and it was only in the 1930s, following the great depression and the spread of unemployment, that it overhauled the Socialists, first in Paris and then in the other industrial centers. In 1920 all this was still in the future, and there was no question of the delegates at Tours, or the *militants* in the constituencies, dividing along class lines, for all the effort the Communists made to stick the "petty-bourgeois" label on their opponents. This is not contradicted by the fact that the Socialist rump at Tours at first represented less than 40,000 members, against some 110,000 who joined the new Communist party, for most of the Socialists were veterans of the labor movement, while the Communist majority included a large number of newcomers who dropped out after a few years.[3]

The typical adherent of the Third International in 1920 was either a prewar Syndicalist whose thinking had been radicalized by the war, or a rural neophyte who had never previously belonged to any

[2] Annie Kriegel, *Le Congrès de Tours. Naissance du parti communiste français* (Paris, 1964), pp. 17 ff. The Nord and Pas de Calais departments had followed Guesde for over thirty years, and they did not repudiate him when he joined the government in 1914. Indeed, they remained the principal industrial stronghold of socialism even after 1945. At the leadership level, Guesdists, Jaurèsists, and Blanquists had all backed the *union sacrée* in August 1914, and in December 1920 only illness prevented Guesde from appearing in person at Tours to support the *minoritaires* who refused to accept the celebrated "twenty-one conditions" set by the Executive of the Third International. Kriegel, *Aux Origines*, II, 807; L. O. Frossard, *De Jaurès à Lénine* (Paris, 1930), p. 161.

[3] Georges Lefranc, *Le Mouvement socialiste sous la Troisième République* (Paris, 1963), pp. 241 ff., 292 ff. The first really disquieting signs, from the Socialist viewpoint, manifested themselves in 1924, but it was in 1936 that the "Popular Front" elections enabled the Communists to make headway in the great industrial centers. It then became apparent that in socially homogeneous industrial milieux, where the bulk of the manual workers tended to concentrate, the Socialist party was losing ground to its rival.

political movement, had joined the Socialist party in the first great surge of postwar sentiment in 1919, and now looked for an opportunity to manifest his revolutionary longings and his vague sympathies for Lenin and the Soviet regime. The small nucleus of genuine Leninists was pitchforked into this environment by the urgent desire of the Russians to create a Communist mass movement in France. Most of these Bolshevik sympathizers were radicals who had gone beyond the "internationalist" or "Zimmerwald" position held by a growing minority (ultimately a majority) of the Socialist party: at any rate after 1918, when fear of a German victory no longer inhibited their instinctive revulsion against mass slaughter. It is worth bearing in mind that by 1919-20 this pacifist sentiment had become dominant within the party; so had a vague sympathy for the Russian Revolution and Bolshevism. The true Communists would have none of this flabbiness. Unlike the now dominant pacifist wing headed by Jean Longuet, they regarded their break with the pre-1914 Socialist movement as final and irrevocable. Unlike the surviving Syndicalists, they had no illusions (or had lost them) about the spontaneous revolutionary drive of the proletariat. Their adherence to Leninism sprang from a newfound conviction that a centralized *party* was needed to give direction to the inchoate strivings of the *class*. Revolutionary Syndicalists like Monatte or Rosmer, who before 1914 had been suspicious of Marxism because they distrusted its Kautskyist or Guesdist interpretation (with the stress on the subordination of the unions to the political party), now changed course as well, though in the main they did so because they mistook the Soviet regime for a large-scale exercise in syndicalism.[4]

The circumstances of the split account for the fact that both Socialists and Communists during the interwar period were weighed down by the need to explain their respective attitudes in terms of the two issues which had come to the forefront in 1917-19: proletarian internationalism, and the quite unrelated question whether the Soviet regime could be described as a proletarian dictatorship. These

[4] For details of these alignments see Alfred Rosmer, *Le Mouvement ouvrier pendant la guerre* (Paris, 1959), Vol. II; Kriegel, *Aux origines,* II, 628 ff., 715 ff., 757 ff.; Edouard Dolléans, *Histoire du mouvement ouvrier 1871-1936* (Paris, 1946), 223 ff.; Pierre Monatte, *Trois scissions syndicales* (Paris, 1958).

loyalties left room for disputes over tactics. Thus it could plausibly be held that revolutionaries should remain independent of *all* governments, including the Soviet government, but apart from a small group of dissident left-wing Communists, no one took this line. Again, defense of the USSR did not necessarily imply approval of its peculiar system of government. But here again it was difficult to maintain a balanced attitude without bewildering the *militants.* On the whole, most Socialists managed to steer a middle course between qualified acceptance of the Bolshevik regime as suitable for Russia, and outright rejection, but this position inevitably failed to become popular: it was complicated and called for intellectual distinctions which most people found difficult. Hence in part the gradual success of the Communists in persuading the younger generation of workers that internationalism, antimilitarism and pro-Sovietism went together, and indeed constituted the proper test of proletarian revolutionary sentiment.[5]

It is important to bear in mind that the Socialist rump after Tours included war-time pacifists and internationalists like Longuet, as well as moderate "defensists" like Blum, and all-out patriots like Renaudel and Albert Thomas.[6] The split had been deliberately engineered by

[5] Kriegel, *Aux origines,* I, 45 ff., 235 ff., 275 ff.; II, 661 ff., 791 ff. The Leninist interpretation of internationalism meant a real break with the past even for former Marxists, since Guesde (like Jaurès) had always insisted that national defense was a duty for every Socialist. The Guesdist *Manifesto* of January 23, 1893, had concluded with the words "Vive l'Internationale! Vive la France!" Guesde's disciple Compère-Morel was a bitter-ender during the 1914-18 war, and Guesde's own polemics against Lenin in 1918 reaffirmed a tradition which his Socialist followers (down to and including that orthodox Guesdist, Guy Mollet) have never abandoned. The Communist attempt to transfer the older republican loyalties to the new "fatherland of the workers" never had more than a limited success, and was quietly abandoned during the 1941-44 Resistance period, when patriotism once more became a Communist virtue (though after a period of rather Machiavellian maneuverings in 1939-41, when the French CP leadership, under Soviet guidance, went so far as to flirt with the German occupation forces).

[6] *Ibid.,* II, 808 ff. Thomas, who had held ministerial office during the war, expressed the "Millerandist" viewpoint of the extreme right-wing group in the Socialist party when in July 1918 he called for armed intervention against the Bolshevik regime, and in a debate with Blum shortly afterwards declared that the choice was between Wilson and Lenin; to which Blum characteristically replied: "Je ne choisis ni Wilson ni Lénine. Je choisis Jaurès." (*L'Humanité,* 9 and 15 November, 1918.) The viewpoint of those prewar Syndicalists who regarded the war as a catastrophe for which France was less responsible than was Germany, was expressed by Léon Jouhaux, *Le Syndicalisme et la C.G.T.* (Paris, 1920), pp. 190 ff., where he offered a qualified defense of "social patrio-

the Russians and their French supporters so as to exclude the moderate left-center elements, whose attitude paralleled that of the Mensheviks (and of Kautsky and the Austro-Marxists). The post-1920 Socialist party thus remained a coalition of divergent elements, even though the extreme Left had departed. If Blum—himself a Jaurèsist—was able to hold the party together for a good many years (at the cost of only one major breakaway before the general debacle of 1940), he could do so only with the support of veteran Guesdists who remained attached to the Marxist heritage as they understood it. But then Blum himself always stressed his fidelity to Marx. At Tours he had even declared for "proletarian dictatorship" (though not in the Blanquist or Leninist sense), and as late as 1945 he chose the occasion of the first postwar congress of the reconstituted Socialist party to reaffirm his adherence to "the essential principles of Marxism," including the analysis of capitalism and the general theory of historical materialism.[7]

Léon Blum is the pivotal figure in French Socialist history during the quarter century between 1920 and 1945. His famous intervention at Tours did more than formulate the anti-Bolshevik position which was to remain that of his party: it established him as the successor to Jaurès.[8] He had broken with the future Communists on the question of democracy—ultimately on the issue of political freedom—and he never wavered in maintaining his principled stand on this ground. In the very month of August 1945 in which he reaffirmed his fidelity to Marx's teaching, he emphasized "the indispensable connection of socialism and democracy." At the same time he recalled the dividing line which continued to separate the Socialists from Lenin's French followers: As long as the Communists placed the interests of the

---

tism" as inevitable and proper. This was also Blum's view, and it formed the principal bond between the party leader and his strongest supporter among the union leaders.

[7] Léon Blum, *L'Oeuvre de Léon Blum 1945-1947* (Paris, 1958), p. 66. Address of August 13, 1945, to the 37th national congress of the S.F.I.O.

[8] Blum himself did not doubt the significance of the lead he had given to the faithful remnant at Tours: "C'est sur le fanatisme doctrinaire de quelques hommes dont j'ai été que s'est brisée en 1920 la vague communiste. (Discours prononcé au Congrès National extraordinaire du P.S. le 10 Janvier 1926 [Ed. de la *Nouvelle Revue socialiste,* 1926])." For an intelligent, if rather hostile, portrait of Blum see Colette Audry, *Léon Blum—ou la politique du Juste* (Paris, 1955); for a more balanced appreciation see Kriegel, *Aux origines,* II, 796 ff.

Soviet Union above those of their own country, they might be regarded as electoral allies, but never as comrades in the full sense of the term.[9]

These attitudes were rooted in ways of thought which the Socialists held in common with other Frenchmen brought up on the democratic heritage. The French labor movement shared the traditional republican patriotism of the Left, and beyond this it had long urged the need for Frenchmen of all classes to become genuine citizens of their country. It is not a trivial matter that the traditional term *"citoyen"* had been retained among Socialists before 1914, along with the Syndicalist form of address *"camarade."* Patriotism and democracy went together. These were convictions which Socialists shared with other citizens from whom they were divided by social and economic issues. The same applied to the common heritage of anticlericalism, which indeed was to hamper the S.F.I.O. in 1945, when perhaps it missed the chance to found a democratic labor movement embracing the bulk of the Catholic workers.[10]

But this is to anticipate. Between 1920 and 1945 the problem was how to rebuild the Socialist party in the face of the Communist challenge. On the whole this was done with greater success in the provinces than in Paris. One touches here upon a major cause of the Socialist party's enduring weakness. Even before 1914 it had not been very successful in organizing the workers in the centers of industrial mass production. After 1920, in a country which was experiencing an accelerated changeover from small-scale to large-scale industry, the Socialists continued to be hampered by forms of organization and propaganda—perhaps also by a personnel—which did not evoke an adequate response from the masses of recently arrived, and still rather primitive, workers in the new industrial centers. The party indeed grew numerically, and spread into the provinces on the heels of the

[9] Blum, pp. 83 ff.

[10] Philip M. Williams, *Crisis and Compromise: Politics in the Fourth Republic* (London, 1964), p. 97: "If the Socialists could not satisfy the revolutionary workers, their appeal to the reformists was hampered by the religious quarrel. They could never attract the Christian proletariat because of the fervour with which they clung to the anticlerical tradition. *Laicité* was the hidden reef that wrecked the proposal for a French Labour party which Blum and his friends vainly launched at the Liberation."

industrialization process. But it lost ground in Paris, and its growth elsewhere tended to be at the expense of the Radicals, which in practice meant that its class character was changing. At the same time it could not be said to be making sensational headway in organizing the white-collar stratum, though it continued to do well among the civil servants, notably schoolteachers.[11]

Along with these structural weaknesses there went internal complications and splits which it would be tedious to detail. They were related to an intellectual failure which in the end was decisive. During the 1930s, when liberalism proved hopelessly outmoded both in politics and in economics, thus offering an opportunity to its historical rival, the Socialist party remained wedded to forms of thought which had been barely adequate in 1914. Politically, it was committed to parliamentary democracy at a time when the system was clearly failing to work satisfactorily; it had no answer to the new set of problems suggested by the "end of laissez-faire," save a generalized belief in the superiority of socialism over capitalism. In particular, it had no clear and detailed concept of economic planning as a workable alternative to the market economy. Its propaganda thus tended to remain abstract —parliamentary politics apart, which in the nature of things could not inspire enthusiasm among either the masses or the intellectuals. In the 1920s these weaknesses had not mattered greatly. In the later 1930s, with economic crisis and political upheaval knocking at the door, they proved fatal.[12]

[11] Daniel Ligou, *Histoire du Socialisme en France 1871-1961* (Paris, 1962), pp. 331 ff.; 369; Lefranc, *Le mouvement socialiste,* pp. 250 ff. The elections of 1924 had already sounded a warning: in the Seine department the S.F.I.O. was beginning to trail behind the Communist party. The latter, then going through one of its periodical purges, was losing members (some of whom returned to the Socialists) and made a very feeble showing outside the capital. But in Paris it had established itself, and in the long run this was bound to be decisive, as the elections of 1928, 1932, and especially of 1936, were to show (though in 1932 the Communists, through sheer obstinacy and sectarianism, managed to lose 300,000 out of their previous million votes). It is irrelevant in this context that in 1928 and 1932 the Communists pursued a line hostile to the Socialists, while in 1936 the two parties worked together in the Popular Front. What counted was that the Communists were conquering the Paris region, and at the same time spreading into rural areas hitherto closed to their rivals. Lefranc, pp. 264, 275, 323 ff.

[12] Ligou, pp. 356 ff.; Lefranc, *Le mouvement socialiste,* 270 ff., 286 ff., 302 ff. The basic weakness was in economics: not one among the leaders (with the doubtful exception of Marcel Déat, who was expelled for his pains and later

These debates involved in the most direct manner the status of Marxist theory, notably its economic core. After 1945, with the belated triumph of the *planistes* and the adoption of a mixed economy, it became fashionable to equate socialism with planning. During the interwar period this had been far from being the case. State control and nationalization had indeed been adopted as official policy from 1919-20 onward, but the crisis of the 1930s unveiled a state of considerable intellectual confusion.[13] In the later 1920s the critics of official party policy had questioned the validity of Marxism on the grounds that capitalism appeared to be working quite satisfactorily. For a few years indeed the S.F.I.O. seemed to be going through a delayed repetition of the "Bernstein debate" among the German Social Democrats a generation earlier. Even the neo-Kantian critique

---

turned to fascism) really grasped what was at stake. There was a general failure to understand the nature of the crisis, and specifically the causes of the Social Democratic collapse in Germany. The brief Popular Front experience in 1936-37 did not give the few "planners" among the younger Socialists the opportunity they needed: their hour came in 1945, when even veterans like Blum were no longer able to maintain their sterile refusal to have anything to do with *planisme*. It is only fair to add that some of the party leaders, notably Jules Moch, did see the importance of working out concrete proposals for economic planning. Apart from Blum, the chief obstacle to a timely mental renovation came from ex-Guesdists like Bracke and Paul Faure, who could see nothing in all the talk about planning but a revival of the old reformism they had combated for so many years. For a detailed analysis of the Popular Front episode see Henry W. Ehrmann, *French Labor from Popular Front to Liberation* (New York, 1947).

[13] Ligou, pp. 348 ff. The discussion went back to the pre-1914 period, when Guesde characteristically accused the nationalizers of wanting to complement *L'État gendarme* by *L'État patron*. After 1918—in part under the influence of Thomas and others who had held office during the war—nationalization at last became respectable. By then Léon Jouhaux and the more moderate syndicalists believed in it too. Their conversion seems to have occurred under the impact of the war, when it struck them that "industrial mobilization" might well pave the way towards public control of the economy. See Jouhaux, p. 194, on the impression made upon the workers by the contrast between the military call-up and the continued prevalence of an uncontrolled economy, with scandalous profits being made while men were dying: "La classe ouvrière protesta. Elle demanda que la mobilisation industrielle se fît suivant les principes mêmes qui avaient présidé à la mobilisation militaire, c'est à dire que l'État prendrait en mains la direction effective de toutes les usines, disposerait des patrons aussi bien que des ouvriers, dirigerait également les services des transports." This was state socialism with a vengeance, in the name of patriotism and the war effort. One may doubt whether such sentiments were widespread beyond the narrow circle of union leaders associated with the war-time administration, but they certainly formed a bond between these influential reformists and those sections of the military and civilian bureaucracy who were beginning to wonder whether socialism might not be the answer to their particular problems.

of Marx's ethical relativism was warmed up again: characteristically by writers who had been influenced by the earlier German discussion. This form of revisionism attained its peak in 1929, only to be swallowed up by a new wave of Marxist pessimism and catastrophism in the early thirties. The trouble was that the Marxists proved unable to advance beyond generalities about the failure of capitalism, while their most vocal critics—from Henri de Man to Marcel Déat—tended to discredit themselves by flirting with various forms of authoritarianism, and in the end wound up on the Fascist side.[14] By the time the issue came to a head politically, in 1933-36, the enemy was at the gates, and democratic socialism was under attack as never before. A few years later, Blum himself was in prison, while a former colleague like Paul Faure supported the Vichy regime, and some of the dissident "neo-Socialists" of 1932-33—de Man's pupils, with the gifted but ambitious and unstable Déat at their head—had gone all the way to National Socialism. With them went a good many budding planners and technocrats who had despaired of democracy and the labor movement. The Socialist party seemed to be in ruins. Fortunately it revived under the impulsion of the Resistance movement, which not only restored the moral authority of the faithful remnant, but converted a significant number of its leaders to an outlook transcending the tedious debate over reform and revolution. Socialism at long last became synonymous with structural change, brought about more or less democratically under the impulsion of political collapse, and borne along by a current of national sentiment. In short, it ceased to be a distant aim and assumed the character of a constructive response to a challenge affecting the whole of society.[15]

[14] Henri de Man, *Au-delà du marxisme* (Paris, 1927); André Philip, *Henri de Man et la crise doctrinale du socialisme* (Paris, 1928). For a postwar view of the debate see Georges Lefranc, *Histoire des doctrines sociales dans l'Europe contemporaine* (Paris, 1960), pp. 240 ff. The opposing side was introduced to Austro-Marxist doctrine (Bauer, Adler, Hilferding) by the economist Lucien Laurat who hailed from Central Europe. On the whole his intervention had the effect of confirming the ex-Guesdists (Faure, Bracke, Zyromski), no less than the Jaurèsist Blum, in the fatalistic belief that capitalism could not be reformed and that its collapse would have to be awaited: this although Laurat himself was an early convert to planning.

[15] Ligou, pp. 515 ff.; also Blum. For the confusion of the late thirties, see Lefranc, *Le mouvement socialiste,* pp. 302 ff., 342 ff. Some of the intellectual revisionists of this stormy period rose to prominence after the war, notably Robert Marjolin and Pierre Dreyfus (leading planners and technocrats under

It might seem that in a brief account of the interwar years the central place belongs to the anti-Fascist coalition which came into being between 1934 and 1936, with the left-wing intellectuals forming a kind of unofficial bridge between the Socialists and the Communists.[16] But spectacular though these events undoubtedly were (as was the impact of the Spanish Civil War, which cannot be considered here) they impinged only very indirectly upon the central issues dividing the leaders and the theorists on both sides. When on February 12, 1934, Socialists and Communists in Paris demonstrated (not yet jointly) against the growing Fascist menace, the procession headed by Léon Blum included such prominent intellectuals as André Malraux and Jean-Richard Bloch:[17] the first a future Gaullist, the second shortly to become a leading Communist propagandist. Their anti-Fascism, like that of the left-wing intelligentsia in general, sprang in the main from sentiments held in common with non-socialist democrats. The existence of such an attitude—and of a numerous and influential intellectual stratum to back it up—was certainly important: apart from all else, it prefigured the coming Resistance movement. But in an analytical account of French Marxism, before and after 1945, this theme can only be noted in passing. There was to be a somewhat similar upsurge of feeling among a section of the intelligentsia in the late 1950s, in the form of a protest movement against the Algerian war; and once again it was this element which made it possible for Socialists and Communists to find, or feign, a common language. But such movements of opinion have their place in a general political history of French democracy. Anti-Fascism is not a distinctive political creed, any more than is anti-Stalinism. However estimable such sentiments may be, they are too vague and diffuse to lend themselves to analytical treatment.

---

both the Fourth Republic and the Gaullist regime), and the anthropologist Claude Lévi-Strauss. At one moment the revisionists of the 1930s also had the sympathy of Guy Mollet, but in the end he stayed with the majority (Lefranc, p. 311). That the issue throughout was not simply definable in terms of Marxism and non-Marxism is evident from the fact that some of the early "planners" grouped themselves around the "Combat marxiste" group animated by Laurat.

[16] For a lively account of this subject see David Caute, *Communism and the French Intellectuals, 1914-1960* (London, 1964), pp. 112 ff.

[17] Lefranc, *Le mouvement socialiste,* p. 315.

What needs to be considered rather is whether the failure of the Socialist party between 1920 and 1945 (not to mention earlier and later periods) pointed to a fundamental weakness both in its doctrine and in the human material on which it relied. The term "failure" must indeed be qualified: most of the Socialist program of 1919 (then regarded as utopian) was enacted after 1945, or even earlier during the brief Popular Front regime of 1936-37. The war-time Resistance movement largely grouped itself, if not around the remnant of the S.F.I.O., at any rate around a stratum of intellectuals and workers whose faith in socialism had survived the catastrophe of 1940. Gaullist legislation in 1944-45 comprised a good many traditional socialist themes, and the Fourth Republic (like the Fifth thereafter) consequently differed markedly from its bourgeois predecessor which had collapsed in 1940. In economics at least, socialism after 1945 was quietly rebaptized "planning," and in this new guise became respectable and even orthodox. A whole new stratum of technocrats and planners rose to power under the Fourth and Fifth Republics, on a wave of revulsion against market-economy stagnation and the political cesspool of the Third Republic. In all these respects socialism might be said to have conquered even its enemies, and to have been tacitly accepted as the basis of modern industrial society.

The real failure lay at a different level. One aspect of it may be said to have manifested itself already at the opening of the century, when Jaurès could not secure for his *Humanité* the 100,000 working-class readers who might have assured its independent existence.[18] Socialism and syndicalism offered no effective resistance either to the outbreak of war in 1914 or to the wave of chauvinism which engulfed the country. In 1919 the first postwar elections brought the Socialist party (as

[18] Lefranc, *Le mouvement socialiste,* pp. 143 ff. The paper had been launched in 1904 on a wave of *Dreyfusard* sentiment, with the support of leading Jewish intellectuals; the shareholders included the well-known sociologists Lévy-Bruhl and Marcel Mauss, and the archaeologist S. Reinach. The Dreyfus Affair in fact cured the Socialist movement of its endemic antisemitism, and thus made it possible for Blum to play a leading role in it after 1920. This was largely the heritage of Jaurès, and it was to have lasting consequences. But while it helped to spread Socialist sentiments among intellectuals of bourgeois origin, the *Affaire* did not convert many workers. The S.F.I.O. in 1906 had 35,000 organized members—out of a salaried population of over seven million. The unions numbered fewer than one million, of whom less than 300,000 were affiliated to the *Confédération Générale du Travail.*

yet unaffected by the Communist split) only a modest rise in voting strength compared with prewar (from 1,400,000 to 1,700,000) instead of the expected landslide. During the interwar period Socialists and Communists together never came within sight of winning an electoral majority, and when they briefly did so in 1945, they promptly lost it a year later. In any case the Communists had by then become the stronger force, so that the Socialists had to lean on Catholic elements further to the right in order to safeguard democracy from the Communist threat. Whatever else they may have wanted, the majority of the workers—and a fortiori of the other social groups—plainly did not want democratic socialism.[19]

These disappointments raise the question whether there was not from the start an element of utopianism in the idea of winning a majority of the working class—ultimately of the whole population—for a cause which in the end seems to have commended itself only to an elite of workers and intellectuals. In the particular circumstances of the Third Republic between 1870 and 1940, when democratic socialism took shape, this illusion was capped by another: the belief that parliament would remain the decisive arena of the political struggle. In fact the parliamentary system ceased to function in the 1930s, just when the Socialist party for the first time came within sight of gaining power (albeit with Communist help); and when a majority for radical economic change was briefly won in 1945-46, the national and international scene had been transformed by factors beyond the control of the Socialists, who were consequently deprived of the fruit of their belated victory. Wedged in between their bourgeois-democratic allies and a totalitarian Communist party, most of their energy in the postwar period was inevitably spent on a series of holding operations. Meantime the gradual planification and socialization of the economy proceeded in what seemed almost an automatic fashion, with a new

[19] For figures, see Kriegel, *Aux origines,* I 330; Ligou, p. 534. As already noted, the turning point in Socialist-Communist relations had come with the Popular Front elections in 1936, when the Socialists definitely lost control of the Paris region, and indeed lost votes altogether, while the Communists almost doubled their strength; Lefranc, *Le mouvement socialiste,* p. 323. For the rest one may say that the Popular Front's victory at the polls had come exactly four years too late. In 1932 a Blum government might have transformed France; in 1936 it was helpless and condemned to disaster.

technocratic, or managerial, stratum emerging to take the place of the old bourgeoisie, and without a noticeable growth in working-class activity other than of the most primitive kind. State control had finally been accepted; workers control was as far off as ever.[20]

In strictly political terms the Socialist party would seem to have missed its best chance in the early 1930s, when the Communists were still weak. By 1945 it was uncomfortably placed in an intermediate position between stronger Catholic and Communist rivals—a situation which has endured, though with the difference that in the 1960's the tripartite division into Gaullists, Communists, and left-center democratic groups, gave the S.F.I.O. a more pivotal position, without increasing its numerical strength. An opportunity to rejuvenate the party by fusing it with various left-wing Resistance groups was thrown away in 1945: the rank-and-file did not take kindly to the idea of admitting newcomers who had not worked their way up through the hierarchy.[21] Meanwhile the party's traditional anticlericalism continued to repel the Catholic workers who adhered to their own unions and supported the newly founded Christian Democratic movement, the *Mouvement Républicain Populaire* (MRP); while on the left, ground was still being lost to the Communists, especially in the larger cities. Socialist voting strength fell from 23 percent of the total in 1945 to 14 percent six years later—a proportion which has remained more or less constant. Membership seems in recent years to have oscillated around 100,000. Socialist influence by the 1960s was more marked in medium-sized towns than in the great centers, and stronger in rural communes than in the towns. The party and its affiliated

[20] For the manner in which this situation was interpreted by a Socialist leader who had taken a prominent share in converting his party to the doctrine of planning and nationalization, see Jules Moch, *Confrontations,* (Paris, 1952), especially pp. 365 ff.

[21] Williams, pp. 89 ff., 97 ff. An exception was provided by the Marseilles area, where new leaders who had come up through the Resistance—chiefly Gaston Defferre and Francis Leenhardt—took over the old (and rather corrupt) party organization and remodelled it very effectively, so that it became attractive to middle-class and white-collar voters and electorally successful. However, a price had to be paid: Defferre and Leenhardt stemmed from the Protestant bourgeoisie of Marseilles, and their leadership of the local organization inevitably tended to improve its moral tone at the cost of making it look rather less proletarian. Robert Bonnaud, "Qu'est-ce qu'un Defferre?" *Partisans,* No. 14, (Feb.-March, 1964).

union federation, *Force Ouvrière,* now tended to draw most of their support from civil servants, white-collar employees, and workers in small plants and secondary industries. Few prominent intellectuals in the 1960s were affiliated with the Socialist party, though many counted as supporters of its breakaway rival, the *Parti Socialiste Unifié* (PSU). Lastly, the S.F.I.O. no longer had a significant literature or journals that carried weight in the wider intellectual community.[22]

Since 1945 the S.F.I.O. has thus developed into a predominantly lower-middle-class and white-collar representation, though until 1951 manual workers were found to constitute one-third of its membership, and in some areas they were still dominant.[23] It is remarkably strong at the municipal level, less so in national affairs, though it has retained the loyalty of some very able and highly-placed civil servants who have played a key role in the various European organizations. During the political storms of the 1950s it was unable to accommodate itself permanently either to Mendès-France or to de Gaulle, though at times it supported both. It clung to parliamentary rule long after it had become obvious that presidential government was needed to provide a minimum of stability (and incidentally to make the planned economy work). In short, it gave the impression of having become conservative in the worst sense of the term.

As against this negative assessment it is arguable that in a modern industrial country with a growing tertiary sector, a movement committed to democratic socialism, and friendly to white-collar and professional people, still has an important part to play. The Socialist party is experienced in administration and provides a forum for

[22] This last statement requires a qualification: though the official *Revue Socialiste* is not inspiring, there have in recent years been new publications which reflect a species of modern-minded Socialist revisionism. It is also arguable that the spread of political clubs has indirectly helped to popularize Socialist concepts. An organization such as the *Club Jean Moulin* (named after a prominent Resistance leader) is not formally linked with the Socialist party—and indeed includes a good many high officials and technocrats who might be described as left-wing Gaullists—but in a general way it does represent a socialist attitude, notably in economic matters.

[23] Williams, p. 95, suggests that the preponderance of civil servants at the middle echelons has accentuated a tendency towards long service and "advancement in order of stupidity." It seems to be the case that the Socialist party finds it difficult to recruit young people; its youth organization has frequently been in trouble with the leadership. The party is also less attractive to women than both its Communist and its Catholic rivals.

democratic debate. It is strongly entrenched in the nationalized industries and represents an acceptable alternative to the Gaullist version of economic planning. It is both internationalist and pro-European, and can claim the merit of having anticipated the current forms of supranationalism. It may have passed its peak, but the same can perhaps be said of its rivals.

These considerations lead to the most important postwar change of all: the adoption of a planned economy, in which the major long-term decisions are made at the center. France having pioneered in this respect, the concept of planning had by the 1960s been adopted by the Gaullist regime, as well as by the left-center forces grouped around the official Socialist party, the dissident PSU, and the left wing of the Catholic movement. While the Communists were still holding out, the remainder of the Left had at last realized that the battle for structural change could be waged only on terrain common to the working class and the technical intelligentsia. In practice this meant that the Left could make itself heard nationally—apart from presidential elections—only if it adopted a coherent attitude on the kind of planning it wanted. If the Gaullist regime proposed a rapid growth rate for the second half of the 1960s, and at the same time failed to pursue the logic of its own choice, the Left could in all good faith advance the claim that socialist planning would promote an even faster rate of economic growth and a more equitable division of the national product. The official planning bodies themselves furnished ammunition for this line of approach, inasmuch as their ambitious programs came up against the residual opposition of those sectors of the administration—chiefly the Ministry of Finance—where economic liberalism had entrenched itself. In this manner, planning for faster growth presented itself as a national problem which the Left felt able to resolve.[24]

[24] On this subject see Alfred Sauvy and others, *Le Plan Sauvy* (Paris, 1960); Pierre Mendès-France, *La République moderne* (Paris, 1962); François Bloch-Lainé, *Pour une réforme de l'entreprise* (Paris, 1963); Raymond Boisdé, *Technocratie et démocratie* (Paris, 1964); Michel Crozier, *Le phénomène bureaucratique* (Paris, 1963); Serge Mallet, *La nouvelle classe ouvrière* (Paris, 1963); *Les paysans contre le passé* (Paris, 1962); André Gorz, *Stratégie ouvrière et néo-capitalisme* (Paris, 1964); Marc Paillet, *Gauche, année zéro* (Paris, 1964). See also the discussion of the Fifth Plan (for 1966-70) submitted by the official *Commissariat du Plan* in September 1964, notably the comments in the PSU

What this nation-wide discussion in the 1960s signified was that the prewar dispute over reformism had finally been overtaken by a drive for *structural changes democratically controlled:* a mental innovation of great significance, since it cut the ground from under the stale controversy over ministerialism. The question was no longer—as it had been from 1900 to 1940, i.e., from Jaurès and Millerand to Léon Blum—whether Socialists might participate in a bourgeois government, and on what terms, but rather, how they could promote social changes which were anyhow leading away from liberalism, but which might, if left unguarded, lead to an uncontrolled technocracy, or to a kind of corporate regime. In this perspective, socialism had ceased to be a distant utopia, without therefore becoming "politics" in the pejorative sense of the term. It was now seen as a possible answer to the problems of a mature and literate democracy: something quite different from the forced-draft modernization of backward countries, which was what socialism had come to signify in Eastern Europe or in the *tiers monde.*

If the spread of such pragmatic views through most strata of industrial society—though not among peasants and shopkeepers—presaged a political revival on the Left, after the torpor induced by the collapse of the Fourth Republic and the successful Gaullist solution of the Algerian problem, this process could be facilitated by a factor which had long marked French public life: the leftward orientation of a great majority of the teaching profession. For long the shock troops of the Republic in the struggle against reaction and obscurantism, the schoolteachers by the 1960s were for the most part not merely in the democratic but in the socialist camp—though for many of them the term "socialism" carried the prefix "Christian," or at least a tacit understanding that religious neutrality (*laicité*) need not preclude Christian beliefs and political adherence to the Catholic Left, rather than to the official Socialist party with its Marxist ideology.

---

weekly *France-Observateur* on October 1 and 8, 1964, where the problem of squaring the Left's commitment to a rapid growth rate—even beyond the official forecast of 5 percent annually—with the sectional claims of the unions, was for the first time brought plainly into the open. For a restatement of the traditional Marxist standpoint, in terms derived partly from the Trotskyist movement and partly from the Italian school founded by Antonio Gramsci, see Pierre Naville, *La classe ouvrière et le régime gaulliste* (Paris, 1964).

Against this background the long-term problem was not so much the pursuit of a "dialogue" with the Communists as the gradual construction of a platform on which democratic Socialists and Catholics could meet—and not only during election campaigns.

These considerations served to make French public life in the 1960s a very different affair from what it had been in the age of the Popular Front and the struggle against Fascism. They pointed in a direction already travelled by other West European democracies, away from the issues of the 1930s and 1940s. In this sense the Jaurèsian tradition might be said to have finally come into its own, though the struggle was no longer over the defense of the Republic. Economic and social issues had at last come to the forefront—even in France, where they had long been neglected in favor of political and ideological controversies. The planned and centralized society of the future was casting its shadow, and Socialists could feel that this at least was a subject they thoroughly understood.[25]

The Communist Party

The French Communist party (PCF) had the initial misfortune of having been founded at a moment when the revolutionary wave, which reached its peak in 1919, was plainly on the decline. Moreover, it had come into existence at a time when, to the Soviet government and the newly founded Communist International, Germany seemed a great deal more important than France. This situation lasted until

[25] For a candid assessment of the Socialist party's performance during the Fourth Republic see André Philip, *Pour un socialisme humaniste* (Paris, 1960). See also his *La Gauche: mythes et réalités* (Paris, 1964) in which the decline of classical liberalism, and the parallel rise of technocracy in its Gaullist form, are frankly faced; see especially pp. 171 ff. Himself a prominent figure in post-war political life and for years one of his party's ablest representatives, Philip had the advantage of being a professional economist as well as a parliamentarian. He was thus well placed to realize that the fall of the Fourth Republic in 1958 was largely a consequence of that demagogic *politique de facilité* with which the Socialists had become prominently associated, and which culminated in the 1956-58 combination of financial inflation with a ruinous and senseless colonial war. Though he was expelled for his pains, one may reasonably suppose that Philip—like Mendès-France, whose criticism of the Fourth Republic proceeded from a similar analysis of its weaknesses—has left his mark upon Socialist thinking; not least by stating plainly that the parliamentary system has ceased to function.

the catastrophe of 1933, when German Communism crumbled under the National Socialist onslaught, while at the same time France once more took its place on the international chessboard as a counterweight to a resurgent Germany.[26]

Until then the French on the whole occupied a secondary position within world Communism. France and its labor movement became really important to Moscow only from 1934 onward, and then in the context of an international situation which required an abrupt change of orientation from "ultra-Left" sectarianism to Popular Front tactics. By then the internal Bolshevization of the PCF—which *inter alia* entailed the replacement of intellectuals by functionaries of working-class origin, who could be more easily manipulated and were less inclined to ask awkward questions—had proceeded to the point where the leadership could impose a complete change of "line" almost overnight. Paradoxically, the party benefited from its relative weakness between 1919 and 1934 when its character took shape. It was indeed duly Bolshevized and Stalinized—especially from 1924 onward, when Trotsky's adherents were removed—but it was never as thoroughly wrecked as the German party on whom the most disastrous experiments were practiced by Moscow during those years.[27]

[26] On this subject see Gérard Walter, *Histoire du parti communiste français* (Paris, 1948); Jacques Fauvet, *Histoire du parti communiste français, I, 1917-1939* (Paris, 1964); Jules Humbert-Droz, *L'Oeuil de Moscou à Paris* (Paris, 1964). Humbert-Droz was the official Comintern representative in Paris during the 1920s, and his papers shed light on the internal working of the mechanism. Auguste Lecoeur, *Le Partisan* (Paris, 1963) and *L'Autocritique attendue* (Paris, 1955) (by the CP's former deputy secretary-general in charge of organization) give a fascinating picture of party life seen by a veteran *militant*. The official *Histoire du parti communiste français* (*manuel*) (1964), notwithstanding its title, is not a history, but a mere compilation of texts and authoritative glosses. It has at least the merit of giving a brief *résumé* of the party line, as seen by the Thorezian bureaucracy. The anonymous *Histoire du parti communiste français* (Paris, 1962-65), published by a group of oppositional functionaries, is incomplete, but can serve as a corrective to official legends. The best account of the party's inception in 1920 is to be found in Kriegel, *Aux origines,* a monumental work of documented research written from an independent socialist standpoint. The author (formerly known under her party name as Annie Besse) had access to unpublished material. For an amusing account of her attitudes during the Stalinist period see Edgar Morin, *Autocritique* (Paris, 1959), pp. 167-68.

[27] E. H. Carr, *Socialism in One Country 1924-1926* (London, 1964), Vol. III, part I, pp. 95 ff., 311 ff., and *passim*. Much of the early demoralization of the German Communist party, the KPD, stemmed from the fact that the Russians

The French Communists were not indeed as fortunate as their Italian comrades, who were driven underground or into exile by Fascist persecution, and thus to some degree escaped the worst consequences of Stalinization.[28] But they were not quite as unlucky as the Germans. The latter in 1933 paid for their subservience to Moscow, and their blind adherence to the official line, with a political collapse so total that it left them permanently shattered, traumatized, and unable to offer any further resistance to Stalinization. In France, too, by the 1930s the sergeants had taken over from the officers, but they were given time to learn their job, and in 1934-36 the anti-Fascist wave refloated them, notably on the intellectual and fellow-traveling side. In Germany, where National Socialism in 1933 became the national creed, and where the bulk of the educated class was traditionally hostile even to liberal democracy—let alone Marxism—a breakthrough of this kind had failed to materialize in the 1920s, when political conditions were for once favorable.

In general one may say that the basic problem of all European Communist parties—how to wed the myth of the October Revolution to the traditions of the European labor movement—came nearer a solution in France than elsewhere. It was, of course, powerfully assisted by the ability of the Communists to graft their ideology onto the still living stem of Jacobinism: not least among intellectuals who tended to see the Soviet regime as the continuation of the French Revolution.[29] Yet while this background accounts for the fact that the French Communist party was able from the start to relate itself

---

treated it as a pawn in their relations with the German government and the Reichswehr, notably in regard to Poland and the campaign against the Treaty of Versailles. The French CP was not important enough to be allotted a similar role until the 1930s.

[28] Whence *inter alia* the emergence of a theorist like Antonio Gramsci, who managed to retain his original faith because Mussolini's prisons shielded him from Soviet reality (not to mention the virtual certainty that he would have been liquidated in the Stalinist purges).

[29] A good recent example of this is furnished by Albert Soboul's entirely orthodox (in the Leninist sense) yet quite scholarly *Histoire de la révolution française* (Paris, 1962); see also *Babeuf et les problèmes du babouvisme,* ed. by Albert Soboul (Paris, 1963): a collection of essays presented at an international conference in Stockholm in 1960, when the Babouvist roots of Communism were sympathetically examined at some length by writers from a number of countries, not all of them Communists.

to an important element of the national tradition—and therewith to the *Université* as the guardian of this tradition—it does not explain how and why the party in the later 1930s managed to overcome its selfimposed political isolation. Numerically and tactically, the PCF down to 1934 counted for very little. Its sectarianism had almost wrecked it as an electoral force, though the inner core held together and the grip on the Paris area—decisive in the long run—remained unbroken. It took the anti-Fascist coalition of 1934-36 to turn it into a mass movement.[30]

These fluctuations responded to a complex set of pressures, some of them dating back to the fact that the split of 1920 had been engineered in the expectation of a revolutionary upheaval which never materialized. Like other Communist parties in Western Europe, the French CP had to adapt itself to a postrevolutionary situation, when at first it had imagined itself to be in a prerevolutionary one. This accounts for the fact that the wave of enthusiasm which swept the majority at Tours into the Third International receded very quickly, so that by the late 1920s it almost looked as though the CP was about to dwindle into a sect. Somehow this never quite happened; but the reverse—growth into a movement embracing the entire organized working class—did not occur either, not even after 1945, when conditions were uniquely favorable. The party did in the end become a mass movement, but one that never came within sight of holding effective power. In consequence it eventually began to reproduce all the old internal contradictions of its Socialist rival, down to the quarrel over parliamentarism and the peaceful acquisition of political power.[31]

[30] Williams, p. 71; Walter, pp. 232 ff.; Ehrmann. As an electoral force the CP was severely weakened by its anti-Socialist tactics between 1928 and 1932: it lost 40 percent of its vote on the second ballot in 1928, and some 300,000 votes out of its former million in 1932, when its parliamentary strength fell to a mere ten (and would have fallen to less but for Socialist unwillingness to retaliate). Meanwhile membership went down from 120,000 in 1921 to 56,000 in 1928 and 32,000 in 1932. However, all this did not destroy the party's ability to expand very rapidly from a narrow base when the tide turned in 1934.

[31] Kriegel, *Aux origines,* II, 633, makes the point that Marcel Cachin and L. O. Frossard, who at Tours carried the majority into the Communist camp (though Frossard did not stay long), did not really share the Bolshevik perspective of an imminent world revolution—partly from indifference to theoretical concepts, partly from inbred skepticism. At the same time they and others quite genuinely believed that the impetus given by the Russian Revolution would inject a fresh dynamic into the French workers movement. The Thorezian doctrine and practice of the early 1930s was a good deal more simplistic, but then

Added to this fundamental miscalculation there was the simple fact that down to 1934 the party had failed to overtake the Socialists in elections held at the national level, in the control of the unions, or in the estimation of floating elements stemming from the intelligentsia. The reflux after Tours, and the various internal purges, swept a good many radical elements back into the S.F.I.O., where they linked up with the old Marxist rump. It would have been difficult to say which of the two parties was more resolutely attached to Marxism—even Léon Blum related himself to Marx as well as to Jaurès. The novelty lay in the Leninist concept of a cadre organization directing a more or less inchoate mass of supporters; but while this doctrine was the CP's real strength, and the secret of its survival after the electoral setbacks of 1928 and 1932, it could not be openly proclaimed. The situation therefore remained fluid for some years. More resolute leadership, and the avoidance of splits which eliminated many of the modern-minded *planiste* elements, might in the 1930s have given the Socialists the edge over their rivals. In the event the PCF used the anti-Fascist coalition of 1934-36 to get out of its isolation and turn itself into a mass movement, so that by 1940 it had clearly outdistanced its rival.[32]

Thorez had no education beyond that of the average Communist *militant*. For the misunderstanding of the Russian situation which made veteran Syndicalists treat the "Soviet dictatorship" as the realization of their pre-1914 utopia of proletarian revolution, by way of the general strike and workers control in industry, see *ibid.*, I, 276-81, 285 ff. The "ultra-Left"—i.e., the genuine believers in workers democracy, including the German splinter group known as the KAPD, the Dutch "Tribunists," and Bordiga's faction in Italy—only saw the light after the suppression of the Kronstadt revolt in 1921.

[32] In terms of Comintern history, the sudden reversal of 1934 related back to the earlier "united front" strategy inaugurated by Lenin and Radek in 1921; see Jane Degras, "United Front Tactics in the Comintern in 1921-1928," and Richard Lowenthal, "The Bolshevisation of the Spartacus League," in *St. Antony's Papers, No. 9, International Communism,* ed. David Footman (London, 1961). For the general background to the 1934 turnabout, see Franz Borkenau, *The Communist International* (London, 1938), pp. 386 ff.; for the Popular Front, Ehrmann. The 1936 elections, when the Communists almost doubled their vote, showed how important it had been for them to break with their previous strategy. But the event also demonstrated that, once the word was given, the party could expand very rapidly and mobilize wide support. This was also shown during the 1936 wave of sit-down strikes which caught the leadership by surprise: Lecoeur, *Le Partisan,* p. 54. The manner in which Socialist-led and Communist-led union movements were reunified after 1934 under Communist pressure, and largely to the CP's advantage, is described by Ehrmann, pp. 30 ff. For the intellectual fringe, see Caute, pp. 112 ff.; for the political maneuvers preceding the 1934 "unity of action" pact with the Socialists and Radicals, see Fauvet, pp. 132 ff.

If pacifism was the CP's chief attraction for both workers and intellectuals in the war-weary 1920s, and anti-Fascism in the crisis-ridden 1930s, Stalinism has been its main handicap in recent years. This subject will be considered later, in connection with the general problem of Soviet Marxism and its implantation in France. Here it should briefly be noted that the anti-Stalinist reaction was very late in coming and remained half-hearted even after it had become official in the USSR. Prior to 1945, and a fortiori before the outbreak of war in 1939 (when the Soviet-German pact produced a brief internal upheaval) Stalin's leadership within the USSR was not an issue that concerned the average *militant,* and it was not an important issue for the majority of fellow travelers, notwithstanding the 1936-38 Moscow trials. The latter alienated only a minority of intellectuals, and hardly any workers. They may even have confirmed the average *militant* in his faith that the Soviet leadership was reliably Robespierrist, i.e., terrorist. This conviction was certainly held by the group around Thorez, both before and after the war. Dissident Communists—most of whom had already departed during the 1920s—tended to form sectarian minority groups, or to join the S.F.I.O., where they linked up with Socialist left-wingers and created trouble for the established leadership. At no stage during the 1930s—after the 1934 turnabout, which had in part been precipitated by important defections at the top—did they constitute a threat to the PCF leadership.[33]

Numerically, the most sensational gains were made during the Popular Front period, and then again at the end of the war in 1945, when the party's somewhat belated adherence to the Resistance paid off in a sudden rush to join it.[34] At the same time there was a gradual

[33] Fauvet; Walter; for the 1922-28 period see Humbert-Droz. The Trotskyist group around Souvarine, which included the old Syndicalists behind Monatte and Rosmer, had been expelled in 1924. In the later 1920s the party's tendency towards "infantile leftism" was to alarm the Comintern direction, though to judge from Humbert-Droz's correspondence, its leaders were also thought to err on occasion through excessive concern for "bourgeois legality." In the light of later events it is amusing to find Ercoli-Togliatti in 1927 expressing alarm and indignation over the French CP's "parliamentary cretinism"; Humbert-Droz, pp. 255-56.

[34] Williams, p. 77. Between 1934 and 1937, CP membership rose sensationally from 50,000 to 340,000; after a collapse in 1939-40, there was another sharp rise to an estimated 400,000 at the Liberation. In 1946 a figure of one million adherents was claimed, but this was an exaggeration; the claimed 1954 figure of

strengthening of the CP's hold over the *Confédération Générale du Travail,* though this had to be paid for in 1948-49, when the Socialist-led *Force Ouvrière* split off. If a generalization can be risked, the CP in recent years has been strongest in three areas: the Paris region, the industrial basin along the Belgian frontier (where, however, Socialist strength remains considerable), and the more backward rural departments of the South and Center, where the party's following includes prosperous farmers, as well as smallholders and sharecroppers. In these latter regions the CP has plainly benefited from the enduring strength of the anticlerical tradition, as well as from its demagogic resistance to the social transformation in agriculture. It remains comparatively weak among technicians, white-collar workers, and civil servants, who in general seem to prefer the Socialists, though its fellow-travelling penumbra includes large numbers of elementary school teachers (but few teachers in higher institutions of learning, where intellectual standards are more demanding and Marxism-Leninism in its orthodox form encounters resistance).[35]

The fundamental problem throughout these years remained that of aligning the party's strategy upon the defense of the USSR, a criterion which from 1924 onward had become the prime touchstone of Communist loyalty. The growing favor which the French CP enjoyed in Moscow—notably after Thorez and his group had taken over the leadership around 1930—stemmed largely from its unflinching readiness to execute major turnabouts whenever the interest of the USSR appeared to demand it. The two most dramatic occasions arose in

over half a million may also have been inflated by as much as 50 percent. Since the advent of the Fifth Republic in 1958, the true figure has probably been below 300,000, though more is claimed. The electoral vote (automatically doubled by the postwar enfranchisement of women) rose to over five million in October 1945 (when the Socialists obtained 4,600,000), and by another half million a year later; it fell back a little in 1951, rose once more to 5,600,000 in 1956, and slumped to less than four million with the advent of de Gaulle in 1958—a level only slightly exceeded in the 1962 elections following the termination of the Algerian war.

[35] Williams, pp. 78 ff.; Maurice Duverger, *Les partis politiques* (Paris, 1961); Pierre Fougeyrollas, *La conscience politique dans la France contemporaine* (Paris, 1963), pp. 38 ff. It has never been easy to discover why so many Frenchmen vote for the CP. The prosperous peasants of the Gard department probably do so because as Protestants they are traditionally hostile to their Catholic neighbors; Stuart R. Schram, *Protestantism and Politics in France* (Alençon, 1954), pp. 164 ff.

1934, with the offer to the Socialists (and later to the Radicals) to form a common front against Fascism, and in 1939, when the CP leadership not only reversed its prowar attitude overnight, but deliberately incurred governmental repression by acclaiming the Soviet-German pact and denouncing France's entry into the war. On these and on lesser occasions, the task of striking a balance between the overall strategy, and the tactical requirements imposed by the internal French situation, was formally left to the French CP leadership; in practice it was dictated by the International, in other words by the Soviet government.[36]

Both the 1934 turnabout and its temporary reversal in 1939 were to have lasting consequences transcending the calculations of the CP leadership and the maneuvers of the Comintern. The 1934 change of line made it possible to abandon the sectarianism imposed upon the party from its beginnings by the mentality of the early *militants* and their determination to have no truck with "social traitors." Patriotism became once more fashionable, and the Jaurèsian vocabulary was revived—though it was tacitly understood among the inner leadership circle that the only fatherland worth defending was the "workers fatherland" constituted by the USSR. When this conviction was put to the test in 1939 by the Stalin-Hitler pact, the French CP responded—after very brief initial hesitations—in a manner calculated to gratify both the Comintern (or what was left of it) and the Soviet leaders. A year later the German victory in 1940 became the occasion for an attempt on the part of the CP leadership—clearly at Soviet instigation—to strike a bargaining position vis-à-vis the German occupants,

[36] Walter, pp. 125 ff., 194 ff., gives the official CP line on this subject without mentioning the CP's subordination to Moscow's tactical requirements. Humbert-Droz, pp. 187 ff., documents this for the Ruhr conflict in 1923, when the Comintern had the difficult task of coordinating the activities of the German and French parties. But Soviet supervision also extended to details during less troubled periods. Thus, when in 1928 the then prevailing "class against class" electoral strategy failed to pay off during the first round of the French parliamentary elections, there were agitated sessions in Moscow—attended by Stalin and Bukharin in person—in the interval between the first and second ballot, to consider the possibility of a tactical change. On this occasion Stalin, according to Humbert-Droz, exclaimed "The Soviet Union cannot admit that there should be no Communists in the French Chamber!" Similarly, the 1934 turnabout was directly imposed by Moscow in view of the growing German threat after Hitler's seizure of power, though its timing was probably influenced by the defection of Jacques Doriot from the leadership of the PCF.

while at the same time the Resistance movement was denounced as an imperialist trap, and de Gaulle as a British agent.[37]

For obvious reasons the party's record during the war years became an extremely sensitive subject after 1945, and this despite the fact that many people were willing to forgive the Communists their antiwar stand in 1939. The crucial episodes related to the 1940-41 period, when Communist propaganda in occupied France extolled the Soviet-German alliance, and denounced both the democratic politicians later tried by the Pétain government and the Gaullist or Socialist resistance groups which were then springing up all over France. This line predictably came to an end when Hitler invaded the USSR in June 1941. Until then Communist propaganda was often difficult to distinguish from the German article.[38] After the war, attempts were made to rewrite the record; in particular it was asserted that as early as July 10, 1940, the CP had issued a clandestine tract to the French people calling for resistance to capitulation and the Vichy regime. The fact is that no such appeal was published until the German attack on the USSR, and that the "document" furnished by the PCF in 1947 to sustain its claims was fraudulent. The veritable CP manifesto circulated in August (not July) 1940 contained no condemnation whatever either of the Germans or the Pétain regime, but had much to say about the responsibility of "warmongers" such as Blum and Mandel. As for de Gaulle, he was until 1941 consistently described in Communist

[37] A. Rossi (Angelo Tasca), *Les Communistes français pendant la drôle de guerre* (Paris, 1951); see also the (unofficial and anonymous) *Histoire du parti communiste français,* especially Vol. II, pp. 7 ff.; for details, also Ehrmann, pp. 139 ff. For the effect on Communist and fellow-traveling intellectuals see Caute, pp. 137 ff. For the official Communist view of the Popular Front era and its close in 1939 see Walter, pp. 274 ff.; 341 ff.

[38] Cf. "Les Communistes et la Résistance," in *Contrat Social,* VIII, No. 4 (Paris, July-August, 1964); for fuller documentation see Rossi, *Les Communistes français,* and *Physiologie du parti communiste français* (Paris, 1948), also *Le Pacte Germano-Soviétique. L'histoire et le mythe* (Paris, 1954). It is notorious that immediately after the fall of Paris, in June 1940, the CP leadership approached the German occupying authorities with a request to permit the legal appearance of *L'Humanité.* Former Communist deputies offered in 1940 to testify against Blum, Daladier, Reynaud and Mandel at the trial then in preparation (it was not actually held until 1942, by which time the situation had changed), and Thorez published an abusive attack on Blum which employed the terminology then made familiar by the Germans; *Contrat Social,* VIII, 261.

literature as an agent of the City of London, or of "British imperialism" in general.[39]

With the belated change-over to patriotism, it became important after the war to inflate the actual role of the Communists in the Resistance between 1941 and 1944. This had been considerable, but not as large as was subsequently claimed. Their organization was, of course, more highly centralized than that of the Socialists, who controlled only one major Resistance network, *Libération-Nord,* and for the rest worked jointly with nonsocialist groups. The Communist effort was more spectacular, not least in the "purge" of collaborators which followed the Allied landings. For evident psychological reasons, Communist losses were grossly exaggerated after the war. Perhaps to compensate for the fact that Thorez had been obliged to sit out the war years in Moscow,[40] an attempt was made to represent the Communist party as the main backbone of armed resistance to the German occupation.[41]

[39] For the fabricated "document" published in *L'Humanité,* (December 12, 1947), and the real text of the pamphlet circulated by the CP in August 1940 see *France-Observateur* (June 18 and 25, 1964). In fairness it should be noted that the Communist party had been outlawed in the autumn of 1939 and a number of its parliamentary deputies sent to prison. In January 1940, those Communist deputies who had been exempt from the first wave of arrests, because they had obeyed the military call-up, were formally deprived of their parliamentary status when they tried to attend the session of the Chamber; exceptions were made only in favor of those who broke with the party. On this occasion, Frossard—who in 1920 had led the pro-Communist majority at Tours into the Third International—spoke for the Socialists in urging that Stalinism (as distinct from Communism in general) be not only outlawed but branded as treason and rooted out. This atmosphere of mutual hatred explains, if it does not excuse, the Communist behavior in the summer of 1940. For details see Rossi, *Physiologie du parti communiste français,* pp. 25 ff., 61 ff., 90 ff.

[40] A circumstance not alluded to, or mentioned with polite embarrassment, on the occasion of his death in July 1964, when de Gaulle issued an official message of condolence on the demise of his ex-Minister in the Provisional Government of 1945. When the National Assembly met on October 3, 1964, its Gaullist president, M. Chaban-Delmas, in a lengthy ritual eulogy of the deceased, remarked delicately that in choosing between France and the Soviet Union in 1939, Thorez had only followed his Communist conscience, and that for the rest, in seeking refuge in the USSR, he had safeguarded not so much his person as the Secretary-General of the Communist party; *Le Monde* (October 4-5, 1964). Technically, Thorez had since October 1939 been a deserter from the French army. His return to France in November 1944 was part of an arrangement concluded between de Gaulle and Stalin; Lecoeur, *Le Partisan,* pp. 200 ff.

[41] Whence the fraudulent assertion that the *parti des fusillées* had sacrificed 75,000 of its followers on the altar of patriotism: a claim first made among the general confusion of August 1944, when the number of Parisians executed

The sequel was to show that none of this really mattered to the hard-core *militants* whose spiritual fatherland was the USSR. Most of them stayed loyal in 1939, the more so since the party's return to antiwar propaganda responded to the quasi-anarchist, antigovernmental, and antimilitarist mood from which the Communist movement had originally arisen in 1919-20. If the patriotic and anti-Fascist line of 1934-38 had appealed to the masses—and to liberal intellectuals stirred by the Spanish Civil War—the return to sectarianism in 1939-40 did not shock the *cadres*. The war was unpopular from the start, and after the military collapse of 1940 it was an open question whether Thorez and Duclos might not be overtaken by their erstwhile colleague Jacques Doriot, who had moved from Stalinism to the rival totalitarian camp.[42]

The party in fact had a choice between several lines of conduct: it could either be patriotic and democratic, or pacifist and pseudo-revolutionary, depending on circumstances. Similarly, it could preach class against class intransigence, or enter into tactical alliances, while reserving the opportunity to make an outright bid for power. In the decade between 1934 and 1944 these alternatives were pursued in accordance with the overriding purpose of aiding the USSR, and the subordinate aim of expanding the party's following and seizing whatever positions could be secured through Popular Front or Resistance alignments. Nonetheless, it is evident that by the end of this period it had become difficult to execute major tactical changes in a manner which made sense both to the party functionaries and to the masses,

---

by the Germans was fantastically placed at this figure; A. Dansette, *Histoire de la libération de Paris* (Paris, 1946). The actual figure of executions for the whole of France during the war, furnished by the French authorities at the Nuremberg trial, was 29,660 (*Agence France Presse,* September 12, 1947), of whom perhaps one third or one quarter may have been adherents of Communist groups, the great majority belonging to other Resistance movements.

[42] For the attitude of the *militants* see Lecoeur, *Le Partisan,* pp. 105 ff., 135 ff.; for Doriot see Walter, pp. 265 ff.; Fauvet, pp. 125 ff., 138 ff., and *passim*. The former Politbureau member was potentially as dangerous as Mussolini had once been to his Italian ex-comrades. His *Parti populaire français* (founded in 1936) had a better claim to the "Fascist" label than either the dissident neo-Socialists of 1933 or the right-wing Leaguers who still believed in the outdated nationalism of Maurras and the *Action française*. After 1939 Doriot openly banked on a German victory, while the CP leaders were induced to gamble on the permanence of the Soviet-German alliance. Both were mistaken, but it took Hitler's attack on the USSR, and still more the German military defeat, to decide the competition between them.

while at the same time keeping the support of the intellectuals. The latter constantly tended to mistake tactical slogans for declarations of principle, and thus became disheartened when the party line failed to conform to their notions. The working-class *militants* were less troublesome, but potentially more dangerous. Ultimately everything depended on them, and the leadership had to inculcate habits of military command and blind obedience for fear of encouraging open discussion and the spread of doubt. After 1944 the growth of mass support, and the partial integration of the CP into the national community, in consequence of the Resistance experience, had the additional effect of limiting its freedom of maneuver, since it now became important to maintain these positions, which would be endangered by a renewed affront to popular or national sentiment. Military discipline was ineffective when applied to nonmembers. On Leninist principles this should not have mattered, but a mass movement operating in a democracy cannot in the long run remain Leninist, however hierarchical its organizational structure, and however determined the leadership to impose its policies from the top downward. A balance had to be struck, and from 1945 onward it became evident that the official line could no longer satisfy those *militants* who took Leninism seriously.[43]

Trouble with the intellectuals had been endemic since the early years. The party had come into being in 1919-20 on a wave of antiwar sentiment powerfully reinforced by the pre-1914 tradition of antimilitarism. For intellectuals of bourgeois origin (and how many were not?) Communism at first was almost synonymous with pacifism. After all, had not Lenin broken with the Second International on the issue of resistance to the war? "Zimmerwald" meant something even to people who deplored the Bolshevik seizure of power. This pacifist sentiment, powerfully expressed by prominent writers like Anatole France, Romain Rolland, and Henri Barbusse, prepared the ground for the revolutionary antimilitarism of Raymond Lefebvre and Paul Vaillant-Couturier: both among the earliest adherents to the Third Interna-

[43] Lecoeur, *L'Autocritique attendue,* pp. 24 ff. The anonymous *Histoire du parti communiste français* of 1962-65 is particularly bitter about the Thorezian line in 1944-45, when the Communists entered the government and subordinated everything to the war effort; in Vol. II, especially pp. 265 ff.; the authors hint that the matter was probably settled by Stalin, in accordance with his estimate of the Soviet Union's global interests. For the role of the anti-Fascist intellectuals after 1933 see Fauvet, pp. 261 ff.; for their share in the Resistance see Caute, pp. 147 ff. and Morin, pp. 27 ff.

tional. From 1919 onward the pacifist stream merged with the Communist current. A majority of intellectuals came to the CP by way of antiwar sentiment, at any rate until the middle thirties, when anti-Fascism became the dominant concern. The party in turn made use of pacifist slogans so far as the "defense of the USSR" allowed. It even risked official persecution in the mid-twenties for the sake of its anti-colonial campaign, which condemned military ventures in Morocco and elsewhere in terms derived from a pre-Leninist tradition of hostility to overseas conquests.[44]

At a deeper level the problem was rendered insoluble by the contradiction between the party's rationalist pathos and the oppressive Stalinist outlook it was obliged to defend. There is no need to question the sincerity of the pathos, especially in the case of authentic working-class leaders such as Thorez or Duclos.[45] It was quite in order, and quite in accordance with tradition, for Jacques Duclos in 1938 to extol Galileo, Copernicus and Pasteur as liberators of the human spirit.[46] The entire French Left had been brought up on the Enlightenment, and Communist *militants* were perhaps more profoundly and naively attached to it than intellectuals like Aragon who had graduated to Communism by way of surrealism.[47] In the 1920s these differences in upbringing merely lent additional color and interest to the scene.

[44] Fauvet, pp. 52 ff., 98 ff.; Caute, pp. 59 ff. For Raymond Lefebvre see Kriegel, *Aux origines* II, 767 ff. The pure pacifists of bourgeois origin mostly did not stay long, but many remained sympathizers. See Fauvet, pp. 262 ff. for the role of Gide and Rolland; for the discomfiture of the liberal intellectuals after 1939 see Caute, pp. 137 ff. For the post-1945 atmosphere see Morin. Prominent recruits lost in 1939-40 included Sartre's school friend Paul Nizan, perhaps the most gifted of the group who adhered to the party in the 1920s. After he had broken with the CP over the Hitler-Stalin pact (and joined the ranks to be killed at Dunkirk), his former comrades spread the tale that he had been a police informer: a calumny repeated by Aragon as late as 1949 in his unreadable novel *Les Communistes;* Caute, p. 139.

[45] Maurice Thorez, "Le Front Populaire et l'essor culturel," in *Le parti communiste français, la culture et les intellectuels* (Paris, 1962). Writing in 1937, the party leader not only celebrated the international renown of Romain Rolland, but even hailed the award of prizes to French films (including an authentic masterpiece, Jean Renoir's *La Grande Illusion)* at the Venice *Biennale.*

[46] *Ibid.*, pp. 47 ff.; cf. Marcel Cachin, in *ibid.*, p. 285; "Nous sommes les fils des Encyclopédistes. Nous restons fidèles à leurs conceptions matérialistes, à leur souci du progrès matériel et moral de l'homme."

[47] Fauvet, pp. 98 ff. The whole group joined in 1927, led by André Breton who later broke with the party: in Aragon's eyes an expression of that anarchic "individualism" which it was the mission of the Communist party to root out. The atmosphere is well described by Caute, pp. 93 ff.

Matters changed in the following decade, with the progressive hardening of the Soviet regime, and came to a head after 1945, when Stalinism was seen to represent as great a menace to traditional Western liberties as Fascism had ever done. By the 1950s the Communist party, in France as elsewhere, had plainly taken on the features of a monolithic organization whose rigid discipline, founded on a complex system of esoteric "truths," suggested an unconscious imitation of the hated Roman Church. The party's hieratic language, its obsession with heresy, and the tone of its polemics, all bore the imprint of a Catholic culture, with the additional disadvantage of crudities stemming from the primitive mentality of its Soviet guides and the intolerant narrowness of its own *militants*. Further development along these lines would have resulted in complete isolation. The party, in fact, during these years lost its best minds, while others stayed on in the hope that matters would gradually improve: as indeed they did after the mid-1950s, though even by the 1960s the intellectual climate was still perceptibly less liberal than in the Italian Communist party.[48]

The theoretical side of these debates will be examined presently. Here it remains to single out the main cause of the trouble as it affected the CP leaders from the political angle, which after all was what concerned them most: the failure to come to terms with the intellectuals. Ultimately this went back to the misunderstanding of the Russian Revolution as a proletarian rising, when in fact the Bolshevik party had from the start been a faction, or fraction, of the Russian revolu-

[48] Caute, pp. 197 ff. For the human factor underlying one of the significant differences between the French and the Italian situation see Neil McInnes, "Antonio Gramsci," in *Survey* No. 53, (London, October, 1964). For the general atmosphere of the Stalin era, see Morin, pp. 83 ff. For the official cultural doctrine of these years see Laurent Casanova, *Le Parti communiste, les intellectuels, et la nation* (Paris, 1951). As was to be expected, Casanova was subsequently made a scapegoat for the party's cultural Zhdanovism. The post-1945 euphoria, when for some years it seemed to the Communists that they had won the moral leadership of at least a significant part of the nation, is perhaps best expressed in the first part of Louis Aragon's two-volume essay collection, *L'Homme Communiste* (Paris, 1946, 1953); see also Roger Garaudy, *Le Communisme et la renaissance de la culture française* (Paris, 1945). Eighteen years later, Garaudy had arrived at a rather more sophisticated formulation of his standpoint; see his *Qu'est-ce que la morale marxiste?* (Paris, 1963), in which the party's official philosopher attempted a restatement of Marxism-Leninism in suitably academic terms, and with a few polite bows in the direction of the Vatican and the writings of Teilhard de Chardin.

tionary intelligentsia, and the upheaval it led was subconsciously spurred by a drive to turn Russia into a modern industrial country. Socialism as a substitute for capitalism was not an issue in France, where the labor movement was a reality, so that it was impossible to make *this* aspect of Leninism rhyme with French experience. The resulting gap between ideology and actuality was veiled by a rhetoric which employed the arsenal of Jacobin-Blanquist concepts (themselves pre-Marxist and therefore useless in the long run). If the party wanted to acclimatize Marxism, it had to go back to the real Marx, which in the end it did (though rather halfheartedly) in the 1960s. In the meantime, however, there was the unsolved problem of making communism plausible at least to the technical intelligentsia. This group already formed the core of the Soviet party, and was acquiring importance in a France about to become a major industrial country. The traditional revolutionary rhetoric, which had charmed surrealist poets and painters in the 1920s, made little appeal to a new stratum that did not regard itself as part of either the bourgeoisie or the working class. Yet from the party's standpoint it represented a section of the middle class, which had to be won over without compromising the proletarian class character of the CP: an enterprise in which the S.F.I.O. had already failed. When by the 1960s the problem was at last perceived, it was posed in a manner suggesting an underlying embarrassment: the technical intelligentsia was urged to choose between the "monopolies" (supposedly represented by the Gaullist regime) and the working class, when in reality its orientation pushed it away from the latter—at any rate so long as the CP could be regarded as its main representative.[49]

[49] Léo Figuères, ed., in *Le parti communiste français, la culture, et les intellectuels* (Paris, 1962), pp. 8 ff., where "the intellectuals" are apostrophized in a rhetoric derived from the Jaurèsian era, as though nothing had changed since 1900, and as though the Fifth Republic were really a menace to freedom. This is followed by a lame reminder to the effect that there were in France (in 1962) not only 650,000 teachers, research workers, doctors, artists, etc., but also some 350,000 "cadres supérieurs et ingénieurs du secteur privé et public, auxquels s'ajoutent des centaines de milliers de techniciens." All these were adjured to join, or at least support, the party that would put them in touch with the working class and enlighten them about the march of history: the whole appeal couched in the complacent and patronizing manner proper to an organization which shares with the Roman Church a belief in its own infallibility. See also Georges Cogniot, *ibid.*, pp. 177 ff. For the real nature of the technical intelligentsia and the problem of its relationship to the traditional labor move-

These considerations have a bearing both upon the political problem facing the French Communist party since its founding, and upon the theoretical issues to be examined in the later sections of this study. It has been necessary to treat the Socialist and Communist traditions in isolation so as to bring out the differences between them. At the same time it has to be remembered that when one speaks of French Marxism one cannot ignore the Socialist variant. For not only has the Communist party arisen from an older Socialist tradition, which by 1914 was already heavily impregnated with Marxism, but over the past four decades—and in particular since the 1950s—the contribution made to Marxist theory by independent Socialists and former Communists has been more important than the writings of the orthodox. If therefore in the succeeding parts we now turn to French Marxism properly so described, it is with a tacit awareness that for a majority of the writers under discussion Communism was merely a stage in their evolution towards an independent viewpoint. The latter might be described as Marxist, post-Marxist, revisionist, or simply critical; in any case it represented the end-point of a development in which adherence to the PCF, and to its brand of Sovietized Marxism, was only a passing phase.

Yet as one contemplates the half century since the 1914-18 upheaval shattered Europe's ancient foundations, what stands out is the phenomenon of what for short one may call the "Communist personality." This is something different from mere political convictions; it describes a profound mutation, at a level where beliefs are clothed with flesh and become determinants of action. The Communist personality—and the same is true of its Fascist antipode—was forged in the fires of the First World War and the ensuing Russian Revolution. This statement is not contradicted by the obvious fact that the turmoil of 1917-19 had its prefiguration in the 1848-49 upheaval which produced classical Marxism. So far as Eastern and Central Europe are concerned, this is indeed obvious. It was in the decades between these two crucial dates that the ancient political structure was once more propped up in the three Eastern Empires: force being em-

ment see Mallet, *La nouvelle classe ouvrière*. For the political attitudes of the rural areas see Gordon Wright, "Communists and Peasantry in France," in *Modern France*, ed. by E. M. Earle (Princeton, 1951).

ployed to keep democracy and the labor movement at bay. It was not only in Germany that an attempt was made to refloat the old regime by harnessing to its support the destructive energies let loose by nationalism and industrialism.

The experiment failed. The revolution resumed its course, with a violence proportionate to the degree of repression it had suffered, and at the same time with a new look. When it rose to the surface once more, it had become proletarian and was soon to become Communist. Social Democracy—so patriotic in 1914, to all appearances so completely won over to reform and constitutionalism—was about to disclose its Janus head.

The years of the First World War were Communism's incubation period. For this outcome the governments which launched, and then prolonged, the slaughter of 1914-18 must bear the prime responsibility. It was they who blasted the spark of revolutionary idealism into a raging fire. Without their help Lenin could not have taken power. When the new faith declared itself amidst the wreckage of the Russian Revolution, it showed scant resemblance to the democratic socialism of the prewar period. At best it appeared to revive the earlier drama in France at the close of the eighteenth century. At worst it displayed a sanguinary barbarism proper to the Russian national background. In neither respect could it lay claim to the inheritance of the labor movement. Yet its leaders were able to relate themselves to the past through their highly unorthodox interpretation of Marxism.

This reminder is necessary because the phenomenon of totalitarianism in France—before and after 1945—must be seen in a perspective that relates the French Revolution to its Russian offspring. Only thus do we avoid the academicism which seeks to derive world-shattering events from general ideas, or alternatively from the transformation of social structures under the pressure of technology. In history we have to do with uniquely determined and irreversible events not reducible to mechanical causation. What made Frenchmen between the two wars turn from democratic socialism to totalitarian communism (and in many cases back again after they had experienced the bitter fruits of their choice) was something in their own collective personality, and this something had been formed by a historical experience not shared with other European nations, though all of them responded in some fashion to the challenge of 1917. It is necessary to bear this in mind before one takes the plunge into French Marxism properly so called. What goes by this name is not understood unless it is seen as the intellectual counterpart of a phenomenon linking the France of today with the heritage of 1789 and 1793. The phenomenon itself was that of a revolutionary movement in a non-revolutionary situation: a movement founded in the expectation of an eschatological event which in the end never materialized. The tension between the reality and the vision discharged itself on the plane of thought and action, in the theory and practice of an organization which in the end became for its members a substitute for the promised land they were not destined to see. If it has been said of the early Christians that they awaited the coming of the Savior and instead got the Church, it may be said of the French proletariat that it expected the Revolution and instead got the Communist party.[50]

[50] For the philosophical implications of this theme see the following chapters of this study. Party literature is not a safe guide to the CP's actual history since its founding, but the monthly *Cahiers du Communisme* may be described as essential source-material, so far as the orientation of the middle-level *apparat* functionaries goes, and occasionally this literature also supplies a glimpse of new intellectual trends, e.g., in regard to the perennial problem of finding a *modus vivendi* with the intellectuals. The official *Manuel* (already cited) is consciously addressed to the lower levels in the party hierarchy, and should be read in conjunction with the anonymous three-volume *Histoire* (1962-65) put out by an oppositional group of party functionaries. The spirit of the Thorezian era, which ended in 1964, is well represented by the official protocol of the XVIIth Party Congress, held in Paris from May 14 to May 17, 1964. (See *Numéro Spécial des Cahiers du Communisme, June-July,* 1964.) Among heterodox publications representing the traditional Leninist (but not Stalinist) viewpoint, the monthly *La Voie Communiste* deserves special mention. The "Italian" form of revisionism was for a while reflected in the student organ *Clarté*. At a higher intellectual level, the monthly *La Nouvelle Critique* represents the nearest approach to a genuine discussion organ. There has never been anything to equal the Italian Communist theoretical journal *Rinascitá* (or, for that matter, any French theorist of an intellectual standing equal to that of Antonio Gramsci).

3

The Transformation of Marxist Theory

From Marx to Lenin

The foregoing chapters will have served their purpose if they have made it clear that both the Socialist and the Communist tradition in France had their common origin in the stock of beliefs accumulated by revolutionary intellectuals and workingmen between 1848 and 1871: two political upheavals which severed the labor movement from the republican bourgeoisie, while at the same time implanting a conviction among the workers that they had become the heirs of the revolutionary tradition abandoned by the possessing class. It is a matter of the first importance that the formative stage of the workers movement coincided with a political convulsion which pitted bourgeois and workers against one another. In 1871 as in 1848 the bourgeois Republic had been established by civil war and the massacre of armed proletarians. The "birth trauma" of the regime left its mark on both classes. It also placed its imprint on the major socialist intellectual production of the period: the Marxian system. Marx's characterization of the state as the "executive committee of the bourgeoisie" spelled out a conception shared by Blanquists, Proudhonists, and reformist socialists alike: with the difference that the latter hoped to transform the state into a politically neutral arena of democratic debate. There is no sense in asking whether it is this or the Communist interpretation of the common legacy which "really" represents Marx's views on the subject. Different conclusions could be reached by men who regarded themselves as Marxists. If the French Communist party fell heir to the Guesdist tradition, the latter continued to dominate the rhetoric of the S.F.I.O.'s left wing. In this sense, both parties after 1920 continued to be "Marxist," though not "Marxist-Leninist."

The phenomenon of French Communism is best understood when it is seen in the perspective of a working-class tradition profoundly marked by the traumatic experience of defeat in civil war. After 1880 the trauma gave way to a twofold development: democratic reformism on the one hand, revolutionary syndicalism on the other. The question then was whether the Socialist party would prove able to synthesize these conflicting tendencies, and its failure to do so—consequent upon the 1914-18 war, the split of 1920, and the gradual rise of a Communist mass movement—reinforced the alienation of the working class from the remainder of society. Yet the Communist party, having become the main repository of the ancient tradition of *ouvriérisme,* also fell heir to the dilemma of a revolutionary movement in a nonrevolutionary situation: its eschatological language was out of tune with reality. Since there could not in fact be a "proletarian revolution" in France, the hope was transferred to the USSR as the "fatherland of the workers."

The real faith of the Communist *militants* after 1920 was syndicalist. Insofar as the working-class member of the French CP had a vision of the future, it was the old anarcho-syndicalist dream of a factory without bosses, a society without exploiters, and a nation without a state. That this utopia had not by any means been realized in the USSR, was a circumstance of which he remained in ignorance. *Les Soviets partout* summed up a distinctively proletarian world-view which fastened upon the October Revolution as the symbol of a hoped-for transformation ridding the worker of all the parasites sitting upon his back: from the plant manager and the local official to the bankers and "their" state. In the ideology of the *militant*—an amalgam of syndicalist hostility to employers, faith in history, and pacifist revulsion from military carnage—the October Revolution signified the triumph of the workers over the exploiters. It also represented a revenge for 1848 and 1871. The annual procession to the *Mur des fédérés,* to mark the anniversary of the Commune and its bloody suppression, had always possessed a quasi-religious significance for men and women profoundly alienated from Church and State. The October Revolution gave a new direction to these sentiments: if the successors of the *Versaillais* continued to govern France, at least it might now be said that the heirs of the Commune were in the Kremlin. To the *militant,* the Soviet Union appeared as the embodiment of a revolution which France had missed, and as the realization of a dream which the bourgeoisie had filched away from him.

Communism thus inserted itself into a situation where a significant minority of the working class was already hostile to bourgeois democracy and everything that went with it—including parliamentary socialism. In this respect the instinctive anarcho-syndicalism of the average *militant* (itself a carry-over from the older *ouvriériste* outlook associated with Proudhon) had consequences no different from the Blanquist tradition, though the latter stemmed from the radical intelligentsia rather than from the industrial proletariat. This must be kept in mind if the Leninist version of Marxism, and its practical import in France after 1917, is to be understood. The Communists were able to graft Leninism upon the Blanquist stem because both traditions were hostile to reformist socialism and bourgeois democracy. But this synthesis concerned the leadership and the party theorists rather than their working-class followers, who at heart retained the anarcho-syndicalist faith in proletarian democracy as they understood it. The *militant* accepted the necessity of dictatorship because it was represented to him as the (temporary) rule of a proletarian vanguard, in the interest of dispossessing the bourgeoisie. He did not associate it with totalitarianism or the one-party state, but conceived of it as the extension of the primitive but real camaraderie of the workshop with which he was familiar. It did not occur to him that the Leninist faith in minority dictatorship might portend the political rule of a self-appointed elite: ultimately of a new ruling stratum. When he made the discovery—as many Syndicalists did in the 1920s—he drew back. The choice then lay between leaving the party or staying and hoping for the best. If he turned his back on the party, he might still remain in whatever trade-union organizations it controlled, and from the mid-thirties the CP had won control of the *Confédération Générale du*

Travail, which included the majority of unionized workers in the mass-production industries. The Socialist party—always weak in these centers of heavy industry—could not compete with the CP, once the latter had learned to talk the syndicalist language which the average *militant* understood and liked. Hence the broken unity of the political and the industrial movement was partially but effectively restored by the Communists from 1936 onward. They could now claim to have superseded the ancient division between a union movement hostile to "politics," and a political wing divorced from the industrial proletariat. The claim was not wholly fraudulent; and to the extent that it was based on fact, it represented a new phenomenon: for the first time in French labor history, the mass movement and the political party were brought together, with the party in the controlling position, instead of being a barely tolerated adjunct of the "real" workers movement.

A position of this kind could be sustained only if the political wing reflected the intransigent hostility to state and society which the working-class vanguard had come to associate with revolutionary purity. Communism satisfied this requirement and thus won the allegiance of the *militants.* What it could not do was to gain power in a society which after all formed part of the Western world, and moreover had evolved beyond the stage where Blanquist—or Leninist—tactics were applicable. In the event the CP was transformed into a permanent opposition movement, with a pseudorevolutionary ideology divorced from the circumstances of the political struggle. The latter dictated a strategy of compromise and an attempt to build a coalition of labor and the "new middle class" of technicians and white-collar employees. Instead the CP for many years banked on an alliance of workers and peasants: a piece of romanticism only explicable in terms of the hold which the Russian Revolution had gained over so many minds. It was the old illusion that "producers" could be opposed to "nonproducers." This transposition of Russian populism, in its Leninist form, to French conditions enabled the CP to score electoral gains in the countryside, among peasants disillusioned with their traditional leaders; but the strategy which followed from this orientation was once more one of negative intransigence, and it entailed active resistance to the inevitable transformation of French society. It did not lead toward the conquest of power; it merely increased the size of the Communist vote, thereby involving the PCF in all the paradoxes and contradictions imposed upon an antidemocratic movement compelled to pursue democratic policies.

The root tension between Leninism and syndicalism was fought out at the level of the party apparatus. The masses hardly noticed it, since the party always managed to retain a minimum of the syndicalist vocabulary required to hold the loyalty of the *militants*. For the inner core of leaders and functionaries, the process of "Bolshevization" after 1924 signified above all the shedding of vestigial illusions about the revolutionary spontaneity of the masses, and their replacement by the Leninist faith in the party—meaning the self-appointed leadership core of "professional revolutionaries." The formation of the PCF in 1920-21 had been made possible because Moscow was willing to make some concessions to the older tradition: Trotsky in particular, having lived in France during the first half of the 1914-18 war, understood very well that nothing could be done with the French workers unless an appeal was made to the syndicalist faith. When he fell from power, his French supporters fell with him. This involved a double equivocation: on the one hand, the new Stalinist leadership shed its inhibitions and imposed the Bolshevist orthodoxy, without quite renouncing the traditional language dear to the *militants*. On the other hand, the more clearsighted former Syndicalists left the CP and rallied to Trotsky: quite oblivious of the fact that the man who had crushed the Kronstadt rebellion was as authoritarian as his rivals. One may say that they mistook the Trotskyist opposition—a rebellion within the Soviet bureaucracy, led by a man who had become a doctrinaire Leninist—for a reincarnation of their own naive faith in proletarian democracy. The equivocation lasted just long enough to win the Trotskyist sect a foothold on the fringe of the French workers movement.

The French Communist party, like its sister organizations in Europe, had arisen after 1920 from an interpenetration of two different social strata. Functionaries of working-class origin, with a syndicalist or Guesdist past, made up the inner core; around them there assembled radical intellectuals who had detached themselves from established society and joined what they conceived to be the party of the proletariat. While this situation had parallels elsewhere, the social prominence of the French left-wing intelligentsia created a special problem.

Historically, the socialist movement, in France as elsewhere, had been the meeting point of organized labor and the radical intellectuals, with the latter tending to take over the control posts to the degree that they monopolized the necessary function of generalizing the aims of the movement. Bolshevism, with its emphasis on the "union of theory and practice" and its heavy stress on organizational centralism, appeared to favor such a development. Yet the outlook of the French workers was passionately *ouvriériste* and suspicious of intellectuals drawn from the professional middle class. The Communist ideology moreover consciously promoted the idea of a purely proletarian dictatorship, and allowed no more than an advisory function to the intelligentsia. Ideally the two groups were supposed to come together in the party, the latter being conceived not as a neutral meeting ground of workers and intellectuals, but as a higher unity synthesizing their divergencies in the creation of the true Communist: a being in whom the functional separation of physical from mental labor had already been overcome, at least in principle. Once inside the party, workers and intellectuals were to leave their separate identities behind: the vanguard was to be truly classless.

That was the theory of the matter. In practice the intellectuals surrendered their corporate identity only insofar as they were able to persuade themselves that the party genuinely executed the "will of history." Otherwise their self-abnegation would have been senseless, the more so since it involved a frequent sacrifice of the critical function in favor of semi-educated bureaucrats who held the actual control. As long as it was credible that a movement so constituted held the key to the riddle of history, participation in it was tolerable to intellectuals; otherwise they would rebel, or grow skeptical (on the model, perhaps, of Catholic intellectuals in a church governed by a dull and mediocre clergy). Either the Communist party was the predestined executor of history's purpose, or it was not. If it was, passing mistakes and aberrations might be endured, much as a loyal Catholic might put up with the strange behavior of the hierarchy. If it was not, there was no sense in deferring to the whims of the Kremlin or to the political chicaneries of the party bureaucrats. Hence the problem of political consciousness was crucial. Depending on how the situation was viewed by intellectuals equipped with a Marxist interpretation of history, they would either stay loyal to the party or—in a phrase made familiar in another context—consign it to the dustbin of history.

The party was the crucible in which the Communist consciousness was forged. By the same token it was also the breeding ground of countless doubts and heresies. Every Communist at some stage had to ask himself whether Marxism-Leninism really stood the test of truth. For the hard core of Communist workers this question usually resolved itself in a practical manner: as long as the party remained in the van of the class struggle, their doubts were silenced. To the intellectuals the matter presented itself in a different light. Since they did not participate in the daily industrial struggle, which helped to persuade the *militant* that the party was fighting his battle, they required theoretical arguments. Communist belief did not come spontaneously to them; it reached them via the traditions of a radical intelligentsia which had learned to identify itself with "the people" against its oppressors. The difference lay in the fact that the new creed demanded total submission to a party which claimed to possess the key to the secret of history.

It was perhaps inevitable that, in a country profoundly impregnated by the traditions of Catholicism, a movement originally descended from the Enlightenment should have adopted habits of thought proper to the Church: down to the elaboration of an Index of prohibited literature. But the original commitment was never renounced, whence the uneasy conscience which afflicted the official ideologists even at the peak of the Stalin era. These ideologists, moreover, could not help being aware that the truth of their doctrines had to pass the pragmatic test of political success, failing which the theory would have to be revised. This consideration certainly weighed with the party leaders, most of whom had at one time been working-class activists, before becoming bureaucrats in charge of an increasingly fossilized organization. Unconditional loyalty to the USSR—the first principle of Stalinism—was all very well: it made possible the mixture of fanaticism and fatalism displayed by most French Communists in 1939-40, when they clenched their teeth and bore the storm of rage unleashed by the Hitler-Stalin pact. Such loyalty might also, after 1945, serve to maintain their morale in the face of defeats, disappointments, and private doubts about the Soviet regime and the East European "people's democracies." Even intellectuals might silence their conscience as long as they could equate the party with the cause of inevitable progress towards socialism. The real test came with the dawning awareness that the current of history was moving away from them. It was this, rather than the enormities disclosed by the gradual de-Stalinization of the USSR, that shook their faith and produced the spiritual and moral crisis of the late 1950s and early 1960s, on which the confusion engendered by the Sino-Soviet split superimposed itself.

For Communists who thought about the matter at all, Marxism signified the "union of theory and practice": with the emphasis on the individual's commitment to the task of changing the world. This union presupposed the existence of a social class able and willing to undertake a complete reconstruction of society. Failing this, the intellectuals would be thrown back upon their traditional role of furnishing a more or less critical interpretation of an unchanging reality. Such an outcome signified more than the loss of political hopes: it had implications for theory as well. Having once grasped the Marxian notion that men perceive the nature of reality in the act of trying to change it, the intellectuals who had invested their hope in the party could not lightly renounce it. Their political faith was based on that vision of an alliance between philosophy and the proletariat which Marx had conceived in the 1840s. Trouble arose—as it had done a generation earlier in Central Europe—when the vision was clouded by skepticism. Was the proletariat in fact capable of fulfilling the "mission" imposed upon it by "history"? The October Revolution was held to have supplied the answer. But that revolution had been led by a vanguard of radical intellectuals who substituted themselves for the proletariat, and in due course it had given birth to a society dominated by a new stratum which had indeed arisen from the working class, but had now plainly emancipated itself from it. Thus doubt inserted itself into the fabric of faith. It did not as yet affect the corpus of doctrine known as Marxism-Leninism (notably its more abstract philosophical formulations), but it impinged upon the belief that the Soviet Union embodied a new and higher form of social organization. Yet if it did not, the allegiance given to the Russian Communist party and its French offshoot rested on a misunderstanding of what history was about.

With the preceding remarks we have crossed the invisible border line dividing Leninism proper from its subsequent Stalinist codification, to which Trotskyism supplied the heretical counterpoint. French Marxists might in principle have sympathized with any one of the factions involved in the internal disputes which rent the international Communist movement; in practice those of them who were Communists—for it must not be forgotten that in France it was possible for a Marxist to remain a Socialist: an option precluded elsewhere by the habitual association of Marxism with the Soviet regime—for the most part followed the lead of their party and accepted the Stalinist interpretation. Since Stalinism deliberately subordinated the interests of the International to those of the USSR, there were bound to be rebellions; and to the extent that Trotsky's personality lent itself to a revival of the romantic and utopian themes prominent in 1917-24, it was inevitable that Trotskyism should develop a following both among intellectuals and among former Syndicalists (if they were able to forgive Trotsky his part in suppressing the brief experiment with genuine workers democracy after 1918). In this sense Trotskyism can be said to have stood for a particular version of the Communist faith: one centered upon the concept of world revolution. The trouble was that the world revolution failed to come—at any rate in the industrially advanced countries. Instead, the political struggle polarized itself for Communists in the defense of the USSR against Germany, and after 1945 in the conflict between the Soviet bloc and the Western democracies. In consequence some of Trotsky's followers tended to drift back to the main body, while others broke with Communism altogether. The sole theoretical interest of the mountainous literature produced by these alignments—to say nothing of the political and personal drama surrounding the 1936-38 Moscow "trials"—lay in the demonstration that an independent Communist movement (i.e., one not dependent on the USSR) was not possible: at any rate not until the Soviet bloc had itself dissolved. The self-styled Fourth International founded in 1938 remained a sect. On the other hand, individual Communists might use Trotsky's criticism of the Soviet regime as a starting point for critical reflections of their own. Depending on their evolving political and intellectual standpoints, such reflections might land them in a quasi-anarchist repudiation of politics, or bring them back by a circuitous route to the Marxist socialism from which Lenin had originally branched off.[1]

The counterpart of this oppositional literature was the immense output of the official Leninist-Stalinist school: with the obvious proviso that from the mid-1950s the Stalinist content was progressively diluted. The difficulty here is that an analysis of these writings would be equivalent to an account of all the quasi-intellectual disputes in which the party's official ideologists were involved over a period of several decades. In practice this would reduce itself to a wearisome rehearsal of such well-worn themes as the gradual discovery of the truth about Stalinism and its political practices at home and abroad. It would then be necessary to go once more over the ground ploughed up by the controversialists of the 1950s: from the first rumors about forced labor in the USSR, to the upheaval produced in the minds of loyal Communists by the official revelations about Stalin, followed by the Polish and Hungarian events of 1956. And finally we should be left with the task of estimating the respective strength of pro-Russian, pro-Italian, and pro-Chinese currents in the French Communist party, before and after the death of Thorez in July 1964 and the concurrent installation of a leadership subjected to disturbing winds of doctrine from south of the Alps.[2]

[1] Politically, "left-wing Communism" went back to Kronstadt and the establishment of the Communist party dictatorship as a "dictatorship over the proletariat." But in the later 1920s, and especially in the 1930s, it was more commonly associated with Trotsky's critique of the Stalinist regime as "bureaucratic" or "Thermidorian." The *locus classicus* is Trotsky's *La Révolution trahie* (Paris, 1937) which rang the changes on this theme. In some ways he had been anticipated by his former adherent Boris Souvarine, whose *Staline: Aperçu historique du bolchévisme* (Paris, 1935) had already written the whole Soviet "experiment" off as worthless from the libertarian and democratic viewpoint. But it was only in 1939 that a former Italian Communist, Bruno Rizzi, dismissed communism itself as an illusion in *La bureaucratisation du monde* (Paris, 1939). Most left-wing Communists retained the belief that while the revolution had been perverted, its original aims might yet be realised; Victor Serge, *Mémoires d'un révolutionnaire* (Paris, 1951). For a postwar analysis of Stalinism and fascism as variants of totalitarianism see Jules Monnerot, *Sociologie du Communisme* (Paris, 1949), especially pp. 334 ff. For the syndicalist critique of Leninism see Michel Collinet, *Du Bolchévisme: Évolution et variations du Marxisme-Léninisme* (Paris, 1957).

[2] For the more important of these topics see the collection of documents entitled *Pour la vérité sur les camps concentrationnaires* (Paris, 1951) and the antecedent writings of David Rousset; M. Merleau-Ponty and J. P. Sartre, "Les jours de notre vie," *Temps Modernes* (January, 1950); also M. Merleau-

Instead of plunging more deeply into this morass we take leave to abandon it, with a brief reminder to the effect that—so far as the immense majority of fellow-travelling intellectuals were concerned—they hardly came across anything but the polemical literature already noted. Its importance was in this sense enormous, but the topic is familiar, and the theoretical content too thin to warrant sustained attention. What has to be considered rather is the attempt to frame a new intellectual synthesis.

Orthodoxy and Revisionism

Before turning to the theoretical disputations properly so described, it may be useful to attempt a brief summary of the situation hitherto outlined. The major dividing line is clearly that between the prewar and the postwar period. Although the assimilation of ordinary Marxist concepts went on for some time after 1945, that date represents the peak of Communist influence, though if one likes one may argue that the real reflux came only in 1948. Thereafter it was plain that France would remain a democracy and would not undergo even a temporary Communist dictatorship. Although it took the PCF some years to realize this—the full awareness may be said to have sunk in by 1964, which accidentally brought both the fiftieth anniversary of the First World War and the twentieth anniversary of the 1944 liberation—it had been evident to others for some years. Indeed one may say that from about 1960 the party's erstwhile sympathizers had given up hope,[3] while its official philosophers were quietly abandoning their

Ponty, *Humanisme et terreur: essai sur le problème communiste* (Paris, 1947) and *Les Aventures de la dialectique* (Paris, 1955); J. P. Sartre, Preface to Louis Dalmas, *Le Communisme Yougoslave* (Paris, 1950); "Les Communistes et la Paix," *Temps Modernes* (July, October-November, 1952; April, 1954); "Réponse à Albert Camus," *Temps Modernes* (August, 1952). Edgar Morin, *Autocritique* (Paris, 1959); Lucien Laurat, *Staline, la linguistique, et l'impérialisme russe* (Paris, 1951).

[3] Thus, for example, in Sartre's Preface to the 1960 edition of Paul Nizan's *Aden Arabie* the experience of the years between 1940 and 1960 is written off as a story of lost illusions. In this perspective, Nizan's soldier's death in 1940 had by 1960 acquired a paradigmatic value: it was the only genuinely heroic—because stoical and disillusioned—gesture that Sartre felt able, after twenty years, to cite as an example of moral behavior proper to be commended to the young. Nizan, the target of so many Stalinist calumnies, had been "l'homme qui a dit non jusqu'au bout. Sa mort fut la fin d'un monde."

Stalinist posture and adopting the conciliatory manner proper to an unending debate with non-Communists.[4]

But although politically it is true to say that the peak of Communist influence had been passed by 1948, it does not follow that the same applies to Marxism. The main reason has already been indicated: the French intellectual world was still catching up, just as France as a whole was making up for lost time in other domains. That is why the post-Stalin disclosures of 1953-56 produced such immense confusion: they discredited Communism just when *Marxism* was gaining fresh ground—albeit in the revised version suggested by theorists who had finally absorbed the German-Austrian inheritance of the prewar period. Hence for some years it became quite impossible to say whether Marxist influence was growing or declining. Around 1955 the dissociation of Communism from Marxism had not yet occurred, and the debacle of the Communist myth involved an agonized reappraisal of everything that intellectuals of the Left had been taught to believe about the proletarian revolution.[5]

It is worth remembering that in terms of French political history the twenty years between 1940 and 1960 (when the Fifth Republic may be said to have stabilized itself) constitute a single upheaval which in the end failed to produce the revolution the Left had been waiting for: as indeed Sartre recognized in 1960. By then French society had found a new political balance and was moreover undergoing a rapid and successful industrial transformation. It was a suitable moment for looking back, and not accidentally it was at this juncture that revisionism really took shape, politically and intellectually. It

[4] Roger Garaudy, *Perspectives de l'homme: Existentialisme, Pensée Catholique, Marxisme* (Paris, 1961) and, *Dieu est mort: Étude sur Hegel* (Paris, 1962). These and other contributions to the philosophical debate of the 1960s will be considered later.

[5] The *locus classicus* is Merleau-Ponty's bulky pamphlet, *Les Aventures de la dialectique* (1955): in form a dispassionate critique of Sartre's interpretation of Marxism, in substance a rejection of the Communist myth of the October Revolution; much of it in fact is not concerned with Sartre but with Lukács. One may say that from this moment the French discussion had recovered the level of the earlier German one, with the advantage of additional political experience (not to mention the greater familiarity of French writers with the moral problems raised by revolution and dictatorship). For Merleau-Ponty's earlier qualified defense of Leninism and the Soviet dictatorship see his 1947 work, *Humanisme et terreur*.

could do so because two preconditions had now been fulfilled: Marxism had been absorbed, and the Communist party had ceased to be dangerous. There was no longer an obstacle to the efflorescence of an undogmatic, or—if one prefers it—eclectic socialist doctrine and practice. Marxism was no longer uniquely identified with the Soviet Union, and by the same token it ceased to be the private property of the PCF. It could now become the common medium of the left-wing intelligentsia, and in some measure of the educated stratum in general. The age of revolution—for those who did not transfer their hopes to China or Cuba—was closed.

The new situation was a function of external and internal changes over which the intellectuals had no control. It reflected both the easing of the Cold War, and the fact that France was belatedly turning into a modern country. This modernization had, however, for one of its aspects the assimilation of foreign—notably Central European—concepts. To this degree the rise of a new and more sophisticated understanding of Marxism was part of the larger transformation which the society was undergoing: a transformation which the Communist party had done its best to prevent. From 1948 onward, and increasingly from the late 1950s, the situation was characterized by the successful absorption of intellectual currents not reducible to the old simple-minded antitheses. The older alignments did not disappear, but the debate was raised to a higher level. Marxism was no longer automatically identified with its Soviet version, and an attempt could now be made to construct a new theoretical model. This might take one of two forms: the Marxist-Leninist assumptions could be retained, on the understanding that Stalinism was to be regarded as a temporary phenomenon due to the backwardness and isolation of the USSR. Alternatively, the Leninist element might be extruded and the original Marxist theory recast to take account of the real state of affairs in the Western world since the close of the Second World War. In practice both solutions were tried: the first by the *Temps Modernes* group (at any rate until the defection of Merleau-Ponty); the second thereafter by the genuine revisionists around the periodical *Arguments*. In addition there remained of course the official CP theorists around *La Pensée* and *La Nouvelle Critique;* but their influence never became again what it had been in the late 1940s, when the CP—with its

Resistance halo still more or less intact—participated in the government of the Fourth Republic and set the tone for the postwar debate on East-West relations. Such development of Marxist theory as took place during this period—principally the early and middle 1950s—was tied to the self-examination of left-wing intellectuals who had gone through the Resistance and learned to regard it as a stage on the road to a possible socialist revolution. The question for them was whether France was ripe for such a revolution, and if so, whether the CP was fit to lead it. Even Communists might come to doubt this—in which case they had additional cause to focus their interest on the USSR and the East European regimes.[6]

There was then in the later 1950s something like a "crisis of Marxism," or at any rate of Marxism-Leninism. But—and this can never be stressed sufficiently—revisionism went parallel with the spread of Marxism among intellectual circles who before 1939 had been shielded from contact with subversive, because non-French, doctrines. The collapse of 1940 and the Resistance had broken down ancient barriers against foreign, specifically German, influences which now came pouring in; Hegel, Kierkegaard, Marx, Freud, Weber, Husserl, and Heidegger, were assimilated almost simultaneously. The process had indeed begun on a small scale in the 1930s, but the major intellectual barriers only came down in 1945, just as economically they came down a decade later. The effort to overcome intellectual chauvinism and provincialism—an aspect of the country's modernization in all spheres of life, which was to produce dramatic results in the 1960s—thus favored the spread of a diluted Marxism in the universities, just when the real Marxists began to doubt the relevance of their doctrines. Once this complex situation is under-

[6] It is perhaps significant that the only major intellectual enterprise associated with the CP during these years—A. Cornu's massive three-volume biography of the founders of Marxism—was the work of an historian who occupied a chair in East Berlin; see Auguste Cornu, *Karl Marx et Friedrich Engels* (Paris, 1955-58-62); also, *Karl Marx et la Révolution de 1848* (Paris, 1948); *Karl Marx et la pensée moderne* (Paris, 1948); and *Essai de critique marxiste* (Paris, 1949). Cornu somehow managed to be both orthodox and scholarly. The same might be said of Émile Bottigelli's three-volume edition of the correspondence between Engels and the Lafargues, *Friedrich Engels—Paul et Laura Lafargue: Correspondance 1868-1895* (Paris, 1956-59). These were philological labors of love rather than philosophical enterprises. However, Cornu's third volume, which dealt with Marx's stay in Paris in 1844-45, did take up the delicate subject of the "Paris Manuscripts."

stood, no particular mystery attaches to the phenomenon of a belated introduction of traditional Marxian concepts parallel with a deepening crisis of faith among Communists.[7]

If it is borne in mind that Marxism and revisionism spread simultaneously, the former in the academic world, the latter among Marxists, it becomes a little easier to grasp what happened in areas relatively shielded from political shocks, e.g., the writing of history. It was quite possible for historians to assimilate Marxian concepts—as indeed they had been doing since the 1920s—without identifying themselves either with the Communist party or with one of its offshoots.[8] The same applied to socio-economic studies on the industrial revolution, or on the social history of France. Their authors might be —and in most cases were—Socialists rather than Communists. No matter, they employed a sociological apparatus, and to that extent helped to make Marxism respectable in the academic milieu.[9]

[7] Frenchmen of the liberal persuasion were less surprised than foreigners by this overlap, since they realized well enough that it represented a time-lag in the country's social development; see Raymond Aron, *L'Opium des intellectuels* (Paris, 1955). Where they went wrong was in supposing that the coming dissolution of the Marxist-Leninist school signified the end of Marxism *tout court*. This was to underrate the enduring relevance of Marx's critique of capitalism to socialists dissatisfied with the political and spiritual atmosphere of industrial society. But the empiricist school did recover its self-confidence and produced an analysis which could be called post-Marxian. In sociology there was above all the work of Georges Gurvitch, notably, *La Vocation actuelle de la sociologie* (Paris, 1950-1963); *Déterminismes sociaux et liberté humaine* (Paris, 1955-1963); *Dialectique et sociologie* (Paris, 1962). The Marxist counterpoint was provided by Georges Friedmann, in *Machine et humanisme* (Paris, 1946-1954); *Où va le travail humain?* (Paris, 1950-1963), and other writings; see also his *Leibniz et Spinoza* (Paris, 1946-1962).

[8] So far as the study of the French Revolution was concerned, Georges Lefebvre's great work, *La Révolution française* (Paris, 1930-1957) could be described as Marxist only in a rather diluted sense. But the dilution mattered: it signified that the synthesis of traditional Jacobin, or Jaurèsian, thinking on the subject with historical materialism was now complete. Lefebvre's authority in the academic world was immense, and his work paved the way for the more rigidly Marxist interpretations of Albert Soboul and Daniel Guérin: the latter a Trotskyist sympathizer; see his *La lutte de classes sous la première république* (Paris, 1946). An amusing sidelight is provided by the fact that Guérin himself was directly descended from a Robespierrist family, as well as from the Saint-Simonian Gustave d'Eichthal; see his essay collection *Jeunesse du socialisme libertaire* (Paris, 1959). For Soboul's work see, in particular, *Les Sansculottes parisiens en l'An II* (Paris, 1959).

[9] A good instance is furnished by Professor Jean Lhomme's learned study *La grande bourgeoisie au pouvoir: 1830-1880* (Paris, 1960), which dealt in the most dispassionate manner possible with the social and political role of that class during the era of triumphant liberalism: this despite the fact that the author

Revisionism could not become a major influence until Marxism in its orthodox form had been absorbed and then discredited by the failure of the Communist party to institute the "union of theory and practice." Meantime the neo-Marxist current was sustained by intellectual insights already gained in Central Europe a generation earlier. The intermediaries were for the most part refugees who had gone through the experience of discovering that the Communist form of Marxism was too closely linked with the Soviet regime to be translated into practice elsewhere. This disillusionment ran parallel to the discovery that "what Marx really meant" corresponded neither to the actual outcome of the Russian Revolution nor to the philistinism of Central European Social Democracy. In its prewar German setting this realization had originally taken the form of a revived interest in the Hegelian sources of Marx's thought: an approach stimulated by the discovery of his early writings. These writings became known in France from 1933 onward—a turning point in Western European political history as well. The practical fusion of Marxism and Existentialism—which was to become the central experience of the French intelligentsia during the Resistance—had already been anticipated in theory before 1939. But it needed a new understanding of Hegel to provide French philosophers with the categories required to relate their growing interest in Marx to their more strictly professional concerns. This fusion was achieved between 1933 and 1939, not by the Marxists, but by a Russian-born emigré scholar for whom Marx was merely a guide to what seemed essential in Hegel's philosophy of history. French neo-Marxism came to birth in the lecture hall of the *École des Hautes-Études,* which in those years provided a select audience for Alexandre Kojève's course on Hegel's *Phenomenology of Mind.*[10]

differentiated his model of class analysis from that of Marx (p. 3). This undogmatic attitude had come down to numerous *universitaires* by way of Jaurès and the Socialist historians whom he influenced, notably C. E. Labrousse; for the post-1945 literature see also Charles Morazé, *La France bourgeoise* (Paris, 1947) and *Les bourgeois conquérants* (Paris, 1957).

[10] On this subject see, in particular, A. Kojève, *Introduction à la lecture de Hegel,* ed. by Raymond Queneau (Paris, 1947). Jean Hyppolite, *Genèse et structure de la Phénoménologie de l'Esprit de Hegel* (Paris, 1946); *Études sur Marx et Hegel* (Paris, 1955). M. Merleau-Ponty, *Sens et non-sens* (Paris, 1948). J. P. Sartre, *Matérialisme et Révolution,* in *Situations III* (Paris, 1949); *L'Exis-*

Some of the difficulties inherent in this situation will be examined later. What needs to be retained here are the personal circumstances linking the prewar discussion (which was mainly philosophical) with the postwar dissensions (which were predominantly political). In this context it is sufficient to remark that Kojève in the 1930s lectured to an audience which included Merleau-Ponty, and that these were likewise the years when Sartre first made the acquaintance of German philosophy: though his interest then centered on Husserl and Heidegger. The point which both he and Merleau-Ponty retained was that the thinking of Marx—or at any rate of the young Marx—had been "existential" rather than determinist. With this discovery a flood of light was let in, and it became possible to confront the orthodox with an interpretation clearly superior to, because more authentic than, that on which they had hitherto relied.

But there was more to it than authenticity: as has already been suggested, the French were repeating the experience of the Germans. Specifically, they were coming up against the fundamental shortcomings of the Leninist orthodoxy, now officialized as Soviet Marxism. The difficulty here—for old-fashioned Social Democrats as well as for new-fangled Communists—was that on its philosophical side this orthodoxy was quite in accordance with Engels, if not with Marx. Hence it could not be dismissed as a Russian importation into Marxism. If the libertarian message of Marxism was to be retained, the doctrine had to be freed from the accretions of late nineteenth century positivism and scientism. In practice this meant going back to the early Marx, and then reinterpreting him in the light of the post-Hegelian debate of the 1840s which had already stirred up some of the issues important to Existentialists a century later. But to do this it was necessary at long last to take the plunge into Hegel, and this was accomplished between 1933 and 1939 under the guidance of

tentialisme est un humanisme (Paris, 1947). Tran-Duc-Thao, *Phénoménologie et matérialisme dialectique* (Paris, 1951). Henri Lefebvre, *L'Existentialisme* (Paris, 1946); with N. Guterman, *Morceaux choisis de Hegel* (Paris, 1938); *Problèmes actuels du marxisme* (Paris, 1958); *La Somme et le reste* (Paris, 1959). Maximilien Rubel, *Karl Marx: Essai de biographie intellectuelle* (Paris, 1957). Lucien Goldmann, *Recherches dialectiques* (Paris, 1959). Lucien Sebag, *Marxisme et structuralisme* (Paris, 1964). Needless to say, this brief list does not exhaust the subject of neo-Marxism.

Kojève: himself a fairly orthodox Hegelian and quite indifferent to the revolutionary aims of his pupils.[11]

Here a brief historical retrospect is once more in order.[12] So far as philosophy is concerned, the formation of the first Marxist-Leninist group in France may be said to have occurred between 1929 and 1934. Its members, Georges Politzer, Henri Lefebvre, Norbert Guterman, Georges Friedmann, Pierre Morhange, and Paul Nizan, kept out of factional disputes, and hence attracted less attention than the Surrealist *literati* who a little earlier had moved en bloc to Communism. What held them together was the rejection of academic philosophy in both its aspects—classical rationalism and Bergsonian mysticism—and the urge to unify theoretical thought and political practice. This need not have entailed a break with the traditional interpretation of Marx, but on the philosophical side this interpretation was rather rudimentary. Prior to 1914 Marxism had been identified, by its defenders as well as by its critics, with economics, and specifically with a determinist interpretation of history which did not seem altogether dissimilar from positivism. Debates with adherents of Durkheim's school turned on the respective merits of Comte and Marx. After 1920 Communism presented itself as a "total" world-view unifying philosophy and politics, and the old prewar eclecticism, which had permitted Socialists of the Jaurèsian persuasion to combine Kant with Marx, was no longer acceptable. Its spirit continued indeed to linger on, and this was just why the Socialist party failed to attract

[11] For the earlier German discussion see Georg Lukács, *Geschichte und Klassenbewusstsein* (Vienna-Berlin, 1923), translated as *Histoire et conscience de classe* (Paris, 1960). Karl Korsch, *Marxismus und Philosophie* (Leipzig, 1930). Herbert Marcuse, *Hegels Ontologie und die Grundlegung einer Theorie der Geschichtlichkeit* (Frankfurt, 1932); "Neue Quellen zur Grundlegung des historischen Materialismus" *Die Gesellschaft,* IX, No. 8 (Berlin, 1932). Of course no discussion ever repeats what was said in another context, but the German debate had already established the philosophical starting point for the subsequent French controversies.

[12] On this subject see Georges Politzer, *Critique des fondements de la psychologie* (Paris, 1928), I; *Le Bergsonisme, une mystification philosophique* (Paris, 1946); *Principes élémentaires de Philosophie* (Paris, 1948, 1963). Henri Lefebvre, *Le Matérialisme dialectique* (Paris, 1939; 4th ed., 1957; 5th ed., 1962); N. Guterman and H. Lefebvre, *La Conscience mystifiée,* (Paris, 1936) and *Cahiers de Lénine sur la dialectique de Hegel* (Paris, 1939). Georges Friedmann, *De la Sainte Russie à l'U.R.S.S.* (Paris, 1938).

recruits who were aiming at a complete break with bourgeois society and its modes of thought.[13]

In retrospect one can see in the emergence of this group of youthful Marxists a prefiguration of the post-1945 concern with the human situation, as reflected in the writings of Sartre, Merleau-Ponty and others associated with the monthly *Temps Modernes.* Technically the prewar generation was not yet committed to Existentialism, but its understanding of philosophy differed significantly from that of the editors of *La Pensée: Revue du rationalisme moderne,* which began to appear in 1939 under the patronage of distinguished scientists such as Paul Langevin, Marcel Prenant, Henri Wallon, and Frédéric Joliot-Curie. The *Pensée* group was clearly in a positivist tradition which the older Marxists (if they came from the natural sciences) shared with the generality of the Left. Their journal was to become an important link between the PCF and the academic world, notably after 1945, when its reappearance coincided with the peak of Communist influence. Its founders were not merely leading physicists or biologists in their own right, but adherents of a "mechanical" materialism which plainly owed more to the Encyclopaedists than to Hegel.

The tension between Marxism and Existentialism has remained a constant theme in the work of the only considerable survivor of the original *Philosophies* group: Henri Lefebvre.[14] The Marxian concepts of "alienation" and "total man" were already central to his prewar reflections from the time he came across Marx's early philosophical

[13] Some of these themes were developed in Georges Politzer's writings, and in those of Paul Nizan; see the criticism of official Cartesianism, as represented by Léon Brunschwigc, in Nizan's *Les Chiens de garde* (Paris, 1932). Nizan had joined the Communist party as early as 1927, but it was only in 1929 that he and his friends issued their own journal, the *Revue Marxiste.* When in 1924 the same group had briefly published a periodical with the title *Philosophies,* they were not yet Marxists, though Friedmann had adhered to the pro-Communist *Clarté* organization since 1920; Jacques Fauvet, *Histoire du parti communiste français, I: De la guerre à la guerre, 1917-1939* (Paris, 1964), pp. 102-3; David Caute, *Communism and the French Intellectuals, 1914-1960* (London, 1964), pp. 263 ff.

[14] H. Lefebvre, *L'Existentialisme,* also *Marx et la Liberté* (Geneva, 1947), and his *autocritique* in the March 1949 number of the CP's official philosophical journal *La Nouvelle Critique, revue du marxisme militant.* For Lefebvre's current standpoint, following his break with the CP and with Soviet Marxism in 1957, see the Preface (dated April, 1957) to the 4th ed. of his *Le Matérialisme dialectique,* and the even more heterodox Preface to the 5th (1961) ed.

writings.[15] The "Paris Manuscripts" of 1844 had been a revelation for Marxists of Lefebvre's generation; and the echo of this discovery resounds throughout the concluding chapter of *Le Matérialisme dialectique:* first published in 1939, when—as the author remarked in 1957—Communists still tended to express disdain for the topic. Though politically orthodox, Lefebvre in 1939 was already going against the official line, which in those years was based on the Leninist interpretation of Marxism as a doctrine centered on the analysis of capitalism's political and economic contradictions. In fairness it has to be remembered that this was itself a reaction to the academic habit of treating Marx as the author of a heretical philosophy of history. Under the impulsion of the Russian Revolution and Leninism, this approach gave way after 1917 to the realization that Marxism was meant to be a theory of the proletarian revolution. As usually happens in such cases, the discovery was accompanied by an impatient rejection of all nonpolitical interests, and in particular of long-range philosophical speculation centered on Marx's youthful writings. When Lefebvre in 1957 recalled that between 1925 and 1935 French Marxists like himself had discovered the immediate political relevance of their own doctrine, he went on to note that the great economic crisis of 1929-33, and the practical problems facing the USSR, reinforced the stress on the politico-economic theme: not indeed "economics" in the conventional academic sense, but the political economy of capitalism and socialism. A writer concerned with topics such as *aliénation* and *l'homme total* could not in the circumstances expect a sympathetic hearing even from political friends.[16]

But there was more to this indifference than ordinary philistinism. Insofar as Marxism counted as a philosophy, it was interpreted by Communists—in accordance with the already established Leninist orthodoxy—as a comprehensive world-view embracing the natural cosmos as well as human history. It was just this which made it attractive to the influential academic group around *La Pensée,* as well as to working-class *militants* in search of a faith that could take the place of religion. People like Lefebvre were thus ground between the

[15] The first translation of which into French, by N. Guterman and H. Lefebvre, had appeared in the journal *Avant-Poste* in 1933.

[16] H. Lefebvre, *Le Matérialisme dialectique,* Preface to 4th ed., pp. viii-xii.

upper and lower millstones. It took the full-scale assimilation of contemporary German philosophy after 1945 to render Existentialism popular, even fashionable, among *Marxisants* intellectuals.[17]

The Return to Philosophy

What was involved after 1945 was the acclimatization of Hegel in the French academic world, and the critique of Soviet Marxism from a viewpoint corresponding to that of Central European writers who had rediscovered the philosophical roots of their faith. However abstract this may sound, it implied a series of political choices. Both the German and the French critics of Soviet Marxism were revisionists, in the political as well as in the philosophical sense. The Central European group—with the major exception of Lukács, who in 1924 capitulated to the hierarchy and became a rigid upholder of Leninism (temporarily even of Stalinism)—steadily evolved in a direction which by the late 1930s brought about the severance of its links with the Communist movement. The postwar French revisionists repeated the process, with a time-lag which reflected the difference in external circumstances, as well as the fact (referred to earlier) that the assimilation of Marxism in France had come later and was only achieved in the 1950s: a decade corresponding in some respects to the 1920s in Weimar Germany. Ultimately both groups completed the same trajectory, with the important difference that the Germans passed through emigration, the French through the Resistance movement. The upshot was different also in that the political division of postwar Germany froze the ideological battle lines, while in France they remained fluid. By the early 1960s, the prewar alignments had given way to a tripartite division: (a) orthodox Communists, (b) dissident Communists, and (c) revisionists; (a) and (b) were Marxist-Leninists, though they quarreled over politics; (c) grouped ex-Marxists who had gone through the Communist experience, and writers like Lefebvre who continued

[17] For Lefebvre's subsequent development see his *Critique de la vie quotidienne* (Paris, 1947; 2d ed., with new and "post-Stalinist" Preface, 1957), and his essay in *Rencontres internationales de Genève, 1948* (Paris-Neufchatel, 1949) when he still defended the orthodox Communist position. See also his *Pour connaître la pensée de Karl Marx* (Paris, 1948, 1956) and its rather less interesting companion volume, *Pour connaître la pensée de Lénine* (Paris, 1957): both still fairly orthodox in tone.

to regard themselves as Marxists, but were no longer Communists.[18] It is arguable that Sartre's followers should be classified under (d) as an independent subsection, more Existentialist than Marxist, but one must guard against pedantry. What mattered was the division between Communists, i.e., adherents of Soviet Marxism, and libertarians who used as much of Marx (and as little of Engels) as they needed. Most revisionists were socialists of one kind or another, though few adhered to the official Socialist party (itself rent by new splits since the Algerian war and the coming of the Fifth Republic).

Of course all this is too simple; it is not possible here to do more than sketch an outline. The relevant point in any case is that the postwar assimilation of Marxism had upset the old intellectual division on the Left into Marxists who were mostly Communists, and fellow travelers who remained Cartesians; though it could be argued that the latter had achieved a rejuvenation with the help of Sartre, and blossomed out as Existentialists.[19] However that may be, the ensuing literary and philosophical controversies—between Sartre and Merleau-Ponty, between Sartre and Albert Camus, between the *Temps Modernes* group in general and the Communists—were conducted in terms of rival interpretations of Marxism, while prior to the war it had been quite in order for intellectuals of the Left to ignore Marx. Needless to say, the Marxism at stake in the disputations between Sartre and his colleagues was not that of the Communist party. It was not, that is to say, the political doctrine of a totalitarian organization heading a mass movement and obliged to maneuver on the national and international scene. Rather it was an alembicated extract from the

[18] This had political implications, since from the new standpoint the dispute between Stalinists and Trotskyists was no longer important. So far as philosophy was concerned, Merleau-Ponty had already anticipated this in 1948 when he impartially condemned the Stalinist Roger Garaudy, and the Trotskyist Pierre Naville for their attachment to rationalism and scientism. See Merleau-Ponty, "Marxisme et philosophie," in *Sens et non-sens,* pp. 221 ff. For Garaudy see *n* 4. For Naville see his *Psychologie, marxisme, matérialisme* (Paris, 1946, 1948); *La vie de travail et ses problèmes* (Paris, 1954); *Le Nouveau Léviathan. I: De l'aliénation à la jouissance* (Paris, 1957).

[19] The prewar Cartesians of the Left had their spokesman in Julien Benda, whose *Trahison des clercs* (Paris, 1927), though ostensibly a defense of traditional liberalism and rationalism, was in some ways already a forerunner of the Popular Front: its main implications were anti-Romantic and anti-Fascist. But Benda never accepted Marxism in any of its forms. With Sartre, the attempt was made to graft both Marxism and Existentialism upon the Cartesian stem.

writings of Marx, Lenin, Trotsky, Rosa Luxemburg, Lukács, and anyone else who happened to catch their attention.[20] But it was not an academic issue while there was a chance of a new Popular Front constituting itself around the CP, for in that case the left-wing intelligentsia would look to the theorists of the *Temps Modernes* group to furnish the appropriate slogans.

In reality, the hypothetical chance of a postwar Communist seizure of power by quasi-democratic means had already vanished by 1948, just as it had in Italy. In both countries the Communists were being driven into a prolonged isolation as a consequence of the *coup de Prague* of February 1948; and by the time they emerged from the shadows into the light of the post-Stalin era, the whole character of West European politics had been radically altered by the industrial boom of the 1950s and the integration of the labor movement into the new social order. But it took time for this to sink in. In the early 1950s the debate between Communists and fellow travelers was still conducted in terms set by the former: the question appeared to be how intellectuals could best give their allegiance to the proletariat. That it was their duty to do this, as the only valid riposte to the restoration of the prewar society, neither side questioned—until Merleau-Ponty came along in 1955 and did just that, though he did it in the form of a critique of his erstwhile fellow-editor. What he had to say about Sartre's fellow-traveling went home because by 1955 it was already becoming evident that the CP was doomed to remain in isolation as long as it clung to the myth of proletarian revolution. But in a narrower sense his critique was effective because it laid bare Sartre's chief theoretical weakness: his injection of an extreme subjectivism and voluntarism into what he was pleased to call Marxism. To Merleau-Ponty, who had digested his Lenin, but who was also aware of the prewar debate in Central Europe, Sartre's position appeared hopelessly idealistic.[21]

[20] See Merleau-Ponty's polemic against Sartre in *Les Aventures de la dialectique,* especially pp. 81 ff., 131 ff., and Sartre's own antecedent dispute with Claude Lefort in the columns of *Temps Modernes,* No. 89 (April, 1953).

[21] Merleau-Ponty, *Les Aventures de la dialectique,* pp. 213 ff.: "Ce qui distingue Sartre du marxisme, même dans la période récente, c'est donc toujours sa philosophie du cogito": a justified observation which anticipated subsequent comments on Sartre's magnum opus, the *Critique de la raison dialectique* (Paris, 1960). Cf. Georges Lukács, *Existentialisme ou Marxisme?* (Paris, 1948).

It might seem that we have wandered away from our starting point, which was the assimilation of the German heritage. But the central fact about the postwar debate is that it was both philosophical and political. The intelligentsia could either accept or reject the Communist claim that 1917 represented the fulfillment of 1789, that Marxism-Leninism stood in the tradition of the French Enlightenment, and that it was the philosophy (or "ideology"—the two terms were never clearly distinguished) of the new revolutionary class, the proletariat. If the claim was accepted, their duty was clear: whatever their reservations about the CP, (not to mention the USSR), the intellectuals had to identify themselves with it; or if—like Sartre and his friends—they could not bring themselves to do so, they were bound at least to side with it against its enemies. The issue was debated in these terms because the central question was still the historic status of the Russian Revolution. Acceptance or rejection of Marxism was identified with acceptance or rejection of Leninism. The subversive character of Merleau-Ponty's operation lay in his pointing out that Marxism posed questions which Lenin had not answered, and that in any case it transcended the horizon of the party faithful. What he called "Occidental Marxism" was plainly more suited to the needs of the intellectual stratum than the ready-made doctrines handed down from Moscow. In particular, his interpretation took account both of the new understanding of Hegel which Kojève had introduced in France, and of the Central European discussion of 1923-33, which reflected an awareness that the participants were caught up in a crisis of culture. At this level it was not possible for the CP theorists to follow him—at any rate not before the 1960s, when the more intelligent among them had quietly absorbed some of the heresies of their critics.[22]

Once the question was posed in this fashion, the intellectuals could no longer be content with the lead given them by the CP theorists: not merely because the party itself looked less and less like a revolutionary force, but because its understanding of history—and indeed

[22] Merleau-Ponty, *Les Aventures de la dialectique,* especially his observations on Max Weber and the problem of intellectual and moral relativism, pp. 16 ff., 43 ff. This was the heart of the whole matter, as Lukács had perceived in 1923, and as his French interpreter was to point out again in 1955.

of its own doctrine—was shown to be defective. The revisionism of Merleau-Ponty led to that of the *Arguments* group which ultimately went beyond him. In the writings of this group the theory of revolution gave place to the critique of industrial society, whether capitalist or socialist, though the socialist solution was preferred. At the same time the political standpoint became frankly neutralist. This development belongs to the post-Stalin era; it took definite shape in the 1960s, when it became difficult to say whether the adherents of the new school were still Marxists, although most of them continued to employ Marxian concepts (but likewise Hegelian, Husserlian, and Freudian ones). In their case the assimilation of Hegel and Marx had been pushed to the point where both or either were seen as major thinkers of the nineteenth century, rather than as guides to the future. Something of this had indeed already been implicit in Kojève's belief that after the breakthrough of rationalism in the French Revolution it was, in the strict sense, no longer possible to stem the march towards a rationally organized planetary society, and that all further upheavals would have something secondary and repetitive about them.[23]

All this may seem rather remote from the political scene, and typical of the intellectuals' tendency to overrate their own importance. That there was some remoteness compared with the Central European situation of the 1920s and early 1930s is undeniable. The difference extends even to personalities. After all, Lukács had been a leading figure among the Hungarian Communists, quite apart from his participation in the brief Hungarian revolution of 1919. His philosophical heresies had a bearing upon the internal politics of the International, and when he was solemnly denounced by *Pravda* in 1924, it was not for having questioned Engels' interpretation of Hegel, but for having by implication challenged Moscow's claim to the custodianship of the true doctrine. For the imposition of Leninism entailed just that. If there was only one orthodox interpretation of Marxism, and if it was

[23] Kojève, p. 505. For the later development of the *Arguments* group see Henri Lefebvre, *Introduction à la modernité* (Paris, 1962). Kostas Axelos, *Marx: Penseur de la technique* (Paris, 1961) and *Vers la pensée planétaire* (Paris, 1964). The group had previously sponsored the translation of Lukács' 1923 work, as well as the publication of writings centered on the analysis of industrial society and its cultural problems. For its increasing absorption in anthropological questions see *Arguments* Nos. 18, 22 and 24 (1960-1961).

to be found in Lenin, then any reservations—even if initially confined to the philosophical domain—were bound to have an unsettling effect on Communists in Central and Western Europe who were not yet reconciled to Russian guidance. To be anything but a Leninist signified in the circumstances that it might be possible for Communists to be orthodox without following the Moscow line—which was just what was not wanted.[24]

Yet it would be erroneous to suppose that the issue was simply one of political control. That is what it became in the later years of the Stalin era, but it was emphatically a different matter for East and Central European Communists: notably before they had themselves come to power in 1945-48. This is always misunderstood by people who fail to grasp that when Communists argue about "consciousness" they are talking politics, even though they may appear to be carrying on a dispute over philosophy. Communist thinking (theoretical and practical) centers on the idea of "the party," and this concept cannot be understood in organizational terms alone. It entails a whole series of more or less generalized philosophical notions about the historical process: specifically about the relation of the party leadership to its followers, and of the party itself to the proletariat. It is of the essence of Leninism to believe that there are certain *theoretical* problems (notably that of political morality) which can only be resolved in *practice*—specifically in the practice of the Communist party. Unless this is grasped, the peculiar status of philosophy in Communist theorizing must remain a mystery.

It was no mystery to Sartre and Merleau-Ponty, who realized quite well that the *theoretical* dispute was an intensely *practical* matter: if the Communists were wrong in their interpretation of the world, they would never come to power—at any rate not in Western Europe, where they were not helped by Soviet arms and could not exploit the

[24] Merleau-Ponty, *Les Aventures de la dialectique,* pp. 81 ff. Korsch, pp. 2 ff. The Lukács of 1923, whom the French revisionists of the 1950s adopted, had been the hope of Korsch and other German "ultra-leftists" who wanted a "West European Communism" independent of Moscow. This last was never Lukács' attitude, and when the political implications of his heresy were brought home to him in 1924 by the barrage of Soviet criticism, he fell silent, as did most of his Hungarian followers (including the future arch-Stalinist, Revai). But then politics were directly involved. In France this had not really been the case since 1948.

tensions inherent in a backward, pre-industrial setting where the "bourgeois revolution" had not yet occurred. It was not enough to say that Western capitalism might once more slide into an economic depression, as it had done in the 1930s: there was no guarantee that this would result in a proletarian revolution, any more than it had on the earlier occasion. What needed to be shown was that the Communist party possessed a true understanding of the epoch: that the dialectic of history was indeed such as to promote the polarization of society into hostile camps, with the working class increasingly grouped around the CP; and this in turn entailed an examination of the Leninist view of politics. If it was basically determinist, there was no essential difference between Leninism and the older Social Democratic orthodoxy represented by Kautsky. If, on the other hand, it was voluntaristic and secretly elitist, the question arose whether Communist theory was really adapted to its own practice. Might it not be that the Communists misconceived their own purpose when they placed so much weight on the laws of history and even of nature? Did not a truly dialectical approach entail the recognition that there was no such thing as a material situation independent of the human mind that comes to grips with it?[25]

Clearly this was the point where the revisionist assault on Communist orthodoxy met the Existentialist critique of rationalism and scientism. Both had the same theme: human freedom, specifically freedom to shape the future. The new interest in Marx's youthful writings sprang from the realization that he had himself encountered this problem in the process of emancipating himself from Hegel, and —temporarily at least—resolved it in what appeared to be an Existentialist manner. True, he had subsequently abandoned this promising line of approach and exchanged it for another, difficult to distinguish from positivism (especially after Engels had got to work on it). But

[25] Merleau-Ponty, *Les Aventures de la dialectique,* pp. 82 ff. The question had to be posed in these seemingly abstract terms because Lenin's writings—notably *Materialism and Empiriocriticsm,* with its pre-Hegelian, indeed pre-Kantian, doctrine of cognition—had become the foundation of Communist philosophizing. Though Lenin's *practice* was voluntaristic, his philosophy implied a belief in immutable laws impervious to human volition. This was something the Existentialists found impossible to accept. They could also—once Kojève had clarified the point for them—appeal to Hegel and to the young Marx.

the initial spark had never been extinguished: it was there even in Lenin's voluntaristic concept of "the party" as the focus of rebellion against the mere facticity of events. All that was needed—or so it seemed to Merleau-Ponty in 1955, as it had seemed to Lukács three decades earlier—was to abandon an inadequate notion of cognition which had given rise to the curious medley of science and metaphysics characteristic of "orthodox Marxism."[26]

But was the matter really so simple? Might it not be that Marx had been wise to sacrifice his youthful idealism, and that the Communists were right to prefer Lenin to Lukács? Merleau-Ponty himself was troubled by doubt. If Marx had not been able to resolve the tension between dialectic and materialism, and had finally settled for an uneasy compromise reminiscent of the rationalism of the later Hegel,[27] might this not be because the problem was inherently insoluble, at any rate with the conceptual tools available to Hegel and Marx? Both thinkers had in the end adopted what amounted to a determinist attitude: Reality unfolded as a process whose logic could be grasped by the mind, but not in any significant way altered by conscious volition. Yet the dialectic of the subject-object relation carried a different implication. Who was right—the youthful Marx who had aimed at the "realization" of philosophy, or the author of *Capital* who appeared to believe that the historical process went on, as it were, under its own steam? Was consciousness a mere epiphenomenon? The Communist answer—already suggested by Lenin and rendered explicit by his successors—was to the effect that this was true only of bourgeois consciousness. In addition there was also the collective consciousness of the Communist party and—at a remove—of the proletariat. *This* consciousness was no epiphenomenon. It not only reflected the world, but also remolded it. And the locus of this conscious reflection-cum-remolding of the world was none other than the party itself: a collec-

[26] Merleau-Ponty, *Les Aventures de la dialectique,* p. 87, where the conflict between Leninism and "Occidental Marxism" is traced back to its original source in Marx.

[27] The Hegel of 1827, not the one of 1807, in Merleau-Ponty's terminology; cf. his essay "L'Existentialisme chez Hegel" (1947) in *Sens et non-sens,* pp. 109 ff. This took up a theme suggested by J. Hyppolite in a lecture on Hegel which reverted once more to the subject of his (and Kojève's) interpretation of the *Phenomenology*. See also Merleau-Ponty, "La querelle de l'existentialisme," in *ibid.,* p. 137, for the comparison of Marx and Kierkegaard.

tive philosopher, as well as the instrument of mankind's resolve to recreate itself.[28]

But if this was so, then everything depended on the party's ability to rise to the occasion. The fate of mankind was, quite literally, entrusted to its keeping: a solemn thought, but also an alarming one. What was to happen if the collective philosopher failed in its duty? Moreover, there remained a nagging doubt whether the whole idea of such a fusion of thought and action might not be an illusion possible only on the eve of an approaching revolution: whether of the 1789, the 1848, or the 1917 type. Korsch had already pointed out in 1930 that the Marxian "union of theory and practice" had fallen apart in the years following the failure of the 1848 risings. Thereafter, Marx and Engels had developed a scientific materialism which—at any rate in the formulation it received from Engels in the 1880s—implicitly denied any subject-object dialectic.[29] It was indeed arguable that the Russian Revolution had made it possible to restore the original vision of a transformation in which the Communist party would, deliberately and of set purpose, undertake the task of "changing the world." But this idealist formulation (first put forward by Marx in the 1845 *Theses on Feuerbach*) was difficult to reconcile with scientism. Moreover, the revolution had not—in the USSR—led to the "realization of philosophy," and in the West it had not occurred at all. Was this merely another pause, or did it suggest that the idea of a total transformation had to be abandoned, along with the legacy of pre-1848 Romanticism in general?

That Merleau-Ponty was able to pose the question in this form testified to his assimilation of the theoretical and practical lessons sug-

[28] This was also Lukács' standpoint in 1923; hence his surprise at the indignation caused by his book. He had in fact made explicit the subject-object dialectic inherent in Lenin's conception of the party as the (conscious) vehicle of the (unconscious) process; and this became the esoteric doctrine of most leading Communists in the Stalin era, though Lukács himself repudiated his own insights, at any rate for public consumption. The trouble was that the masses needed a faith, and this could only be supplied by a rigidly determinist doctrine which deduced the certainty of victory from the "scientific" understanding of causal processes embracing nature and history.

[29] Korsch, pp. 5 ff., 15 ff., and Merleau-Ponty's very similar suggestions in *Les Aventures de la dialectique*, p. 85. So far as philosophy was concerned, this change entailed a naively realistic doctrine of cognition which abandoned the insights gained by German idealism, but it also had implications for the understanding of history and its "laws."

gested by the fate of Leninism (and of Lukács). His immediate postwar writings[30] were already distinguished by a thorough appreciation of the issues posed by the Central European debate of the 1920s: notably the critique of scientism in its quasi-Marxist form. But in 1945-47 it had still been possible for him to believe that the "realization of philosophy" was around the corner. By 1955 this faith had evaporated: history quite plainly refused to be rewritten, and the philosophers had returned to their studies. Sartre was the inheritor of this failure. Paradoxically, his influence grew as that of his erstwhile fellow combatant declined, and this although (or because) he was less of a Marxist than Merleau-Ponty: indeed in a fundamental sense no Marxist at all. His star rose over a landscape which left little room for hope that the world might be shaped (or shape itself) in accordance with the heart's desire. This was all he needed. Sartre had always been at his best in fighting hopeless battles. Indeed it is arguable that the whole of his gigantic intellectual *oeuvre* is proof of the capacity of the human mind to engage itself *contra mundum*.

The point where Sartre diverged from Marx was indicated by Merleau-Ponty when he noted that, for all his verbal employment of Marxian concepts, Sartre had at heart remained a Cartesian.[31] The subject-object relation appeared in his writings—all of them, including his political tracts—as a confrontation between the individual ego and an external situation which receives its meaning from and through the ego. In this way he set up a counterpoint to the determinism of the orthodox Marxists, but only at the cost of dispensing with the real historical process altogether. The Sartrean dialectic is that of a spontaneous will pitted against the inert resistance of the material world. Sartre's libertarianism is absolute because the objective relation has been suppressed. History is *causa sui*. It comes about because it is willed. Revolutions are made by those who understand that men are

[30] In particular, "Marxisme et Philosophie," in *Sens et non-sens*, pp. 221 ff.

[31] *Les Aventures de la dialectique*, pp. 131 ff., in particular p. 178: "Le même terme de praxis que les *Thèses sur Feuerbach* employaient pour désigner une activité immanente à l'objet de l'histoire, Sartre le reprend pour désigner l'activité 'pure' qui fait être dans l'histoire le prolétariat. Le 'je ne sais quoi' sartrien—la liberté radicale—prend possession de la praxis." And p. 227: "Le prolétariat dont parle Sartre n'est ni constatable, ni contestable, ni vivant, n'est pas un phénomène, c'est une catégorie déléguée pour représenter l'humanité dans la pensée de Sartre."

free to shape the future. The Communist faith in history is an illusion; but Communism is not an illusion. It can be made real, once the proletariat is driven to revolt against the "alienation" imposed on its existence: provided its leaders—on whom in the last resort everything depends—have the ability and the will to break through the barriers imposed by bourgeois society.[32]

The more technical aspects of Sartre's work need not concern us here. His conclusions can be anticipated, notably insofar as they have a bearing upon the theme of "revolutionary humanism."[33] They may be conveniently summed up as follows:

a) Sartre's basic aim is to "reconquer man inside Marxism" and in particular to liberate the Hegelian-Marxian dialectic from the dead-weight of determinism. This theme is pursued through the introduction of teleological notions. What M. Aimé Patri has called Sartre's "existentialized Marxism" is a doctrine which restores to man the freedom to transcend the historical situation in which he finds himself. At the logical and epistemological level, this theme is worked out with the help of a concept of "intentionality" which Sartre owes to Husserl: the German thinker who, with Hegel and Marx, made the deepest impression on him.

b) The formal coherence of the doctrine is secured with the aid of concepts which ultimately go back to the great age of German idealism (and romanticism). At the same time the link with Marxism is retained by way of the notion that the proletariat is the bearer of a universal truth. This is because its existence manifests in an extreme form the "alienation" imposed upon the whole of mankind. As long as this state of affairs lasts, Marxism is "une évidence indépassable." When the union of philosophy and the proletariat (of which Communism is the political form) has brought about the liberation of mankind from material bondage, Marxism will disappear. "A philosophy of liberty will take its place. But we possess no means, no intellectual

[32] Merleau-Ponty, *Les Aventures de la dialectique,* pp. 214 ff., and *passim.* For a critique of Sartre, and indeed of the whole Hegelian tradition, from a radically empiricist standpoint see Gurvitch, *Dialectique et sociologie,* especially pp. 157 ff.

[33] See, in particular, the first part of Sartre, *Critique de la raison dialectique: Question de méthode* (Paris, 1960); this is a self-contained essay originally published in *Les Temps Modernes* (autumn, 1957). See also Sartre's essay *Matérialisme et révolution,* in *Situations III* (Paris, 1949).

instrument, no concrete experience, which permits us to conceive either that liberty or that philosophy."[34]

c) Sartre considers that orthodox Marxism has become a scholastic system incapable of reaching the concrete reality of history, or of perceiving the nature of individual experience. Being deterministic, it is morally neutral, that is, in practice immoral. There is no Marxist ethic, but there can be a humanist ethic which incorporates Marx's insights. Such an ethic must proceed from the self-evident truth that man is a free and responsible being, not the instrument of a process over which he has no control. Consciousness is not an object among others. Materialism is a metaphysic, and an unattractive one at that. There is no "materialist dialectic," and the study of nature does not yield universal laws applicable to man. One must choose between materialism and freedom, and Sartre has chosen the latter.

d) Communist materialism is a revolutionary myth which at one time had a certain practical value, in that it freed the proletariat from religious superstition and gave it the confidence needed to challenge the established order. But its mythical character has now become evident, and it is thus no longer acceptable as an explanation of the world, nor can it serve any longer as a source of moral energies. Its place must and will be taken by a revolutionary humanism which will dispense with determinism and restore the true dialectic of subject and object, action and cognition.[35]

By way of conclusion it may be said that Sartre's enterprise retains the notion of ontological speculation as a permanent and insurmountable requirement of the human mind, while the early Marx had envisioned a "fulfillment of philosophy" which does away with this particular mode of being: the mode of isolated thinkers reflecting upon the world, while the ordinary man merely experiences it. For the rest, it is plain enough that Sartre—in this respect following the example of Merleau-Ponty—resumed the attempt made by Lukács

[34] Sartre, *Critique de la raison dialectique,* p. 32.

[35] Sartre, *Situations III,* pp. 135 ff.; also Raymond Aron, "Existentialisme et Marxisme" in *L'homme, le monde, l'histoire: Cahiers du Collège Philosophique* (Paris, 1948). For a critical comment delivered from an independent Marxist vantage-point see Henri Lefebvre, "Critique de la critique non-critique," *Nouvelle revue marxiste* (July, 1961). For an early explication of Sartre's standpoint see Dionys Mascolo, *Le Communisme* (Paris, 1953).

in 1923. His speculative construction operates with a notion of history which turns the empirical proletariat into an entity endowed with metaphysical traits: principally the union of subject and object, realized by the Communist party—not the French CP (with which he was never on the best of terms) but an ideal Communist party, such as has never existed anywhere. The practical aspect of this ultra-Leninist vision comes to light when it is considered that, for the party to approximate such a mission, it would have to be composed of philosopher-kings, or at least allow itself to be guided by them. In short, the whole conception is at the furthest possible remove from the actual empirical working class and its political organizations, including the Communist party.

The actual development of the revisionist movement from the late 1950s followed a different line. Sartre's grandiose synthesis having disclosed its speculative character, the true revisionists pursued the direction already suggested by Lefebvre in his writings, culminating in his *Introduction à la modernité* (1962). Following a lead given from across the Rhine by the postwar neo-Marxists (Bloch, Horkheimer, Adorno) they turned away from system-building towards empiricism. Instead of trying to construct yet another universal synthesis, they undertook the more modest task of reconstructing traditional sociology with the help of Marxian insights. Conversely, Marxism was itself subjected to critical treatment in the light of modern anthropological, sociological, and psychological studies. In the main, this was the work of the *Arguments* group, in which Pierre Fougeyrollas and Kostas Axelos took the lead, though still following in the wake of Lefebvre. But even orthodox Marxists like Pierre Naville and Ernest Mandel (both Trotskyist sympathizers) gave increasing weight to empirical investigations.[36] At the political level, the task of revising the ancient formulas was pursued with some success by writers like Yvon Bourdet and Gilles Martinet.[37]

[36] Pierre Naville, *Vers l'automatisme social? Problèmes du travail et de l'automation* (Paris, 1963). Ernest Mandel, *Traité D'Économie marxiste* (Paris, 1962). The latter work, a massive and enormously learned, though somewhat doctrinaire, exposition of Marxist economic thought, had the incidental merit of bringing the Franco-Belgian intellectual world up to date on a traditionally somewhat neglected subject, since its author was at home with German-Austrian and Anglo-American literature.

[37] Pierre Fougeyrollas, *Le marxisme en question* (Paris, 1959); Martinet, *Le*

This summary account anticipates a more considered treatment of some of the main themes. For the moment we are obliged to conclude our survey of the postwar scene with some remarks on the encounter between Marxism and Christian Socialism.

Marxism Versus Christian Socialism

A discussion of this subject must from the start relinquish any hope of dealing adequately with the metaphysical dimension: perhaps an inherent impossibility, quite apart from the problem of coping with the literature.[38] The latter in any case ranges over the entire field of social philosophy, and in addition takes in a large sector of French public life since the 1930s when the Popular Front witnessed a major Communist attempt to win sympathizers within the Catholic fold.[39] The failure of this experiment was soon swallowed up in the greater disaster of 1939-40, followed by the Resistance movement which threw Christians and Communists together, with the Socialists in

marxisme de notre temps (Paris, 1962); tr. as *Marxism of Our Time* (New York, 1964). Yvon Bourdet, *Communisme et marxisme* (Paris, 1963). See also Jean Marchal, *Deux essais sur le marxisme* (Paris, 1955), for an attempt to salvage the core of the doctrine from the dissolution of the system.

[38] For further reading on this subject see, in particular, Gabriel Marcel, *Existentialisme chrétien* (Paris, 1947). Jacques Maritain, *La Philosophie morale* (Paris, 1960). Emmanuel Mounier, *Le Personnalisme* (Paris, 1949). Jean Lacroix, *Marxisme, existentialisme, personnalisme* (Paris, 1949, 1951). A. Mandouze and others, *Les chrétiens et la politique* (Paris, 1948). Jean-Yves Calvez, *La Pensée de Karl Marx* (Paris, 1956). Georges M.-M. Cottier, *L'Athéisme du jeune Marx: ses origines hégéliennes* (Paris, 1959); *Du romantisme au marxisme* (Paris, 1961). Pierre Bigo, *Marxisme et humanisme: Introduction à l'oeuvre économique de Karl Marx* (Paris, 1953, 1961). Henri Desroche, *Marxisme et religions* (Paris, 1962). For the Marxist side of the debate see Garaudy, *Dieu est mort*. Lucien Goldmann, *Le dieu caché* (Paris, 1955); *Recherches dialectiques*. See also *Esprit*, notably of May-June, 1948; December, 1950, and July-August, 1951.

[39] Following Thorez' public appeal to this effect in a broadcast on April 17, 1936; see Gérard Walter, "La main tendue aux catholiques," in *Histoire du partie communiste français* (Paris, 1948), pp. 293 ff. For the Catholic response see G. Fessard, *Le dialogue catholique-communiste, est-il possible?* (Paris, 1937). Some of the non-Communist sympathizers grouped themselves around the periodical *Terre Nouvelle*, Louis Martin-Chauffier being prominent among Catholic writers willing to envisage a limited collaboration. The whole movement soon came under a hierarchical ban, doctrinally supported by the Encyclical *Divini Redemptoris* of March 19, 1937 with its uncompromising condemnation of "atheist Communism."

many cases providing the link between them. The upshot was Léon Blum's abortive attempt in 1945-46 to found a French Labor party embracing Socialists and left-wing Christian Democrats: an initiative wrecked by the intransigence of his own followers. In the postwar period Christian Socialism consequently signified the growing rebelliousness of the Christian Democratic party's own left wing: a rebellion within the framework of Catholicism, though the Vatican's ban on all aspects of socialism was only lifted by the promulgation of the 1961 Encyclical *Mater et Magistra.* This document, by implication anyhow, legitimized socialism, though not Communism (i.e., Marxism), thereby at last facilitating political cooperation between democratic Socialists and the Catholic Left (especially among trade unionists). But whereas the Socialist party had for years offered a welcome to believing Protestants, including some prominent laymen, it remained *de facto* closed to Catholics, however progressive in their general orientation.[40]

The counterpart of all this activity on the far Left was the formation in 1947 of the *Union des Chrétiens progressistes* whose ideologists (notably A. Mandouze and the Abbé Boulier) virtually accepted the Communist program minus its atheism. Parallel with this heresy ran the attempt made by some prominent Dominicans to launch a species of Christian Communism: an experiment which ended with a split in the worker-priest movement and the adherence of a considerable number of its members to the Communist party. An intellectual reflex of this movement is to be found in the writings of Henri Desroche.[41]

[40] Philip M. Williams, *Crisis and Compromise: Politics in the Fourth Republic,* pp. 103 ff. G. Suffert, *Les Catholiques et la Gauche* (Paris, 1960). Pierre Fougeyrollas, *La conscience politique dans la France contemporaine* (Paris, 1963), pp. 90 ff. suggests that the Christian Democratic (M.R.P.) electorate was rather more conservative than the *militants,* let alone the movement's anti-capitalist ideologists. But the biggest stumbling block has always been education. For the left-wing orientation of many French Protestants see Stuart R. Schram, *Protestantism and Politics in France* (Alençon, 1954), pp. 238 ff.

[41] *Marxisme et religions;* some of the author's earlier writings reflected the hope of a "Christian Communism." His subsequent position could perhaps be described as "Christian Socialism," in which respect it did not differ much from that of some contemporary German, Swiss, Dutch, and French Protestant theologians. For the worker-priest movement see Adrien Dansette, *Destin du Catholicisme français 1926-1956* (Paris, 1957), pp. 165 ff. For an impressive

Against this background it is understandable that conservative Catholic theologians (notably G. Fessard and Henri de Lubac) should have regarded the "personalist" philosophy of the influential *Esprit* group (E. Mounier, Jean Lacroix, P. Ricoeur, Jean-Marie Domenach) as a staircase leading to the netherworld of progressivism and Christian Communism. In actual fact the editor of *Esprit* and his friends shared with the heretical *Chrétiens progressistes* only the rejection of capitalism, which they tended to identify with liberal individualism. This, however, was balanced by repudiation of Communist collectivism and materialism, so that, unlike the *progressistes,* the circle around Mounier always maintained its essential independence. Moreover, by the 1960s, when Mounier himself had long left the scene, his followers had absorbed the sociological concept of "industrial society" as a reality comprising both capitalism and socialism, and potentially dangerous to human freedom, whatever the political regime and the control of property. Their philosophy now acquired a post-Marxian tinge which brought it into the general stream of revisionism and socialist humanism. While fully accepting the Marxian critique of capitalist society (notably under the aspect of human alienation) they did not feel obliged to treat Marxism as a seamless web, to be accepted or rejected *in toto*. The *Esprit* group had become socialist without being Marxist.[42]

If Desroche represented the extreme left within the Catholic camp,

---

statement of the Christian Socialist position by a prominent Dominican theologian who did not conceal his sympathy for Marx, see M. D. Chenu, *Pour une théologie du travail* (Paris, 1955). For the link between the pro-Communist theologians and the radical wing of the worker-priest movement, see Dansette's comments, in *Destin du Catholicisme français,* pp. 225 ff., on the role of Boulier, Desroche, and Montuclard in launching the *Union des Chrétiens progressistes* at the end of 1947: a date which not accidentally coincided with the outbreak of the Cold War. Montuclard, one of the prime animators of the worker-priest movement even after it had run into trouble with the hierarchy in 1953, had pioneered the Christian Communist position since 1936, when a small radical group known as *Jeunesse de l'Église* came together under his patronage. See Dansette, *ibid.,* p. 234.

[42] For this interesting development see, in particular, the writings of François Perroux, notably his preface to the *Pléiade* edition of Marx's economic writings, Vol. I, ed. by M. Rubel (Paris, 1963). Perroux's public standing as head of a major academic institution (the *Institut de Science Économique Appliquée*), and his intellectual distinction placed the official seal upon a doctrine previously associated with a group of rather obscure philosophers, of whom E. Mounier (1905-1950) had been the founder and leader.

and Mounier's group the left-center, the right wing found an able and learned spokesman in Fessard, who had already won his spurs in the prewar controversies over the Communist "united front" tactics.[43] Like the *Temps Modernes* and *Esprit* groups, Fessard had come to his understanding of Marx by way of Kojève's interpretation of Hegel: specifically, of the celebrated passage on "master and servant" in Hegel's *Phenomenology*.[44] This had been an important link between Hegel and the young Marx, with the difference that Hegel had placed the emphasis upon the unequal status of master and servant, whereas for Marx the true historical dialectic involved man's relationship to nature, which latter he transforms by his labor, thereby at the same time transforming his own nature. It was this notion which provided the main theme for the Existentialist neo-Marxists, once Lefebvre and Merleau-Ponty had translated it into terms proper to the French tradition. And it was likewise this humanist aspect of Marxism which rendered it attractive to the Christian Socialist group around Mounier and *Esprit*. For Fessard, on the contrary, Marx had merely isolated one element of the dialectic and thereby unwittingly provoked a reactionary countermovement which made an absolute of the other: the mastery of nature and society by "supermen" or "ruling races." The source of the whole confusion was to be found in Hegel's philosophy, which was the root of both Communism and Fascism. The weakness of Communism, in Fessard's view, was its neglect of the political element, though (following Lenin) the Communists had surreptitiously smuggled it back into their doctrine, where strictly speaking it had no place. Fascism, on the other hand, misunderstood society and had nothing to say about economics. Uniquely concerned with the political struggle for domination over lower classes and conquered races, it supplied the antithesis to Communism with its obses-

[43] For G. Fessard's postwar publications see, in particular, *France, prends garde de perdre ta liberté* (Paris, 1946); *Par delà le fascisme et le communisme* (Paris, n.d.); "Le Mystère de la société. Recherches sur le sens de l'histoire," in *Recherches de science religieuse,* Nos. 1 and 2 (Paris, 1948).

[44] Kojève, "Hegel, Marx et le christianisme," in *Critique,* No. 3-4 (Paris, 1946), where incidentally he paid Fessard the ironical compliment of suggesting that he might have become the leading Marxist theorist in France if he had so desired (p. 308). Kojève's own position was Hegelian rather than Marxist, in that he viewed the struggle between Fascism and Communism as a conflict between right-wing and left-wing Hegelians.

sion about economics and class conflict. Thus the two opponents were busy tearing each other and mankind to pieces, in the name of one-sided doctrines ultimately derived from their common source in Hegel's philosophy.[45] In siding with the servant against the master, while making an absolute of "human labor," Marx had impoverished the Hegelian dialectic, and at the same time, by dissolving the state in society, made it impossible to understand politics. Conversely, the Fascist philosophers had lost sight of all human relations other than the master-servant one. To escape from this mortal combat between the warring sides, mankind must find a middle road, which for Fessard inevitably implied the reconciliation of social conflict in the *corpus mysticum Christi*.[46]

Fessard's critique was directed against the Communist vision, but it could also be turned against Kojève's notion that, with the pacification of the globe and the instauration of social harmony, history as such would end: there would be no further wars and revolutions, indeed no historical action of any kind, and for the same reason philosophy too would come to an end, since it would no longer be necessary to change either the world or the categories of understanding.[47] Not all Marxists accepted this. In the rather more disillusioned perspective of the later Lefebvre and of Merleau-Ponty, the whole idea of a final consummation was extruded as unreal and ultimately theological. From their standpoint (which in this respect at least was close to that of liberal empiricists such as Gurvitch and Raymond

[45] Basically this was also Kojève's view, with the difference that he regarded the ultimate victory of Communism as both possible and desirable, though by no means certain. The originality of Kojève lay in the fact that he combined his Marxist sympathies with the traditional stress on human freedom. It was this emphasis on the indeterminate character of history which so greatly impressed the Existentialists.

[46] *Par delà le fascisme et le communisme,* p. 164. Fessard did not complete this lengthy essay, possibly because the Encyclical *Humani Generis* had meanwhile pronounced an official condemnation of Hegel's philosophy; see Iring Fetscher, "Der Marxismus im Spiegel der französischen Philosophie," in *Marxismusstudien* (Tübingen, 1954), I, 207.

[47] *Introduction à la lecture de Hegel,* p. 434 n. Kojève refers to Marx's vision of the "realm of freedom" in *Capital,* Vol. III, ch. 48, as an anticipation of such a state of affairs: a questionable interpretation, since human freedom from material pressure, once attained, might be supposed to release dormant energies not confined to the mere "pursuit of happiness" that Kojève treats as the probable goal of the process.

Aron) the Hegelian eschatology, even in the form given to it by Kojève, failed to take account of the limitless possibilities of human freedom.

The practical relevance of these seemingly abstruse controversies must be judged in the light of the contemporary situation, which in France was characterized by the presence of two great totalitarian rivals: the Catholic Church and the Communist party. Both made an appeal to *l'homme total;* both controlled wide-ranging mass organizations enrolling millions of Frenchmen; not merely as voters, but as trade unionists, political activists, civil servants, school and university teachers, students, artists, scientists, and even philosophers. Both claimed to possess not *a* truth, but *the* truth. Catholics were fully aware that Communist rule would signify the complete secularization of French culture (already far advanced under democracy) and the relegation of their church to a status similar to the one it held in Poland. Communists for their part could not fail to realize that the Catholic hold over a sizeable minority of the working class—not to mention the peasantry—was the biggest obstacle to their political progress. Against this background, philosophical tournaments between Catholic and Communist writers had an implicit political content, the more so since both sides were aiming at the middle ground occupied by the free-thinking intelligentsia of the traditional non-Communist (and non-Catholic) Left. It was not an idle matter that Communist, Socialist, and Catholic unions competed for the loyalty of school teachers and civil servants, as well as for the support of industrial workers. In the long run, the orientation of the intellectuals was bound to be decisive. The Communists knew this as well as their opponents, whence the importance they attached to the "ideological" struggle.[48]

If it were possible to abstract from the religious issue—a peculiarly

[48] In particular Roger Garaudy, *Perspectives de l'homme,* where Existentialism and Catholicism are treated as the only serious rivals of Marxism. For the Thomist school, Maritain repaid the compliment in *La Philosophie morale,* especially pp. 263 ff.; at a more polemical, though still scholarly level, Cottier, in *Du romantisme au marxisme,* struck back at Hegelians and Marxists alike, chiefly on the ground of their atheism, while at the same time denouncing liberalism in general, and the liberal economists in particular, as being responsible for the rise of a godless protest movement. For a more sympathetic approach see Bigo, where the "truth" of Marxism is located in its sociology, its "error" in its metaphysics; also Calvez, pp. 536 ff.

unreal notion in a country like France, where theology has been a political matter for so long—it would be tempting to follow Garaudy's example[49] and list the rival schools somewhat as follows: (a) Existentialism (with a subdivision to take account of the differences between Sartre and Merleau-Ponty); (b) Neo-Hegelianism (Alexandre Kojève, Jean Wahl, Jean Hyppolite); (c) Christian Existentialism (Gabriel Marcel) and Personalism (Emmanuel Mounier, Jean Lacroix); (d) Christian humanism (Teilhard de Chardin); (e) traditional Thomism (Etienne Gilson, Jacques Maritain, H. de Lubac and others); (f) Marxism, meaning of course the Marxism of the Communist party, i.e., Marxism-Leninism. In fact, as has been shown, these distinctions are subsidiary to the major ideological currents; but they are inadequate also from a theoretical viewpoint. Nor does it help much to narrow the field by substituting a tripartite distinction between Catholics, Existentialists, and Marxists, for some of the Marxists are in fact positivists, and others Hegelians, while yet others have accepted the Existentialist critique of Hegel. Moreover, no place would be left for liberal empiricism and "post-Marxian" socialism—the dominant trends of the 1960s. Thus it is not possible, on the basis of these distinctions, to account for a phenomenon such as Christian Socialism. Lastly, the obsession with the Catholic-Communist debate obscures the fact that both Hegelianism and Existentialism were imported from a predominantly German-Protestant environment. Some of the difficulties which manifested themselves in the assimilation of these concepts were quite simply due to the intellectual climate of a country which had "missed" the experience of the Protestant Reformation.[50]

The analysis of doctrines belongs to a subsequent chapter. Here

[49] Garaudy, *Perspectives de l'homme,* and also his *Dieu est mort:* a less satisfactory work, though considerably superior to the author's writings during the Stalin era, when his tone was hardly distinguishable from that of embattled party propagandists such as André Stil, André Wurmser, *et autres Kanapas.*

[50] For the rather similar case of post-1945 Poland see Z. A. Jordan's important work *Philosophy and Ideology: the development of philosophy and Marxism-Leninism in Poland since the Second World War* (Dordrecht-Holland, 1963). It can hardly be thought fortuitous that the French controversies had deeper repercussions in Poland than in neighboring Germany (East and West) where both orthodox and revisionist Marxists tended to take it for granted that philosophical debates with Catholics were unlikely to be fruitful (whereas the same did not apply to Protestants).

we may provisionally summarize the conclusions that seem to impose themselves if abstraction is made, for the time being, from the irreconcilable clash of rival world views.

As noted earlier, the French Communist party had since 1920 developed in response to a situation which constantly called in question its original purpose: that of effecting a total revolution. No such revolution could ever in France have won the assent even of the entire working class, let alone the peasantry, or the professional middle class. Yet Communism as a faith made sense only on the assumption that a total revolution was possible, and that it corresponded to the undisclosed purpose of "history." Since these assumptions were mistaken —at any rate so far as France was concerned—the Communist party was obliged to transfer its loyalties to the "socialist fatherland" of the USSR. This in return reacted unfavorably on its national standing, and in particular deepened the gulf which already separated it from the Catholic masses. The latter were themselves divided between democratic and authoritarian currents, but in either case were not willing to support a Communist bid for power, though they might cooperate with the CP for limited purposes in defense of democracy. In the end, therefore, the growing Christian-Democratic current gave rise to a Christian-Socialist offshoot based on an increasingly militant Catholic labor movement: no longer controlled by the hierarchy, and socialist in all but in name. Hence after 1945 the Communist party found itself blocked, not as before by a purely conservative Catholicism rooted in the preindustrial world, but by a modernized Christian-Democratic movement with roots in the urban working class. The emergence of a Christian-Socialist ideology—which gradually developed from the familiar (and tiresome) clerical moralizing to principled rejection of liberal economics and bourgeois property-relations —presented itself as the intellectual counterpart of this modernization. Here Catholicism profited from the fact that—unlike the Protestant churches and sects, notably in the English-speaking world—it was never completely identified with individualism. Having preserved the notion (though at some cost to its understanding of the modern world) that noncapitalist social relations were possible, it could sponsor a guarded critique of bourgeois society, and even identify itself with a quasi-socialist labor movement, so long as religious values were respected.

The totality of these traits constituted an effective hindrance to the spread of Communist influence among an important section of the working class, though the bulk of that class—notably the manual workers in heavy industry—continued to follow the Communist lead, and rejected Christianity as an apology of the constituted order. At a higher social and intellectual level—among technicians, civil servants, salaried employees, teachers, and professional people—Socialist influence (now predominantly associated with these strata) worked in the same direction. By the 1960s, therefore, the basic problem for the Communist party had become that of adapting itself to a multi-party democracy: and this irrespective of the structural changes introduced by the authoritarian Gaullist regime. Conversely, for Catholics the main problem was still that of coming to terms with the modern world: a world of rapid technological progress, industrialization, and technocratic planning. The erosion of Catholicism's traditional rural base underlined the urgent need to shift to an urban-industrial environment, if this could be done without sacrificing certain values hitherto identified with Catholic doctrine and practice.[51]

On a somewhat schematic view of the situation, the tripartite division of intellectual life into Catholics, liberals, and Marxists—insofar as the manifold controversies could be reduced to this denominator—reflected the circumstance that all three schools were trying to work out an attitude proper to a rapidly changing industrial environment. The political alignments cut across these divisions and tended to confuse them: for it was plainly impossible to say where Gaullism stood on what to social theorists were basic issues, since its following included both planners and liberals, whereas the ideological cement was provided by a mixture of nationalism and quasi-Jacobinical republicanism. In principle the Gaullist coalition might come to include some Christian-Democratic and Christian-Socialist elements (though

[51] Dansette, *Destin du Catholicisme français,* pp. 46 ff., and *passim.* The "post-Marxian" approach of the Christian Socialist school is very marked in Perroux's work, and plainly represents the link connecting this school with the revisionism of the former *Arguments* group, notably as represented by Lefebvre; see the latter's *Introduction à la modernité.* But it also has affinities with the thinking of Marxist sociologists such as Naville and Friedmann.

at the cost of shedding its liberal-bourgeois wing). In this case it was likely to become associated with a "third force" position in home and foreign affairs, for which ideological sanction could be found in the writings of the Christian Socialist school.[52]

These considerations were not extraneous to the philosophical disputes, or merely superimposed on them: they formed their political substance; much as in Italy the rapprochement between democratic Socialism and the Catholic Left had given a new political and intellectual complexion to the 1960s. In both countries the problem continued to reside in the totalitarian character of the Communist party, which had not genuinely shed its Stalinist attitudes, and in France at least had perhaps become so fossilized as to have lost much of the capacity for mental renovation. The new phenomenon of Christian Socialism was itself an index to Communism's failure to make good its claim to represent the "live forces of the nation."

[52] Perroux, Preface to Marx, *Capital,* ed. by Rubel (Paris, 1963), especially pp. xliii ff. For the Communist attitude to religion, and specifically to the position of Catholicism in contemporary France, see C. Hainchelin, *Les Origines de la religion* (Paris, 1955; 1st ed., pseudonymously signed L. Henry, 1935). G. Mury, *Essor ou déclin du catholicisme français* (Paris, 1960). M. Verret, *Les Marxistes et la religion* (Paris, 1961). For the sociology of religion see Desroche, "Socialisme et sociologie du christianisme," *Cahiers internationaux de Sociologie* (1956), and the studies published regularly in the *Archives de Sociologie des Religions.*

4

State and Society

Some General Considerations

The distinction between state and society lies at the root of modern political thought. Every theorist who defines the subject of politics—and a fortiori every practitioner who concerns himself with the exercise of power—makes the primary assumption that the two spheres are separable, react upon each other, and are definable in ways that are immediately obvious to everyone. Indeed the very notion of politics depends on the ability to make such a discrimination. In this as in other matters, etymology is not a useful guide, for although the classical *polis* produced the first coherent attempt to define a rational and systematic theory of politics, its fundamental assumptions differed radically from ours. Ancient thought draws no distinction between society and the state, or between the individual and the citizen. In current parlance classical political theory is totalitarian, though it permits free discussion among citizens on ways of governing the *polis* (not, however, on its *raison d'être*). Concerned as it is with the nature of citizenship, Greco-Roman thinking is quite innocent of sociological notions about the interaction of economics and politics: the latter not being regarded as a separate realm, but as the ensemble of relations which, taken together, constitute the polis or republic—that is, the commonwealth of free citizens who by their activities (and by their soldierly virtue) maintain the life of the state. Because the commonwealth is not yet separated from its political organization (every full citizen is a soldier, there is no military and police power standing over and above him), the theory of society is not separated from that of the state. In the modern sense indeed, the state as an independent power comes into being only on the ruins of the ancient commonwealth, much as in postmedieval times it emerges only after the typical feudal decentralization of power has given way to the rise of absolutism.

The assumptions proper to a situation where "politics" forms a separate activity were common to all the movements and parties which arose in nineteenth-century Europe, once the French Revolution had given the signal for the reorganization of the social order. This reorganization might be conceived, on the idealist model, as the conscious rearrangement of society by the political authority (the state); or materialistically, as the refashioning of the state by social forces working from "below," i.e., from the economic sphere. In either case it was taken for granted that state and society are separate and distinct realities. Their interaction takes place in the public sphere, where the individuals appear as citizens of the body politic, without for this reason relinquishing their essential nature as private persons acting for the common good. The privacy from which they emerge, and to which they return when their work as citizens is done, is rooted in economic relations which in the last resort arc grounded in the institution of property. The latter guarantees the individual's independence from the state and is therefore held inviolable by the dominant liberal school. But socialism too assumes a rigid separation of the two spheres, though it seeks to employ the political institution for the purpose of controlling the economic order. The early socialists did not doubt that the problems posed by the industrial revolution called for state intervention; but they regarded the state as the servant of the new industrial society that was about to establish itself on the ruins of its predecessor.[1]

While the notion of society as an intelligible whole appeared almost simultaneously in the thinking of the Saint-Simonians and their German contemporaries during the third and fourth decades of the

[1] Georges Gurvitch, *Les Fondateurs français de la sociologie contemporaine. I. Saint-Simon sociologue,* (Paris, 1955). For a different view see F. A. Hayek, *The Counter-Revolution of Science* (Glencoe, 1955), pp. 105 ff.

nineteenth century, they differed in their respective attitudes to the state. In France the Revolution had laid bare the social roots of the political organism and thereby helped to "de-sacralize" the language in which public affairs were traditionally discussed.[2] In Germany a similar process of demystification had to await the upheaval of 1848-49, and the failure of the brief liberal-democratic upsurge restored the authoritarian tradition which treated the state as a realm independent of and superior to civil society. Hence the "materialist conception of history" (which Marx in the 1840s extracted from his study of the French historians) had a distinctly more subversive ring in Germany than it ever possessed in France. This is why one cannot treat the Marxian doctrine as simply an amalgam of Comte and Hegel, quite apart from the fact that Marx's intellectual debt to Saint-Simon was qualified by his disdain for Comte and his pupils. The Hegelian view of the state as the embodiment of rationality—as against the conflict of material interests which make up the life of civil society—is at odds not merely with Marxism, but with Saint-Simon's and Comte's vision of the social whole. It is one thing to say that Comte's authoritarian doctrine shares certain features with Hegel's political philosophy. It is quite another matter to suggest that both men saw the relation of state and society in the same light. In fact Comte was able to sketch a rudimentary theory of society precisely because, unlike Hegel, he had been taught by Saint-Simon to regard the political sphere as in some sense secondary and derivative.[3]

[2] Whence Saint-Simon's celebrated *Parabole* (1819), with its scandalous suggestion that France could get on very well without the whole caste of official dignitaries of church and state. This is clearly one source of Marx's (and more particularly Engels') contempt for the state. It is a very un-Hegelian idea and could not conceivably have occurred to Saint-Simon's German contemporaries.

[3] Hayek, pp. 191 ff., describes a fusion of Hegelianism and Comtean positivism as the common characteristic of all the later socialist doctrines, while Gurvitch rightly stresses the indebtedness of Marx to Saint-Simon, whose libertarian idealism had been abandoned by Comte and by the latter's French and German followers. These included right-wing Hegelians like Lorenz von Stein, whose home-grown authoritarianism blended easily with the Comtean variant. Even so, the Germans were preserved by their Protestant inheritance from the more grotesque conclusions to which Comte was driven in the effort to demolish individual liberty: conclusions which stemmed from his Catholic upbringing and in some measure anticipated the totalitarian streak in Russian Communism. Paradoxical though it may sound, Hegel's doctrine was at once more metaphysical and less utopian than Comte's. Or perhaps one should say that his conservative Lutheran pessimism guarded him against the idea of a total transformation imposed by an infallible authority.

Saint-Simon being the chief originator of socialist thought in France, the fact that he can be seen as a distant ancestor of Marx makes it comparatively easy to account for the role of Marxism in the subsequent development of the French socialist movement. The French did not have to be converted to the doctrine that the industrial revolution called for a rational scientific reorganization of society. This Saint-Simonian idea—the starting point of all socialist criticism of liberal economics and bourgeois society—had by the later nineteenth century been so fully absorbed that virtually every political school in France paid at least lip-service to it. Across the Rhine such notions had a more subversive ring, unless dressed up in the Fichtean or Lassallean language of "state socialism," with its implied critique of bourgeois liberalism from the standpoint of the Prussian bureaucracy and its academic fuglemen. Inasmuch as Marxism was associated with radical democracy—it had after all taken shape in 1848, the "year of the barricades," and Marx himself in some sense always remained the man of 1848, at any rate to his German followers—its doctrines transcended the familiar context of the German situation. The latter—from the Restoration of 1815 to the Bismarckian era—encouraged a constant stress upon the assumed responsibility of the state for the moral guidance of the body politic. Since it was widely held that the social and moral well-being of the community was the proper business of the government, the state might be called upon to perform all sorts of services not dreamed of in the comfortable philosophy of Western bourgeois liberalism. Here was a possible meeting point of conservative and socialist thinking, not to mention the religious strain whose roots went back deep into the medieval past. As against the rising liberal current, capitalism might be denounced as immoral and un-Christian (because subversive of the "natural order") and dangerous to national solidarity as well, since it gave rise to class conflict. In this conservative perspective, liberalism and Marxism had something in common: both—though for different reasons—were committed to a transformation which signified the death of everything the traditionalists held dear. That the liberals described as paradise what the Marxists denounced as purgatory made little difference in the long run. Both schools were at one in taking a fatalistic view of the transformation in progress once the market economy had been unshackled. Liberals indeed welcomed the result, while the Marxists consoled themselves with the belief that the reign of capitalism would be brief. Yet from a conservative viewpoint, liberalism and Marxism looked and sounded remarkably alike.

The practical relevance of these seemingly abstract disputes is made evident by the impact they left upon the nascent labor movement on both sides of the Rhine. Here the German Social Democrats took the lead, from the 1880s onward, with a thorough assimilation of Marxian concepts. In the process, however, they transformed Marxism from a revolutionary doctrine of political action into a fatalistic analysis of society. In the original Marxian view the conquest of political power is the decisive act whereby the working class establishes a socialist order (ultimately a classless communist one). The transformation, even though already prepared by the growing socialization of the economy, is brought about by a political revolution in which the workers employ the state for the purpose of abolishing the old property relations and extruding the former ruling class from the centers of power. In the Social Democratic version of Marxism, as institutionalized in Germany by Kautsky and others, the conquest of power drops out of sight. In its place one finds a sociological analysis which treats politics as a reflex of social change. This analysis was indeed grounded in Marx's doctrine of the state as an instrument of class rule, but Marx had never intended long-range sociological considerations to serve as a guide for political action. From the belief that the state is, historically speaking, an aspect of class society, it does not in the least follow that it is a mere epiphenomenon, or that politics are irrelevant. If the Social Democratic movement worked on the assumption that the political struggle is always necessarily subsumed under economics, it misread both Marx and the evidence of the facts.

From this fateful misunderstanding, which accounts for much of the subsequent misfortunes of German Social Democracy, the French movement was comparatively free. Having grown up on revolutionary soil, it could not well fail to perceive that bourgeois society had come into being through a momentous political struggle against the old regime. Moreover, the Republic was constantly menaced, from the Right as well as from the Left, and the working class was occasionally called upon to defend it against the common enemy. Under these circumstances, sociology could never take the place of politics even for the most doctrinaire French Marxists. At most they might assert that the fate of the bourgeois Republic was none of their concern. That the struggle for its control was being fought out at the political level—i.e., at the level of institutions such as the government, the army, the judiciary, and the educational establishment—they could not well ignore. The fact was drummed into them by the repeated crises of the regime, and not least by the manner in which the Third Republic—since the 1890s and especially after the Dreyfus Affair—stabilized itself through a series of political and educational "purges" of antidemocratic elements.[4] Whatever their shortcomings, Marx's French disciples did not fall into the trap of treating these issues as a mere reflex of the "real" socio-economic process. They knew quite well where the power lay, and were not going to be tranquilized with sociological analyses which evaded the question of political control. Even the Syndicalists did not pretend that the matter could be ignored: they merely regarded the state as hostile and refused to be drawn into a campaign for reforming it through the electoral process. The Guesdists did, it is true, share the general Social Democratic illusion that the numerical growth of the working class must automatically bring about a redistribution of political power in its favor. But even they did not altogether succumb to the temptation of recasting their doctrine in sociological terms. It was left to the German Social Democrats to equate social reformism with political action, in principle as well as in practice, and to rationalize this evasion on the grounds that the superior reality of the economic domain must assert itself in the long run.

If Marxism signified that political relations could be dissolved in economic relations (not only under socialism, but already in the here-and-now), then clearly there was no need for a specifically socialist theory of politics. In Germany, both before and after the aborted revolution of 1918, this comfortable notion was paralleled by the traditional idea of the state as a realm superior to and independent of

[4] These involved *inter alia* the extrusion of religious teaching from state schools, the institution of courses in civic consciousness, and the attempt—in which prominent educators like Durkheim took a share—to establish a normative ethic not dependent on traditional religion. In such an atmosphere it would have been paradoxical for Socialists to treat the "ideological" realm as unimportant.

the social sphere. This idealist view—popular not only among conservative bureaucrats but also in the liberal milieu—formed the counterpart of the "materialist" doctrine which saw politics as a mere function of economics. Incompatible though they were, these misunderstandings concurred in diverting the Socialist movement from the crucial problem of gaining control of the "superstructure." The state as a neutral arbiter of socio-political conflict was an even grosser delusion than the state as a reflex. That both notions were entertained simultaneously by men who regarded themselves as Marxists can be explained only in terms of the German labor movement's fundamental inability to transcend its sectional origins. People who do not understand politics—and the German working class had never really come in contact with the political sphere above the level of municipal administration—are easily persuaded that the whole thing does not matter. Hence the gap between the confident determinism of the German Social Democratic movement and that movement's real weakness when confronted with rivals who had grasped the central importance of the political struggle.

In France, as noted before, such illusions were more difficult to sustain. The Republic had "de-sacralized" politics and torn the veil off the class struggle, which in Germany lay hidden behind a façade of bureaucratic rule and legal-philosophical verbiage. The elaborate mumbo-jumbo of the German professorate (itself an appendage of the state bureaucracy, and committed to its spurious neutrality) had no precise counterpart in France, where officialdom under the Third Republic was actively engaged in promoting the republican ideology in the teeth of royalist and clerical resistance. The relevance of political power was not in doubt, nor was its connection with the party struggle. The difficulty lay rather in rendering the Marxian analysis compatible with the traditional republican-democratic ideology which quite deliberately abstracted from class considerations. That the state should serve the needs of society was not in dispute, but who or what was society? Conservatives, Liberals, and Socialists had different answers to this question, and after 1918 they were joined by Communists and Fascists, who for all their mutual antipathy concurred in believing that the state could and should reshape society, once it had been captured by a party which "knew what it wanted": in other words, by a political elite with a totalitarian program and a terroristic organization to back it up. If this new vision obliged the Communists to reformulate Marxian doctrine in Leninist terms, it also encouraged their Fascist rivals to believe that the proletarian revolution could be headed off by a "national-socialist" conquest of power. Neither side doubted that the political issue was crucial. In this respect the Russian Revolution, and the series of Fascist coups d'état in post-1918 Europe, had a similar effect: they combined to make official liberalism and Social Democracy seem equally old-fashioned. Political relations, it turned out, could *not* be dissolved in legal (or economic) relations. The political sphere was *not* a mere reflex. It was autonomous and might even generate sufficient power to make possible the forcible reorganization of the "material infrastructure." With the fusion of Bolshevism and Fascism in the fully developed Stalinist doctrine around 1940, the process was complete: totalitarianism now had attained both a political form and a theoretical instrument.

In what follows we pursue the implications of this change for the renovation of Marxism in postwar France. The political aspect would require separate treatment. Here we simply register the doctrinal efforts spurred by the dawning realization that orthodox Marxism had come to stand for a political practice no longer in tune with the realities.

Social Class and Political Power

Although the concept of "class" stands at the center of Marxian theorizing about politics, it has never been easy to determine what exactly its significance was for Marx himself in those parts of his work where he extrapolated from the analysis of capitalism with the intent of formulating a more general statement of his viewpoint.[5] There is no doubt that he regarded class relations (themselves rooted in production relations) as constitutive of bourgeois society, in the

[5] For additional reading on this subject see Georges Gurvitch, *Le Concept des classes sociales* (Paris, 1954); Raymond Aron, *Les grandes doctrines de sociologie historique* (Paris, n.d.), pp. 99 ff. Emile Durkheim, *Le socialisme: sa définition, ses débuts, la doctrine Saint-Simonienne,* ed. and with a Preface by Marcel Mauss (Paris, 1928). R. Dahrendorf, *Class and Class Conflict in Industrial Society* (London, 1959).

sense that property in the means of production, or exclusion therefrom, was the basic constituent of the socio-political order. But precisely in what sense "class" differed from stratification according to noneconomic criteria was never clearly spelled out, and his followers were left with the half-solved problem of accounting for the dialectic of state and society (or politics and economics) in terms of class struggle, without quite knowing whether "class" was to be understood in economic terms, or treated as a historical concept. In the former case, there was little difference between the Marxian viewpoint and the procedure familiarized by empirical sociology. On the alternative assumption, the concept of class served as the key to the historical transformation of feudal into bourgeois society. On this second and more philosophical reading, which on the whole was adopted by the more theoretical Marxists, a class was to be regarded as an ensemble of social relations embracing politics and culture as well as economics: a veritable microcosm from which in due course a new society might be expected to arise, as bourgeois society had gradually arisen from its modest beginnings in medieval Europe. A class then was fully developed only when it had become conscious of its historic role, so that the factor of consciousness entered as a constitutive element into its very being. In this perspective, the coming displacement of the bourgeoisie by the working class acquired the dignity of a principle, inasmuch as it signified the advent of an age in which men would at last emancipate themselves from rule by a privileged exploiting stratum. Under socialism, the "political economy of labor" would triumph over the "political economy of capital": not in the banal sense of a reversal of roles within an unchanging structure of domination and exploitation, but in the sense that "labor" would at long last be recognized as the unique source of social wealth, and "surplus labor" as the origin of those (now defunct) class relations which had enabled a privileged minority to monopolize both power and culture.

As against this quasi-philosophical vision, which transcended the horizon of empirical thinking, the positivist sociology of Comte and his successors (down to Durkheim and his school), had familiarized the French public with an approach that treated social classes as strata arising from the functional division of labor; and since this division was conceived, on the biological or organicist model, as a permanent necessity imposed upon society by the growing complexity of functions rooted in the work process, it followed that the most one could hope for was a more egalitarian distribution of economic tasks and material rewards. On these assumptions, which could without difficulty be extracted from the Saint-Simonian doctrine (though the same was true of some aspects of Marxism), class conflict appeared not as the prime motor of social progress, but rather as a regrettable departure from the normal equilibrium, which latter in turn might easily be identified with the *status quo*. If this was questioned, as by those reformist Socialists who followed Jaurès, it was plausible to suppose that the replacement of bourgeois by socialist property relations would be the work of the public authorities—acting in the interest of the social whole—rather than the revolutionary accomplishment of the labor movement. In its Jaurèsian form this kind of socialism (like its Fabian parallel in Britain) signified the tacit abandonment of the Marxian notion that the working class would undertake the reconstruction of society. That task, it was thought (and sometimes said), devolved rather upon the growing stratum of public officials, scientists, technicians, and intellectuals in general, whose emergence into full view around 1900 underpinned the revisionist critique of orthodox Marxism, at the same time that it suggested a practical means of replacing capitalism by a new and more egalitarian system.[6]

The theoretical difficulties inherent in the Marxian approach were indeed obvious. In the *Communist Manifesto*, and to a lesser extent in his later writings, Marx had credited the working class with the ability to replace the bourgeoisie, while at the same time stressing its descent from the submerged strata of preindustrial history: the slaves of antiquity and the serfs of the European middle ages. There was a latent contradiction between this vision of the proletariat as an ex-

[6] For the British counterpart of these discussions see the voluminous Fabian literature. Of course the Fabians never said in so many words that the working class was unfit to exercise power, and that the task of administering the coming collectivist order would devolve upon the intelligentsia: specifically the managerial and technical intelligentsia. But this was what their theoretical and practical approach implied from the start. The very composition of the group—a loose assemblage of men and women drawn from the educated professional class—and its system of admitting new members by cooptation, signified a quite evident desire to guard against pressures from below. All this was only half-conscious. It became politically relevant when the British Labour party, for lack of any alternative, had to accept Fabian direction. For a critical view of the subject from an orthodox Marxist standpoint see E. J. Hobsbawm, *Labouring Men: Studies in the History of Labour* (London, 1964), pp. 250-72.

ploited class destined in the end to triumph over its oppressors, and his more mature formulations, in which the industrial workers appeared as the pioneers of a new society freed from the dominance of capital. Moreover, this second and less apocalyptic view had been qualified by the implied suggestion that capitalism was giving birth to a "managerial" stratum in control of industry: a stratum secreted by the economic process itself.[7] These perspectives lent themselves to different interpretations, not all of them favorable to the belief that the "emancipation of labor" would be synonymous with the instauration of democratic equality in the workshop. More damagingly, the question might be asked whether the whole analogy between the respective roles of bourgeoisie and proletariat was not seriously misleading, inasmuch as it credited the proletariat with the ability to perform a task hitherto reserved for groups associated with the emergence of new modes of production. Unlike the bourgeoisie, which even in its early beginnings was already the bearer of a new form of economic organization, the proletariat performed a subordinate role, comparable perhaps to that of the peasantry in an agrarian order of society. Like the latter, it was indeed an indispensable element of the production process, but scarcely one destined to rule. The Marxian construction, with its dichotomic view of society, might be suspected of having underrated the significance of the fact that the conflict of landowner and peasant had been resolved in the latter's favor only with the rise of an entirely new form of economic organization: that of industrial capitalism. The bourgeois revolution had indeed emancipated the serfs, but it had done so by bringing the bourgeoisie to power. If the socialist revolution was envisaged on the model of the bourgeois one, might it not result in the growth of a new social hierarchy, with the working class at the bottom of the pyramid and a new dominant stratum on top? Was it not indeed very likely—precisely on the analogy of the bourgeois revolution which had served Marx as the model for his own construction—that the emancipation of labor would be the achievement of a new directing class?[8]

[7] *Capital,* III. 374-80, 427-31 (Moscow, 1960 ed.).

[8] Raymond Aron, p. 149. "Le prolétariat ne constitue pas des forces ou des rapports de production nouveaux au sein de la société capitaliste. . . . Dès lors, l'assimilation de la montée du prolétariat à la montée de la bourgeoisie est

The point can be clarified by recalling that the role assigned by history to the proletariat during the early phase of the bourgeois revolution had been that of fighting the battles of the bourgeoisie. The new capitalist order of society (which was also the new industrial order) mobilized an array of social forces comprising both the early entrepreneurs and their salaried work force. In launching itself against the old regime, with its agrarian base and its autocratic state, the nascent proletariat served the cause of the rising industrial-capitalist stratum; in other words, it fought for the triumph of capitalism. Unlike other Socialists of his time, Marx discerned this historical mechanism and candidly described it as both inevitable and progressive. He was enough of a Hegelian to savor the bitter irony of the situation he was describing, for Hegel had taught him to regard history as a procession of stages whose true meaning is concealed from the participants (though plain to the philosopher). He was also sufficiently in tune with the positivist temper of his age to believe that the secret of the whole drama had at last been pierced. In future there would be no more "world-historical masquerades" on the model of the French Revolution, whose principal actors had costumed themselves as ancient Romans. Mankind had come of age. In particular, the modern working class, having at long last emancipated itself from the trammels of bourgeois ideology, would now enter into its inheritance: the new industrial society, which it had helped to create, was there to be administered by the actual producers. Though not strictly speaking a clash between two different modes of production, the alternative capitalism-socialism represented a choice between different ways of organizing the economic process, and the dichotomy arose from the system's *modus operandi* itself. The latter was kept going by the appropriation of surplus value produced by the workers under conditions where their only property (their own labor) was controlled by the capitalist class which monopolized the productive apparatus. Hence class conflict was built into the structure of the system. Yet the conclusion drawn by Marx—that the workers could and

sociologiquement fausse." The least one can say is that this argument is more in tune with Marx's own manner of posing the problem than with the convoluted mazes of sophistry in which his orthodox disciples tended to get lost when confronted with such awkward questions. See Raymond Aron, *Main Currents in Sociological Thought,* tr. by Richard Howard and Helen Weaver (New York, 1965), especially part III, section V.

would reverse the relationship—did not necessarily follow. At any rate it did not follow from his analysis of the bourgeois revolution, but rather introduced a new factor: that of class consciousness.

It is to be observed that this criticism leaves intact the Marxian concept of class, both in its narrower and in its wider sense. What it renders questionable is the thesis that the industrial proletariat will play a role in the transition to socialism similar to that played by the bourgeoisie in the antecedent rise of capitalism. Yet though the Marxian analogy is faulty (at any rate in the way it is formulated in the *Manifesto,* before Marx had succeeded in fusing historical and sociological concepts), the mistake may not be as damaging as it appears at first sight. For even though the rise of the working class within the new industrial pyramid provides no analogy to the construction of that pyramid by the class of industrial capitalists, it may reasonably be held that a fully developed industrial society can dispense with social control by a privileged stratum of bourgeois entrepreneurs. The workers might then at last enter into their inheritance and take over the edifice they have constructed with so much toil. To the argument that the bourgeoisie is likely to be replaced by a bureaucratic or technocratic elite, there is at any rate the counterargument that in this case the class struggle will assume new forms until socialist democracy has become a reality. Alternatively, the symbiosis of working class and technical intelligentsia within a socialist planned economy may be envisaged on the model of a radically democratized workshop in which the administrators defer to the general will, instead of executing the orders of remote and anonymous financial controllers or shareholders. On either assumption there is adequate scope for the deployment of working-class initiative, even though the final result may fall short of the old anarcho-syndicalist utopia.

With the emergence of a technological stratum tied to the working class by its social origins, as well as by similarities of education and political outlook, it even becomes possible to envisage the transition to socialism as a fairly smooth and painless operation. Given that both the short-term and the long-term interests of the two groups are similar, at any rate in the sense that both are concerned to promote the fullest possible employment of the productive apparatus, it may be said that workers, technicians, and managers stand in a symbiotic relationship to each other, as against the private owners who cling to their irrational privileges. Compared with either the workers, or the managers and technologists in modern industry, the pure capitalists or shareholders appear increasingly as claimants without function. This is the rationale of the kind of socialism which, in any developed industrial country with democratic traditions and institutions, derives its confidence from the observable fact that private property in the means of production is becoming superfluous, while the entrepreneurial function is withering away. Even if it be argued that the process must first pass through a phase of state capitalism—with public administrators in control of the planned economy, and their nominees (the "technocrats") in strategic positions within the industrial hierarchy—it is still possible to hold that this authoritarian form of socialization can be transcended, once the workers, through their unions, have learned to exercise democratic control in industry. From a Marxian viewpoint this conclusion is all that matters. If the resulting picture does not quite fit the eschatological perspectives of the *Manifesto,* it is substantially in tune with the more realistic formulations of *Capital.*[9]

Two Concepts of Revolution

Thus the sociological core of Marx's argument can be salvaged with a little ingenuity, though only at the cost of abandoning the simple dichotomy bourgeoisie-proletariat which he had extrapolated from the social conflicts of his age. The interaction between Marxism as a doctrine, and Communism as a movement, is perhaps nowhere clearer than in relation to Marx's vision of the class struggle, for it was the indelible impression made upon him by the bloody suppressions of 1848 and 1871 that animated the passions flowing into his political writings; and it was from the latter rather than from *Capital* that his French followers deduced the necessity of "proletarian dictatorship" during the transition period. This is about all that needs to be said on

[9] This may be disputed on the grounds that Marx never developed a satisfactory definition of the concept of class. Gurvitch, *Le Concept des classes sociales,* pp. 19 ff. But though this is true, he left the road open for his followers. In any case it is not obvious where socialists in the last century could have obtained a substitute. They certainly could not have found one in either Saint-Simon or Comte.

the subject, so far as the doctrinal aspect of French Communism is concerned; for although the French CP has in recent years become a pseudo-revolutionary movement—in the sense that its representatives no longer seriously contemplate a revolutionary seizure of power and the installation of a minority dictatorship—the style of its propaganda is still infused with concepts dating back to the Jacobin-Babouvist interpretation of the Great Revolution. Marxism, as the link between that heroic past and the inglorious present, conserves a quasi-religious function to the degree that its nomenclature is bound up with memories of the Commune and the *semaine sanglante;* much as Leninism signifies the myth of the October Revolution rather than the drab reality of Soviet society. In this sense the dichotomic view of the class struggle as a contest between a reactionary bourgeoisie and a revolutionary proletariat has become a myth in the Sorelian sense (with the important qualification that, like all genuine myths, it was not manufactured consciously, but arose spontaneously from the collective experience of the believers). The myth is indispensable to Communists; indeed it makes modern Communism what it is. But it no longer possesses even the limited theoretical value it had when Marx formulated it. Hence its obstinate retention is a sign of the French CP's unwillingness or inability to bring itself up to date.[10]

If we now shift back from Communist practice to Marxian theory, what do we find? In the Marxian model, classes are not "income groups," neither are they coterminous with social strata arising from the division of labor. Historically, a new class makes its appearance with the emergence of a new mode of production. At this stage its objective role is still concealed from it, and this circumstances is reflected both in its ideological immaturity and in its lack of political power. The transition to the stage of full domination over the new society is effected by means of the class struggle in its political aspect: as a more or less peaceful confrontation with other classes. In addition to the cur-

[10] Pierre Fougeyrollas, *Le marxisme en question* (Paris, 1959) pp. 51 ff. Yvon Bourdet, *Communisme et marxisme: notes critiques de sociologie politique* (Paris, 1963), pp. 81 ff. Gilles Martinet, *Le marxisme de notre temps* (Paris, 1962), pp. 51 ff. Lucien Laurat, "L'Évolution réformiste du marxisme," *Contrat Social,* Vol. II, No. 4 (July, 1958), pp. 236-42. Aimé Patri, "Saint-Simon et Marx," *Contrat Social,* Vol. V, No. 1 (Jan., 1961), pp. 18-24. Maximilien Rubel, "De Marx au bolchévisme," *Arguments,* No. 25-26 (1st and 2d trimestre, 1962), pp. 31-39.

rent holders of power these may include the temporary allies of the rising class: e.g., in the case of the bourgeoisie, either the peasantry and the urban plebeians (1789) or the immature industrial proletariat (1830, 1848). A class exists as such only in relation to other classes, and it becomes fully conscious of itself only in the politico-ideological struggle to win a place for itself within the social whole. A class which is as yet unconscious of its role cannot exercise political leadership or aim at a revolutionary transformation (whether peaceful or violent is immaterial in this context). A fortiori a class which denies its own existence, and sees itself merely as an assemblage of individuals, thereby proclaims its unfitness to play an active historical part. Such classes are doomed to disappear, leaving the stage to others. Examples might include the peasantry and the urban petty bourgeoisie during the later stages of capitalism. These ancient classes either possess no true consciousness or have lost it, this loss being itself an index to their coming disappearance. On Marx's assumptions it follows that if the industrial proletariat should lose whatever consciousness of its historic role it once possessed, this would be a sign that it was on the point of vanishing as a class, for it is consciousness that transforms a social group from a class *in posse* to one *in esse*. The factor of consciousness becomes crucial during the political struggle, and it is at this stage that the lengthy preliminary effort at self-education discloses its adequacy.

So far as the bourgeoisie was concerned, that effort had culminated in the Enlightenment of the eighteenth century, following a semi-successful trial run during the Renaissance and the Reformation. The French Revolution (and its American counterpart) were the test of the bourgeoisie's readiness to proceed from ideology to politics. Correspondingly, the failure of the liberal-democratic movement in Germany during the 1848 upheaval disclosed that the German middle class lacked the will to attain political power, whence it followed that the destruction of the old regime would have to be undertaken by the workers. The latter, however, could not content themselves with completing the democratic revolution which the bourgeoisie had failed to accomplish. They must transcend the limits of bourgeois democracy or resign themselves in perpetuity to a subordinate role: a possibility Marx did not seriously envisage, since he was convinced that the operation of the economic system would keep the class struggle going. Capitalism was inherently unstable, and moreover subversive of bourgeois democracy, since it did away with its surest foundation: the relatively wide distribution of private property. Hence even the Social Democratic version of Marxism, as formulated by Engels, Kautsky, and the Austro-Marxists, reckoned with the certainty of a socialist revolution arising from the insoluble contradictions of the economy: capitalism and democracy were incompatible in the long run. Whether the final transformation took place peacefully or otherwise was immaterial. Its political content was determined by a conflict rooted in the nature of the system which confronted a growing mass of workers with a shrinking class of exploiters. In the end, therefore, the factor of consciousness, which in the early stages of the process was barely available as a means of constituting the workers *as a class,* was all that stood between the "self-government of the producers" and the maintenance of an increasingly irrational system of domination. As soon as this truth had sunk in, the political outcome could no longer be in doubt.

It is worth stressing that this conception could be formulated in terms not dependent on the Leninist misunderstanding of the October Revolution as a proletarian seizure of power. In principle it was and is possible for orthodox Marxists to dismiss Bolshevism as an aberration (as indeed Kautsky and the Mensheviks had done from the start). This must be stressed because it is frequently asserted, with bland disregard for history and theory alike, that the fate of Marxism is involved in the practice of the Communist movement. Such a proposition makes sense only on the assumption that there have been no Marxists since Trotsky. In actual fact the perspective sketched out by Marx in *Capital,* (and by those Marxists who took their lead from Engels) is quite independent of the relevance which the Soviet model may have for backward societies. Its value depends on what one makes of the transformation which the major industrial countries have undergone in recent decades. Since these countries, not accidentally, are bourgeois democracies, it is important to ask how the Marxian approach has stood up in the light of recent developments.

Now the conclusion—for anyone not blind to the lessons of the past half-century—must surely be that the "conquest of political power by the working class," in the traditional understanding of the phrase, is an impossibility. Neither the Social Democratic nor the Communist form of political activity has led to the establishment of something describable as a workers state, let alone to the state's "withering away." Democratic socialism—whether confined to ordinary reformism or enlarged to include economic planning—falls significantly short of this traditional aim. Communism not merely falls short, but contradicts it, inasmuch as its authoritarian character heightens the antagonism between the state and the workers, enforces rigid discipline at the "point of production," and does away with strikes, self-government, and trade-union autonomy. In relation to backward, pre-industrial countries, Communism indeed has turned out to be a substitute for capitalism; with regard to developed industrial societies it is irrelevant, save as a permanent opposition movement. A Communist dictatorship in a backward country portends an industrialization drive and the political expropriation of the working class for the benefit of an entrenched caste of planners: themselves the leaders of a new privileged stratum. Under more advanced conditions a Communist seizure of power is either impossible, or—if installed from above by outside military pressure—synonymous with social retrogression, cultural barbarization, and the destruction of democracy, including labor democracy. Insofar as Western Communists have tried to evade these contradictions they have been obliged to revert to a species of syndicalism, thus liquidating half a century of Leninist theory and practice. Thrown back upon their working-class origins, they regain the political honesty they had sacrificed to their totalitarian aim, only to find themselves confronted once more with the problem that faces every purely sectional labor movement: the seeming inability of the working class to transcend its limitations and raise itself to the level of a dominant political elite.

The Crisis of Liberal Democracy

In the French setting, this dilemma was sharpened by the delayed impact of Communism during and after the great economic depression of the 1930s. The evolution of the French CP into a mass movement paralleled the loss of faith in the ability of liberal democracy to ensure full employment and an adequate rate of economic growth. Stalinism and Fascism both grew from this root, for calls to proletarian revolution had their counterpart in the political and ideological frenzy of the extreme Right. Both movements proclaimed the need for a total reorganization of society, to be undertaken from above, by the state. Both failed, whereas a genuine transformation was achieved after 1945: in part under the ultrademocratic Fourth Republic, in part by the Gaullist regime, which latter did away with political pluralism, but left the established republican traditions and democratic liberties intact. This outcome did not significantly affect the perspective of traditional democratic socialism, since it could be held that the Gaullist solution was merely one variant among others, and that the matter would in the end by settled along democratic lines. But it undercut the theoretical assumptions and practical expectations of the CP; for the management of a semi-planned economy by an authoritarian regime was not provided for in the Communist texts. These allowed only for a simplified dichotomy, with the class struggle obliging the state to side with the exploiters against the workers, or vice versa. They did not envisage a situation where bourgeoisie and proletariat would both be politically expropriated for the benefit of a state bureaucracy which had become sufficiently autonomous to override the traditional class conflicts. The French CP might indeed have drawn the appropriate lessons from the Stalinist experience: primarily the lesson that situations can arise where the political authority has sufficient power to reorganize society. But it was tacitly assumed that this could be done only after a "proletarian revolution." The Gaullist regime was explained away as a suitably modernized form of Bonapartism: a camouflage for the domination of the great monopolies. It was only beyond the ranks of the CP and its hidebound ideologists that some Marxists began to toy with the notion of a new technocratic regime.[11]

If the class struggle did not result in a clear-cut victory for either side, the outcome must be a temporary stalemate and the instauration of a regime apparently independent of both warring classes. For such a conclusion theoretical warrant could be found in Marx's analysis of Bonapartism. This, however, pertained to an ordinary crisis of bourgeois society, not to the latter's dissolution. In the 1960s, Marx's fol-

[11] Maximilien Rubel, "De Marx au bolchévisme." Since the author was a Social Democrat, his analysis was both scholarly and dispassionate. This could not be said of the numerous Communist writers who worked the topic to death. For the rest, Rubel's essay, a sober historical study, amounted to a restatement of the view that the "conquest of political power" in the Leninist sense is an illusion fatal to the labor movement.

lowers in Western Europe had to confront the possibility that the laws applicable to this society might no longer be operative.[12]

The Marxian analysis presupposed a distinction between society and the state—or between the economic order and the political order—which had been rendered questionable by the series of political upheavals beginning in 1914. Communism and Fascism, in their different ways, challenged the liberal-democratic integration which subordinated the state to (bourgeois) society. But this subordination had also been the premise of Marxian theorizing, which traditionally did not envisage a situation where state and society would be fused, with the state becoming the dominant partner. Yet such a fusion was the open or undisclosed aim of every totalitarian movement. Lenin had taken the first tentative steps towards a theory and practice of totalitarianism, and the advantage of the Communist movement over its Social Democratic rival rested largely upon the fact that it was mentally equipped to promote practical solutions which did away with the old dichotomy between economics and politics. Hence it was not enough for Communists, when faced with the impending collapse of liberal democracy, to fall back upon classical nineteenth century formulations, for the basic presupposition of the Marxian (as of the liberal) analysis—the independence of the social order from the political superstructure—had been called in question: not least by the practice of Stalinism. As a matter of plain theoretical consistency, the Communists ought to have acknowledged that the old formula stood in need of revision. A struggle between classes for control of the state is conceivable only in a situation where state and society can still be clearly distinguished, and where the state is controlled by the economically dominant class. What the Communists ought to have said, but could not say, was that bourgeoisie and proletariat were both losing ground to a third force, the bureaucracy.

[12] Léo Hamon, ed., *Les nouveaux comportements politiques de la classe ouvrière* (Paris, 1962). *Pour une démocratie économique,* in the Jean Moulin Collection (Paris, 1964). Pierre Belleville, *Une nouvelle classe ouvrière* (Paris, 1963). Martinet, pp. 147 ff. Edgar Morin, Claude Lefort, Pierre Naville, Serge Mallet, "Marxisme et Sociologie," *Cahiers du Centre d'Études Socialistes,* Nos. 34-35 (Nov.-Dec., 1963). Pierre Naville, Serge Mallet, Claude Lefort, and Pierre Mendès-France, "Les Travailleurs peuvent-ils gérer l'économie?" *ibid.,* Nos. 23-24 (Feb., 1963). See also the dispute between Sartre and Lefort in *Temps Modernes,* No. 89 (April, 1953), already referred to.

For Socialists wedded to Marx, but not tied to the Leninist mythology, the problem presented itself somewhat differently. They too experienced the need to revise their theoretical model, but having long grown skeptical of the antiquated class-struggle phraseology, they did not have to explain to themselves why the proletariat showed no capacity for taking power. As they saw it, the basic change since the First World War had been the collapse of the unregulated market economy and the gradual introduction of centralized economic planning. This automatically reinforced the authority of the government, and therewith the role of the planners in control of the central apparatus. The goal thus defined itself in terms of capturing the machinery rather than destroying it for the benefit of a hypothetical workers state, which Soviet experience had anyhow shown to be utopian. Socialists did not have to seek far-fetched analogies with Bonapartism to understand the relative autonomy of a regime in charge of a planned economy. They could and did accept the thesis that central planning had become possible, and that it did not necessarily have to be planning "in the interest of the monopolies." The balance of power within society could be shifted by a drastic expansion of the public sector and by stricter control over capital investment undertaken by the business community. This was not reformism: it amounted to a major structural alteration, and the whole experience of France since 1945 had shown that such changes could be introduced democratically.[13]

Plainly, however, both the Socialist and the Communist interpretation of the facts implied a profound modification of the original Marxian model wherein the institution of a new social order was tied to the self-emancipation of the working class. On the Socialist hypothesis, collectivization would come about through the gradual extension of state control and the consequent growth of a stratum allied to the working class, but not identical with it, save insofar as the upper layer of skilled workers and technicians might be expected to merge with the

[13] Cf. Pierre Mendès-France, *La République moderne* (Paris, 1962), and the various publications of the Club Jean Moulin: the major intellectual and political focus of the moderate Left (including the left wing of the Gaullist coalition) after the collapse of the Fourth Republic. See also the *Cahiers du Centre d'Études Socialistes,* around which the left-wing Socialists grouped themselves; and some of the contributions to the semi-Trotskyist monthly *Socialisme ou Barbarie.* The whole discussion operated at a much higher level than the corresponding debate in CP journals such as the monthly *Économie et Politique.*

lower level of the managerial hierarchy. On the Communist assumption, the process would be spearheaded by the party; but the party, though "linked" to the proletariat, was viewed in Leninist theory (and in Stalinist practice) as a self-appointed vanguard which compensated the intellectual shortcomings of the class it was supposed to represent. And while the dialectic of social class and political party was not a Communist invention—it had in fact been an important element in every bourgeois revolution since the sixteenth century—this was all the more reason for suspecting that Communism simply reproduced a state of affairs where the masses were being shepherded in a direction they themselves had not chosen. If the Communist party was an effective instrument of authoritarian control, it owed this advantage precisely to the fact that its internal structure and its ideology prefigured the social hierarchy of the future. The vanguard of professional revolutionaries, which on the morrow of its victory would transform itself into the nucleus of a new ruling elite, was at the farthest possible remove from that autonomous working-class movement which Marx had envisioned after he had emancipated himself from the elitist tendencies of his early years. On either reading of the facts, the central Marxist hypothesis—an organic fusion of socialism and working-class democracy—seemed no longer tenable.[14]

In the light of these provisional conclusions it may be useful to recall the starting point of the discussion: the Marxian concept of class, and the analysis of society in terms of class conflict. It should then be possible to formulate a hypothesis with respect to the next development in Marxist theory and practice.

Marxian sociology—to distinguish it briefly from its positivist rival, which has been the more or less official standpoint of bourgeois society since at least the end of the nineteenth century—operates with a concept of class which seeks to account both for long-term historical processes and for the specific transformation of bourgeois relations into

[14] For some of the psychological consequences of the gradual loss of faith in proletarian emancipation see Andrée Andrieux and Jean Lignon, *L'Ouvrier d'aujourd'hui,* Preface by Pierre Naville, (Paris, 1960). The genuinely tragic aspect of the resulting change of mood is vividly illustrated by the despairing pessimism of veteran Syndicalists, who after a lifetime of struggle have abandoned hope in the possibility of workers control at the point of production. The need for some kind of hierarchy in the workshop, and the resultant authoritarian regulation of the labor process, are now widely accepted as unalterable.

socialist relations. Classes are assumed to be associated with specific modes of production, and class conflict is regarded as the mechanism whereby the evolution of society is carried forward. This approach was linked in Marx's thought with the perspective of an ultimate or final stage when the class struggle would have come to an end. If abstraction is made from the utopian element in this vision, there remains a politically neutral mode of perception which does not differ greatly from the positivist variant, save insofar as it stresses the importance of social conflict during the bourgeois revolution. The Marxian thesis could then be adequately summarized as stating that class conflict has been the motor of social evolution ever since early capitalism made its major impact upon European society in the sixteenth century. This formulation is in principle compatible both with positivist modes of thought and with the belief that class antagonism is an aspect of capitalism. But politically nothing follows from it. In particular, it does not follow that the class relations typical of advanced bourgeois society will necessarily give rise to a classless socialist order.

Insofar as Marx drew conclusions of this kind, he was extrapolating from the experience of an age in which the rise of the bourgeoisie was the social counterpart of an economic transformation resulting in the establishment of modern industry. His thesis could be summed up simply and briefly: capitalism having done its work, there was no further need for the capitalists, who could now disappear and make room for the "associated producers." A formulation of this kind clearly left open the possibility of a different type of centralized direction substituting itself for the capitalist one, and indeed the cautious approach Marx adopted in the concluding volume of his major work did not lend a great deal of encouragement to anarcho-syndicalist utopias. To that extent every socialist who had grasped the logic of his economic doctrine could safely style himself a Marxist.

What the formulation did not cover was the mechanism of the socialist transformation itself. On the model of the bourgeois revolution, the transition period could be envisaged as one of intensified class struggle, and this was the view taken by the Communists: though not by their reformist rivals, who drew different conclusions from Marx. What neither side took sufficiently into account was the change in the relationship between the economic sphere and the "superstructure." The class struggle had been an aspect of industrialization and had reached its fullest expression in the age of the bourgeois revolution. The transformation of the market economy into a regulated one, and the concurrent crisis of liberal democracy, also affected the mechanism of class conflict, inasmuch as the state now appeared as the guardian of the postliberal order, and increasingly as the arbiter of social conflict. At the same time the socialization of the economic sphere, where it occurred, left substantially untouched the structure of the industrial work process itself, as distinct from its legal integument. The net result was to substitute one form of authoritarian direction for another. Lastly, the connection between the managerial hierarchy and the political controllers established itself at the level of a coherent new directing stratum with a theory of its own: that of planning. Since the attitude of this elite converged with that of the increasingly numerous and important technical intelligentsia, and since it could plausibly be asserted that planning served the "general interest," it might be said that bourgeoisie and proletariat were being expropriated for the benefit of a newly dominant group.

The revelance of these considerations for the analysis of Marxism in general, and of Marxian thought in post-1945 France in particular, is linked to the concept of class. In principle it was possible to apply the Marxian apparatus to the new situation, but this could be done only by abandoning the perspective of a proletarian revolution in the traditional sense of the term. If unwillingness to take this step condemned the CP to sterility, excessive readiness to read pessimistic conclusions into the situation might drive some Socialists too far in the direction of technocratic authoritarianism. Notwithstanding the disappointment engendered by the course of events since 1945, it remained possible even in the 1960s to retain some residual faith in the capacity of the working class to operate a socialist economic order.[15]

[15] Jean Poperen, "Unification socialiste ou technocratie autoritaire," *Cahiers du Centre d'Études Socialistes,* Nos. 30-31 (July, 1963). Serge Mallet, "Les luttes ouvrières dans les secteurs industriels avancés," *ibid.,* Nos. 7-8, (September, 1961). Also Mallet, "Pour un programme de l'opposition," in *Temps Modernes,* Nos. 149-151 (July-Aug.-Sept., 1958): the only serious Marxist analysis of the Fourth Republic's dissolution to be published at the time. Mallet made many socialists uncomfortable by pointing out that the parliamentary regime had become an obstacle to economic modernization. In particular, it enabled the most parasitic pressure groups to levy blackmail upon industry and the working

The Economics of Neo-Marxism

It was remarked in an earlier chapter that the original introduction of Marxism in France before the First World War occurred at a time when its exponents lacked an adequate theoretical training in economics. To this indisputable statement another and more controversial one can now be added, namely that the successful implantation of Marxism in the French intellectual world, during and after the 1930s, came too late from the standpoint of economic theory. If the first wave had come before Marx's French disciples were properly equipped to take part in the international debate over liberal and Marxian economics, the second wave found them busy expounding the Marxian system just when its practical relevance had been called in question by the collapse of laissez-faire economics in the Western world, and by the simultaneous rise of centralized economic planning in the USSR.[16]

To grasp what was involved, it is necessary to be clear about what the crisis of the 1930s signified for economic theory. From, roughly speaking, 1870 to 1930 liberal and Marxian economics had developed along parallel lines: the Marxian analysis of capitalism furnishing a critical counterpoint to the liberal defense of the system. This defense rested upon a set of theoretical propositions which were hurriedly abandoned in the 1930s, when—to quote a writer already mentioned—it was no longer a question of expounding the theory of capitalism, but of salvaging its practice.[17] With the unregulated market economy in

---

class alike, the chief beneficiaries being the Poujadist clientele of retrograde *petits-bourgeois* who quite naturally entered into an alliance with the Algerian *ultras* against the rationalizing and modernizing Gaullist regime. See also the article series "La Classe ouvrière et le régime," *La Nouvelle revue marxiste,* No. 2 (Paris, November, 1961). For the belated and hesitant Communist attempt to come to grips with at least one aspect of the problem see Henri Krasucki, "Ingénieurs et classe ouvrière," *La Nouvelle critique* (May, 1964) and Philippe Cazelle, "Notes sur l'idéologie technocratique," *ibid.*

[16] For this subject see Ernest Mandel, *Traité d'Économie marxiste* (Paris, 1962). Pierre Bigo, *Marxisme et humanisme* (3d ed., Paris, 1961). Charles Bettelheim, *Problèmes du développement économique* (Paris, 1957). Georges Friedmann, *Où va le travail humain?* (Paris, 1950). Pierre Naville, *Vers l'automatisme social? Problèmes du travail et de l'automation* (Paris, 1963). Henri Chambre, *Le Marxisme en Union Soviétique* (Paris, 1955).

[17] Mandel, II, 420. Readers of this work—a truly impressive one—will not fail to note that its author bases himself on the great tradition of Central European Marxist theorizing: the only one to have developed the original doctrine further and maintained its relevance, at any rate down to the 1930s.

ruins, and the very existence of bourgeois society—or, if one prefers it, Western civilization—at stake, it was urgently necessary to pull theory and practice together, even if this meant abandoning those aspects of neoclassical doctrine which had departed furthest from reality. The "Keynesian revolution" did just that. It discarded the notion of a self-regulating economic order, thereby providing the rationale for state intervention to maintain full employment. At the same time it scrapped the neoclassical value theory in favor of a purely pragmatic approach. While the dominant academic school had derived practical conclusions from its theoretical model—a model which obstinately ignored the actual condition of the real world outside the classroom—the Keynesian approach started from the recognition that the market economy had broken down, and constructed its new model in accordance with practical policy recommendations. What emerged was something that could be placed in the service of liberalism and socialism alike, provided both parties tacitly agreed not to quarrel over the extent of state intervention required to keep the system in balance. The practical relevance of economic doctrine had been restored—at the expense of classical liberal teaching which held that the free market guaranteed the maximum utilization of economic resources, if not ignorantly interfered with from outside. In short, capitalism had been saved, but its theory had been discarded. In future it would have to get along with a purely pragmatic set of policies calculated to secure a rate of growth adequate to maintain more or less full employment. Failure to perform in accordance with this goal would count against "free enterprise," i.e., against capital investment not regulated by the public authorities. For now that investment had been revealed as the crucial factor, socialists might quote Keynes as well as Marx. If unemployment was a consequence of inadequate capital formation, the responsibility for avoiding it fell squarely upon the owners of capital. To that extent Keynes had weakened the doctrinal defense of the system in the very act of shoring up its mechanism. Of course no socialist had ever believed the claims made for economic liberalism. It was only necessary to look around in order to realize that the market economy could function quite well (from the viewpoint of its controllers) on the basis of permanent mass unemployment. But it was one thing to have this said by Marx, and another matter to have it confirmed by the outstanding representative of the liberal school. After the Keynesian revolution things could never be the same again. In particular it could never again be said that socialism was irrelevant because Marx's value theory was obsolete.

In principle this situation should have been gratifying to Marxists in France as well as elsewhere, and indeed these were the years when Marx was suddenly "discovered" by academic economists who had been roused from their dogmatic slumber by the collapse of the neoclassical doctrine taught in the universities.[18] But this was merely the negative side of the matter. To make good the initial advantage they held as critics of liberalism and laissez faire, Marx's followers would have had to evolve a theory of socialist economic planning applicable to advanced industrial countries. The elements of such a theory existed in the form of scattered contributions to a discussion in progress since the publication of Pareto's *Cours d'économie politique* in 1897.[19] The trouble was that the more interesting of these contributions had been made by socialists who were not Marxists and consequently did not employ the Marxian value concept. Conversely, the Marxist school (as represented by Kautsky and his German and Austrian pupils) did not before 1930 attach much importance to the question of planning in a socialist economy, since it was held that the time for troubling oneself over such matters was still far off. The golden age of Marxist economic theorizing between 1910 and 1925 centered upon macro-economic topics, notably the analysis of finance capitalism and the new phenomenon of imperialism. Neither Kautsky nor Otto Bauer, Hilferding, or Rosa Luxemburg—let alone Lenin and Bukharin—had given sys-

[18] Joan Robinson, *An Essay on Marxian Economics* (London, 1942, 1949), and *The Accumulation of Capital* (London, 1956). The change in the traditional appreciation of Marx affected several of Keynes's followers, but not the master himself, who persevered in the British academic habit of ignoring the author of *Capital*. It is true that Keynes had not read Wicksell either and hence remained unaware of the extent to which his own discoveries had been anticipated by the Swedish school of economics, which since before 1914 had been laying the foundation for the subsequent theory and practice of Swedish Social Democracy.

[19] *Collectivist Economic Planning*, ed. by F. A. Hayek (London, 1935), in particular Enrico Barone's paper ("Il ministerio della produzione nello stato collettivista," 1908) published in English as an appendix to the 1935 volume. See also Oskar Lange and Fred M. Taylor, *On the Economic Theory of Socialism* (Minnesota, 1938). The post-1920 discussion owed its impetus in large measure to the Russian Revolution; its theoretical side was stimulated by L. von Mises' work *Die Gemeinwirtschaft* (1920) published under the title *Socialism* in 1937.

tematic attention to the question how a socialist economy might be expected to operate. After 1917 the Bolsheviks approached the matter in hit-or-miss fashion, and the resultant "command economy," whatever its pragmatic value to a country still struggling with the problem of "primitive accumulation," had little theoretical or practical interest for Western socialists. The Soviet discussions around the first Five Year Plan of 1928 were naturally concerned with domestic problems; insofar as the debates had a more general bearing upon economic theory, they were related to the question of economic growth: in other words, to the problem of industrialization. Moreover, it was readily assumed by Soviet economists that the proper function of theory was to provide intellectual rationalizations for whatever decisions were taken by the policy-makers. The resulting misuse of theoretical concepts to underpin pragmatic policy considerations became especially marked from 1936 onward when it was asserted that the construction of socialism had been substantially achieved: this despite the fact that the existing scarcity economy—with its authoritarian direction, its vast disparities in income, and its reliance on commodity production for the market—bore little resemblance to what Marxist theory had traditionally described as socialism.[20]

In reflecting upon these events, the handful of Marxist economists in France between the 1920s and the 1940s followed in the wake of their colleagues abroad. There was little original thinking, and not much attention was given to what had become a pressing problem for France: economic planning in a milieu where laissez-faire capitalism had ceased to function satisfactorily. While the Central European intellectual discussion after the First World War (Hilferding, Bauer, Henryk Grossmann, Fritz Sternberg) made use of Marx to account for the apparent stagnation of European capitalism, the debate among Socialists and Communists in France remained suspended between planners who were not Marxists, and catastrophists who contented

[20] Mandel, II, pp. 426 ff. Alfred Zaubermann, "Revisionism in Soviet Economics," in *Revisionism: Essays on the History of Marxist Ideas,* ed. by Labedz (London-New York, 1962), pp. 268 ff. While the Soviet discussion of the 1920s involved Trotsky and his Russian followers (notably Preobrazhensky), as well as Bukharin and the representatives of the official Stalinist school, from Varga to Strumilin, its foreign repercussions were more noticeable in Germany and England than in France, even among Communists not belonging to the dominant faction.

themselves with predicting the imminent collapse of the hated system. It took the 1939-45 war to produce some Communist writings which made an effort to come to grips with the new situation, and even then what emerged was not much more than an insistence that the choice for France lay between socialist planning, and planning in the interest of the "monopolies." [21]

In taking account of the post-1945 discussion it is necessary to bear in mind that Socialists and Communists might mean quite different things by "planning." The Socialist party having at long last been converted to the planning heresy, its theorists were concerned to establish the proper balance between private and public investment which would make effective direction from the center possible. The principle had been accepted by all the parties which emerged from the wartime Resistance movement, including the Gaullists; and indeed the "technocratic" wing of Gaullism was sufficiently prominent for a while under the Fifth Republic to cause some alarm in business circles. State planning and Keynesian economics went together; and while they might differ over the role of the central authorities, Socialists, Christian Democrats, and Gaullists could and did agree on *dirigisme,* i.e., central control of investment and maintenance of rapid economic growth. That this could not be ensured by an unregulated market economy was common ground among the political forces which sustained the Fourth and Fifth Republics, though it might be disputed by the more old-fashioned liberals. It was also tacitly accepted that the role of the government involved constant arbitration between employers and trade unions, to keep prices stable and avoid inflationary pressures. Here again the Fifth Republic inherited a situation which dated back to the immediate postwar years, when the Communists were in the government and took their share in operating the economy. That the latter was inevitably a "mixed" one, in that the majority of investment decisions were still made outside the public sector, was taken for granted

[21] Charles Bettelheim, *Les problèmes théoriques et pratiques de la planification* (Paris, 1946). The more usual line of retreat for Marxist writers was to produce sociological studies of imperialism or fascism, in which the responsibility for these phenomena was mechanically attributed to the machinations of the capitalists and their political henchmen. See Daniel Guérin, *Fascime et Grand Capital* (Paris, 1945). The prewar discussion owed something to Lucien Laurat what at least familiarized French readers with what was going on abroad; see his *L'Accumulation du Capital d'après Rosa Luxembourg* (Paris, 1930).

by all concerned. The balance between public and private investment might indeed shift; and a Keynesian liberal like Mendès-France (whose formal conversion to socialism occurred only in the late 1950s) was as determined as any Marxist that this balance should be altered in favor of the public sector: e.g., by nationalizing some of the major industries still under private control. But however important from a practical viewpoint, such measures did not involve major questions of principle. Nor was it necessary to deduce the desirability of "workers control in industry" from a specifically Marxian analysis of capitalism. The proof was that this particular demand came to be associated with the left wing of the Catholic labor movement, as soon as it had emancipated itself from clerical control and adopted a socialist platform.[22]

Hence if the Communists were to differentiate themselves from the general stream of reformist socialism and *dirigisme* (i.e., state control and central planning), they could do it only by stressing the class character of the state and the monopolistic structure of private capitalism. These themes were in fact pursued both in party literature and in the writings of Marxist economists not adhering formally to the CP. What emerged from these studies was the concept of neocapitalism. This became the general formula for defining a state of affairs where, as these critics saw it, the great private monopolies had entered into partnership with the government for the purpose of (a) underwriting their profits (b) "socializing" the losses of the public sector, for the most part composed of the older and less profitable industries (c) channeling public funds into investment areas where private capital lacked the ability or the will to provide the necessary infrastructure. To this might be added concealed inflation as a consequence of Keynesian monetary manage-

[22] For the orthodox Socialist position on this topic see J. Moch, *Confrontations* (Paris, 1952), and the writings of André Philip. For the left-wing Catholic standpoint see Eugène Descamps, "Économie concertée et démocratie économique," in *Socialisation et personne humaine: Semaine Sociale de France, Grenoble 1960* (Lyon, 1961), pp. 365 ff. The then vice-president of the Christian trade-union federation, the CFTC, took the lead in 1964 in persuading his organization to abandon the "Christian" label, while retaining its unofficial Catholic attachments: thereby provoking the departure of the more conservative elements who could not stomach outright socialism; see his interview with Serge Mallet in the *Nouvel Observateur* (Jan. 28, 1965). On this as on previous occasions Descamps made it clear that for him socialist democracy signified not simply central planning, but also democratic decision-making and active workers participation.

ment: a point on which Communists and laissez-faire liberals concurred. The socio-political aspect of the system was occasionally characterized as "technocracy", though the CP's theorists on the whole favored a more traditional terminology: any hint that the state no longer belonged to the capitalist class might disconcert the *militants.* Such disturbing notions were left to writers associated with the various left-wing Socialist or dissident Communist movements outside the fold.[23]

The need to distinguish between Communist and Marxist writing, and the steadily declining relevance of the former, as the CP theorists departed ever further from reality, makes it necessary at this point to dissociate the topic from the political propaganda surrounding it. One may note, however, that in the measure in which the Communist party tried to recover lost ground, it did so by falling back upon the syndicalist strain in its tradition. The industrial conflicts of the 1960s brought out a pragmatic note which doubtless helped to sustain the loyalty of the workers, but had no bearing upon wider issues. While the Socialist and Catholic unions backed their refusal to accept official arbitration by a reasoned criticism of the authoritarian version of planning, the CP and the *Confédération Générale du Travail* contented themselves with the crudest kind of sectional wage bargaining. This was the counterpart of a political propaganda in which the regime was invariably described as the loyal servant of its capitalist masters: a repetition of an old mistake which Communists might be said to share with Marxist Social Democrats of an earlier generation. Occasional references to "state capitalism" did not bridge the widening gap between traditional assumptions and the realities of a situation in which the government

[23] All the above themes are analyzed in Marxist (but non-Communist) fashion by the group of writers cited above; see Ernest Mandel, "L'Apogée du néo-capitalisme et ses lendemains," *Temps Modernes* No. 219-220 (Aug.-Sept., 1964). For the corresponding Italian discussion see Bruno Trentin, "Politique des revenus et planification," *ibid.* See also the articles by Ernest Mandel, Serge Mallet and Oreste Rosenfeld in *Nouvelle revue marxiste* (Nov., 1961). It is noteworthy that these writers did not trouble themselves over the traditional hobby-horse of Leninism in its Russian and French variants: the supposed domination of the state by the monopolies. It was enough for their purpose to note that the working-class organizations possessed no effective control over the central policy-making apparatus. At a more journalistic level the same theme was tirelessly pursued in the weekly *France-Observateur* (later the *Nouvel Observateur*) by Michel Bosquet (pseudonym for André Gorz).

was subject to conflicting pressures from capital and labor, and able to exploit their sectional antagonisms in the interest of its own political strategy.[24]

If the Communist trumpet gave an uncertain sound in the 1960s, the prime responsibility rested with the party leaders who, unlike their Italian colleagues, were neither able nor willing to modernize their political outlook and abandon the more unrealistic assumptions they had taken over from their Soviet teachers during the Stalinist era. But there were also more deep-seated troubles, which reflected the difficulties all Marxists were having in bringing their theoretical apparatus up to date.

The principal difficulty stemmed, paradoxically, from the collapse of traditional free-enterprise capitalism and the partial socialization of the economy (discreetly obscured as "planning"). This might have been expected to generate a renewed interest in Marxian economics, but while it raised the prestige of Marx as a prophet, it did not correspondingly enhance the influence of his disciples. The latter had in the meantime for the most part committed themselves to an elaborate apologia of the Soviet regime as the antipode of Western liberal capitalism. When socialization occurred in the West after 1945, in a manner neither foreseen nor controlled by the Communist movement, the latter lost interest in the subject and fixed itself in an attitude of permanent opposition to democracy. The consequence was a partial revival of syndicalist attitudes—particularly marked in France, where Communist militancy had always drawn emotional strength from the *ouvriériste* understanding of the class struggle as a conflict pitting the manual workers against the rest of society. It was difficult to abandon this attitude in the interest of the now urgently necessary formation of an alliance of workers, technologists, and planners against the conservatism of the business community: the only basis on which socialism could be made to rhyme both with democracy and with the national

[24] In practice this was recognized, at any rate by the leaders of the CGT, whence their irritation over being left out of the major planning decisions. But the "reformist" implications of this attitude were checked by the party's unyielding commitment to a sterile pseudo-revolutionary attitude decked out with Leninist slogans. The resulting cleavage between theory and practice at times recalled the rather similar record of Italian Socialism before the First World War.

interest. The lead in this matter had to be taken by the Socialists, and to some extent by the Catholic Left: neither of them hampered by doctrinaire commitments to Soviet Marxism. Hence the sudden mushrooming of political clubs in which officials and intellectuals came together in an atmosphere unaffected by traditional party polemics. Hence also the formation of a loose but effective coalition ranging from the revisionist neo-Marxists, via the rival Socialist parties, to Christian Democrats and Social Democrats of various shades. The motivational force came from the discovery that the Communist party, while numerically powerful, was intellectually sterile. In the strategic calculations of the democratic Left, the CP's proper function was seen as that of a reserve force; in less flattering language it might be described as a potential supplier of political cannon-fodder.

A Socialist-Catholic alliance could be got under way only on the understanding that democracy and political pluralism were not to be questioned even inferentially. This consideration ruled out the notion of a Popular Front with the CP in the driver's seat. Moreover, there had to be mutual toleration in philosophical matters, i.e., neutrality on the religious issue, rather than strident atheism. These attitudes were the necessary counterpart of the kind of undoctrinaire socialism to which the democratic Left stood committed in the 1960s. They were more or less in tune with traditional Social Democratic Marxism in the style of the First and Second Internationals, but not with Leninism, let alone Stalinism—and the French CP had remained Stalinist, whatever its leaders might profess in public. Neo-Marxist revisionism thus led back, by a circuitous route, to the political conclusions analyzed in the preceding section. Socialist planning in a country like France was conceivable only on a basis of political pluralism. It also implied that effective direction would lie with a social stratum—the "new class" of technicians and planners—beyond the range of Communist propaganda. The economics of socialism were not necessarily reformist in the traditional pejorative sense of the term, for major structural change was not excluded; but they were not catastrophist either. The goal in any case was a planned economy with the public authorities in control: not a syndicalist utopia or a one-party dictatorship. On either count the CP could join such a coalition only with considerable mental reservations—or change its character altogether and acknowledge that the age of total transformations was past.

At the theoretical level the new situation reflected itself in the socio-economic writings already referred to, and more particularly in the defensive character of the only major treatise on economics to bear the orthodox Marxist imprint in recent years: the work of Ernest Mandel.[25]

An apologia of traditional Marxism is more easily delivered by an economist than by a political philosopher. Not only is the topic less controversial, but there are sound theoretical reasons for maintaining that the usefulness of Marx's approach is by no means exhausted. Moreover, the critique of capitalism offers a common meeting ground for Socialists and Communists. So far as France and Belgium are concerned, it may be added that fresh ground could still be broken in the early 1960s by a theorist working with the Marxian apparatus: notably one who was obviously in complete command of his subject, and thoroughly familiar with the entire corpus of Anglo-American academic literature as well.

For all that, a dispassionate reader of Mandel's work might have noticed a certain aroma of scholasticism. His two massive volumes of exegesis, interspersed with straight economic history, brought the French public up to date on the subject, without for that reason adding much to the theoretical side of a debate in progress, in Central Europe and elsewhere, since the opening years of the century. It was doubtless important that French readers should at last be placed in possession of an authentic exposition of the doctrine, instead of having to rely on the grotesque travesties produced by semiliterate Soviet economists. One would like to believe that no one who has access to Mandel will ever again waste his time on the typical products of Soviet *idiotnost*. And no doubt academic critics of Marxism for their part could learn something from an exegesis which did away with some of the misunderstandings traditionally current in polemical exchanges between liberal and Marxian economists: e.g., the notion that all Marxists were com-

[25] *Traité d'économie marxiste*. Mandel's minor writings do not enter into consideration here, any more than does his adherence to the Trotskyist interpretation of the USSR. This last is relevant only insofar as it constitutes a point of departure for critical reflections on Soviet economics, and Soviet Marxism in general. For the rest, Mandel's critique of Western economics follows the general line of left-wing Socialist thinking associated with the dissident Socialist movements in France and Italy, not to mention the British New Left. See the *Temps Modernes* essay already cited, and its English version, "The Economics of Neo-Capitalism," in the *Socialist Register* (London, 1964).

mitted to the doctrine of "absolute impoverishment." But these were mere exercises in clearing the ground. The really important question was whether Marxism could continue to furnish an instrument of economic analysis, or whether it was now to be regarded as the last of the great classical systems whose revelance had been undermined by the disappearance of the market economy.[26]

The strength of Marxism has always lain in the kind of historical sociology which makes it possible to see the rise of capitalism as a movement involving a radical reorganization of society: the steady accumulation of capital furnishing a kind of backdrop to the more visible and dramatic proceedings in the social foreground. The separation of the immediate producers from their tools—in other words the transformation of peasants and artisans into "free" laborers—is an essential part of the process; it is also the aspect from which liberal economists have traditionally averted their embarrassed gaze, preferring to dwell upon the growth of freedom consequent upon the "movement from status to contract." The superiority of Marxian theorizing over liberal economics in this domain is overwhelming, and Mandel makes the most of it. On the other hand, he faces the dilemma of every economic historian who seeks to differentiate between capitalism and industrialism. Historically, the two have marched together. It is no doubt possible in principle to be critical of the capitalist form of development, while treating the change-over from agrarian to industrial society as a step forward in the emancipation of mankind. The fact remains that much of the original socialist protest (and some of the

[26] Even so there is something to be said for getting rid of absurdities. Mandel's discussion of the thorny subject of real wages and purchasing power, in Vol. I, pp. 168 ff, should at least have taught some academic economists to take Marx more seriously, and to temper their own optimism as to the beneficial working of the free market economy. The Marxian argument that capitalism accumulates wealth and poverty respectively at the two opposite poles of society is not contradicted by the observation (which Marx did not challenge) that, with growing productivity, real wages have a tendency to rise. Pauperization relates to the "reserve army," not to the working class as a whole, and it is an ascertainable fact that where the market economy has remained "free," it has invariably produced an immense bottom layer of paupers. This has nothing to do with the fantastic rubbish produced by Soviet propagandists and their Western acolytes, from which it might be inferred that real wages have steadily declined under capitalism, so that e.g., the purchasing power of the American worker was halved between 1850 and 1950! This latter notion was still official doctrine in the USSR as late as 1955. Mandel, p. 179.

current concern over alienation) relates to industrialism as such. It is at least arguable that capitalism and socialism are merely alternative ways of organizing industrial society, and that the difference is less important than was thought at one time. Marx already had to face this awkward topic in the concluding volume of *Capital,* where his earlier optimism is entombed beneath a mountain of argument tending to suggest that the curse of mechanical labor (and the bureaucratization which goes with it) can at best be diminished, but not removed. Since his day the emphasis has increasingly shifted from the indictment of capitalism to the critique of industrialism: including its socialist variant. Moreover, the fact that large-scale organization calls for a hierarchy of supervision in the workshop has obvious implications for socialist practice and Marxist theory alike. In coming to terms with this set of problems, contemporary socialism has been obliged to abandon some of the older libertarian rhetoric, whose muted echo now tends to have a faintly nostalgic sound.[27]

On its sociological side the core of the Marxian argument is emphatically affirmed by Mandel—in those passages of his work where he relates the Marxian vision of the classless society to the theory of economic growth.[28] This is a restatement of what is indeed central in the "materialist conception of history": the notion that the class division of society has its roots in the appropriation of unpaid surplus

[27] This was perceived by Marxist sociologists like Georges Friedmann whose work is cited by Mandel. What Mandel has to say on the subject amounts to a reaffirmation of the classical Socialist doctrine that the "inhuman" aspect of industrialism is due to its capitalist organization. This sidesteps the modern sociological argument (first systematically developed by Max Weber) that the essence of the process is rationalization, and that the capitalist form is irrelevant. We shall see in the final chapter how the neo-Marxist school in philosophy has dealt with this theme, which strictly speaking is extraneous to economic theory. For the increasingly centralized and hierarchical structure of modern capitalism (or should it be industrialism?) see Mandel, pp. 197-99.

[28] "C'est le mode de production capitaliste qui, par l'essor prodigieux qu'il assure aux forces productives, crée pour la première fois dans l'histoire les conditions économiques pour la suppression de toute société de classe." Mandel, I, 215. This at least disposes of the totally un-Marxist notion, familiar from Soviet literature, that the necessary preconditions of human emancipation do not arise from a mature capitalism, but have to be artificially created by socialist industrialization in backward countries. But the return to orthodox Marxism poses a different problem: even though it is true that capitalism lays the foundations, it does not follow that socialism will necessarily take the form anticipated in the nineteenth century.

labor by a privileged group freed from material toil. Once more it is possible for modern Socialists to accept this, and then to raise the question (already suggested by Syndicalist writers early in the century) whether the functional separation of physical from intellectual toil may not contain the germ of a new class division. It is not easy to see how this argument can be disposed of on traditional Marxist grounds, since it makes use of the Marxian approach and then applies it to the analysis of postcapitalist society. In the end one is left with a dichotomy between the familiar Socialist emphasis on rational organization, and the no less traditional Syndicalist demand for workers control. Does this cleavage prefigure a harmonious solution at a higher level, or a steady growth of social and political polarization? No one can say, certainly not an orthodox Marxist, but there is some ground for skepticism.

A similar and related difficulty makes itself felt in those sections of Mandel's work where the planned economy of the USSR is contrasted with the unplanned and crisis-ridden state of the West in general and the United States in particular.[29] It is clearly easier to restate the Marxian theory of cyclical crises than to evolve a new intellectual construction relevant to the semi-planned economies of post-1945 Western Europe. The Marxian doctrine is applicable only to an unregulated market economy and in the 1960s the only major country still committed to such a system (plus a few built-in monetary stabilizers, to prevent the worst from happening) is the United States. The East-West confrontation in this area thus reduces itself to a comparison between the USA and the USSR: an awkward choice for European Marxists, and doubly awkward for a writer who does not accept the

[29] Mandel I, 422 ff.; II, pp. 225 ff. Mandel's account of imperialism (II, 68 ff.) follows conventional Leninist lines. It therefore fails to meet the argument that colonial exploitation has been of genuine importance to Western capitalism only during the period of intensive "primitive accumulation." Once this phase was over, colonial plunder lost its importance. Nor is it the case that developed industrial-capitalist countries were dependent on the possession of colonial markets, though they certainly drew incidental advantages from them. These advantages accrued in proportion to the metropolitan country's ability to outdistance its rivals. The British Empire in India and Africa in its heyday was a by-product of Britain's dominant position on the world market, not (as Hobson and Lenin thought) a major outlet for surplus capital; the latter went (as it always does) to economically developed areas—including the white-settler "Dominions"—rather than to the true colonies.

claim that socialism has already been established in the Soviet Union.[30]

This is more than a passing matter. The problem for Marxists arises not simply from the fact that the urgent drive for capital accumulation sharpens the antagonism between the state and the worker during the transition period to full socialism (notably in a country lacking democratic traditions and an established labor movement). Such a situation could still be blamed on unfavorable historical circumstances. The real trouble is that the industrial revolution as such appears to generate new class alignments, and that it does so under capitalism and socialism alike. One may get around the difficulty by dropping the term "class" and talking of "social stratification" instead; but these verbal maneuvers do not become more attractive when perpetrated by socialists. What is at stake in the end, as every Marxist knows, is control over the means of production. It is one thing to reject the term "state capitalism" as a proper description of the Soviet regime, on the grounds that capitalism presupposes private property and a market in capital values. It is another matter to treat the bureaucratic phenomenon as a mere obstacle to the attainment of socialist democracy, instead of recognizing in it the germ of a new and permanent class division.[31]

[30] *Ibid.*, II, pp. 231 ff., 425 ff. For Mandel the Soviet system is "transitional" and falls short of full socialism as long as commodity production for the market, and major social inequalities, are allowed to continue. In view of the steady growth of these features, this assessment raises awkward questions for the future, even if the theoretical assumption of Trotskyism (bureaucratic deformation due to backwardness and extreme economic shortages) is accepted as a partial explanation of what occurred under Stalin.

[31] In a halfhearted manner this is conceded by Leninist critics of the regime, who yet do not want to abandon their commitment to the notion that the USSR is on the road to full socialism. *Ibid.*, II, 328: "Si l'on peut accuser d'hypocrisie ceux qui prennent prétexte du danger bureaucratique pour refuser ou pour retarder en fait le renversement du capitalisme . . . on ne peut contester que la concentration de toutes les ressources économiques entre les mains de l'État risque de maintenir ou d'étendre les conditions d'inégalités sociales. Le fait que cet État affirme gouverner 'au nom de la classe ouvrière' n'offre qu'une consolation purement juridique." Behind this concession to sociological realism lurks the depressing realization that the October Revolution did *not* in effect give power to the working class, but merely to a party acting in its name. Was this merely due to the political immaturity of the class, or did it hide a deeper incapacity? It is evidently impossible for Leninists (and Trotskyism is simply an offshoot of Leninism) to acknowledge the latter conclusion, but on traditional Marxist grounds there is no good reason why it should not be frankly recognized that political "rule" by the working class is an impossibility.

Inversely one may agree that the replacement of classical political economy by pure economics signifies a kind of intellectual bankruptcy which the Marxist school has avoided: it is alone in having maintained the traditional approach which sees society as a whole. Unfortunately the social whole to which this unified vision applies is the market society of liberal capitalism, with its relatively autonomous economic organization, its cyclical crises, and—its class struggles. The planned and centralized economy now arising before our eyes—with an obvious time-lag for the United States: the only major country to which the Marxian analysis is still more or less applicable—departs from the classical model not only in regard to the familiar decennial cycle: it tends to do away with the rigid separation of political and economic categories. This truly is the end of economics as an autonomous discipline. Marxists may welcome its disappearance, on the grounds that it signals the knell of bourgeois society.[32] It is, however, increasingly evident that the recent evolution of capitalism cannot leave its old antagonist quite unaffected. Liberalism and socialism have grown up alongside each other, and it is at least arguable that they must stand and fall together.

[32] Mandel, II, 430-32.

5

The Logic of History

Historical Materialism

At the origins of Marxism there lies an experience which the founders of the doctrine shared with the leaders of the French Revolution: the discovery that a new idea does not triumph merely because it is rational. After the first flush of enthusiasm in 1789 the revolutionaries had experienced the resistance of the established order, and in the lengthy drama that followed, victory and defeat were closely interwoven. Moreover, the unleashing of popular passions during the second and more radical phase of the Revolution entailed the partial abandonment of the utopian aims prevalent in the earlier stage. A certain disillusionment with the idealist approach to politics was inherent in the Jacobin attitude after 1792, foreshadowing the later emphasis upon economic interests. To the extent that Marx and Engels, like many of their contemporaries, were sobered by the defeat of 1848-49, they too experienced the need to base their hopes on something more solid than the power of ideas or the revolutionary enthusiasm of the exploited. After 1850 they tended to affirm with increasing persistence that the ultimate triumph of socialism was inscribed in the logic of history. Though from time to time they found themselves in the company of men who clung to the earlier standpoint, their general outlook, as the Victorian era wore on, was subtly influenced by the evolutionism of the positivist school. By the 1890s, when Engels had taken over from Marx, it was not easy to distinguish his version of the doctrine from the fashionable evolutionist creed then current among bourgeois radicals.[1]

The materialist conception of history took shape in this atmosphere of mingled political disillusionment and growing confidence in the over-all direction of social development. Its formulation by Marx in 1859, in his well-known Preface to the *Critique of Political Economy*, occurred in the same year that saw the publication of Darwin's research. By 1867 (when Marx seriously considered dedicating the first volume of *Capital* to the author of *The Origin of Species*) his frame of mind had become sufficiently evolutionist to permit the inference that socialism would come about through a process inherent in the operation of the economic system he was analyzing. After the death of Marx in 1883, Engels, Kautsky, and Plekhanov went further in this direction. Engels, beginning and ending as a Hegelian, still thought it right to deduce the "iron laws" of history from a metaphysical conception of the universe. Kautsky dispensed with metaphysics, but did not for this reason revert to the revolutionary materialism of the early Marx. Instead, he virtually adopted the evolutionism of Comte and Spencer, which subjected the whole of history to a single law of organic development. Since the law guaranteed the eventual triumph of reason, there was no need to worry about temporary setbacks.

In principle this was also the attitude of non-socialist evolutionists (including academic sociologists like Durkheim), with the difference that they saw contemporary bourgeois society as the natural and inevitable outcome of a universal process of development from barbarism to civilization. Though in disagreement on this point, all concerned held that Marxism was to be understood as the socialist variant of the common evolutionist credo. In this perspective, the difference between

[1] In 1850-52, when Marx and Engels broke with their former associates, and simultaneously abandoned the hope of an imminent total revolution, there was as yet little to presage this outcome, though some of Engels' early formulations in the 1840s already pointed in such a direction. Moreover (as noted in Chapter 1), Marx permitted himself a final fling in 1850 before relinquishing his original hopes. The *locus classicus* is the Statement of Principles issued in 1850 by the *Société Universelle des Communistes Révolutionnaires*, a document signed by Marx and Engels together with the Blanquist emissaries J. Vidil and Adam, and the Chartist leader Julian Harney, which bound the associates to the Blanquist slogans of "permanent revolution" and "proletarian dictatorship" (though the latter formulation may have been due to Marx). See Karl Korsch, *Karl Marx* (London-New York, 1963), p. 233 *n*.

positivism and socialism reduced itself in the end to a simple matter of personal and political antagonism between Comte and Marx. This was more or less the view taken by Jaurès and his supporters, who were naturally pleased to find in Marx confirmation of their own views. As might have been expected, Sorel adopted the anti-evolutionist stand, though to buttress it he was obliged to fall back on Bergson. The original Marxian approach having been abandoned by all concerned, the debate resolved itself into a clash between positivism and vitalism. As in Germany, where Nietzsche supplied the irrationalists with suitable arguments against scientific materialism, the romantic rebellion fed on a mixture of vague resentments and true insights into the inadequacy of scientism. In the crisis of the 1930s, when faith in liberalism and positivism collapsed, the political Right attracted some disillusioned Socialists who had lost their belief in peaceful progress. Conversely, the more radical positivists now came forward as full-fledged Marxists: if the bourgeoisie was no longer willing to support scientific materialism, these heirs of rationalism would strike camp and join the proletariat.[2]

In point of fact Marx had been careful to stress the historical character of his doctrine, and to differentiate the critical analysis of bourgeois society from the attempt to construct a theory of society as such. Although by the later 1860s he had quietly absorbed as much of positivism as he could use for his own purposes, he stopped short of the notion that the general concept of evolution (which he was quite willing to employ for history as a whole) explained the mechanism of any particular civilization, e.g., the contemporary Western one. From the fact that bourgeois society had arisen from an earlier social formation, it did not in the least follow that its own development exempli-

[2] Hence the evolution of the *Pensée* group. These distinguished scholars—mostly from the natural sciences, with Paul Langevin and Marcel Prenant in the lead—from 1933 onward systematically introduced the study and propagation of "dialectical materialism" in France, not as a metaphysical enterprise, but as a new method of research in the natural and social sciences. Themselves in the great tradition of the Encyclopedists, they firmly believed that Marxism was to be understood as the contemporary form of scientific rationalism. Unlike their predecessors before 1914, they extended this benediction even to Engels' and Lenin's pseudo-Hegelian philosophizing. In this they broke with tradition, for when *Capital* first appeared in print, the Comtean journal *La Philosophie positive* published a critical notice which blamed Marx for introducing "metaphysics" into political economy. E. de Roberty, "Compte rendu du *Capital,*" *La Philosophie positive* (Nov.-Dec., 1868), pp. 507-9.

fied a general principle of social evolution common to all previous stages of history. Still less did it follow that violent upheavals belonged to the past. What was past was simply the *bourgeois* revolution. This had given rise to a society disrupted by class antagonisms, a society incapable of passing peacefully and gradually to the higher stage of communism. Whatever its shortcomings, this approach preserved the insight that every historical phase had its own laws. For the rest, Marxism defined itself quite simply as the revolutionary critique of bourgeois society and of the economic system associated with it—capitalism.

In the later nineteenth century, the evolutionist belief in peaceful progress supplied the philosophical rationale of reformist socialism. In Britain it did so from the 1880s, when the Fabians evolved their characteristic amalgam of Bentham, Ricardo, Mill, Spencer, and Jevons, as an alternative to Marxism. In France, the typical response to Comte's bourgeois progressivism took the form of asserting that Marx had demonstrated the inevitability of socialism. The evolutionary view was conserved—as indeed it had been retained by Marx in relation to human history as a whole—but its conventional political interpretation was rejected. Instead of treating bourgeois society ("civilization") as the predestined final term of history, the new viewpoint postulated the advent of a postbourgeois age as a necessary consequence of capitalism's own development. This took care of the demand for science, while preserving some of the older utopian content. In this perspective the early socialists now appeared as naive prophets of a future whose coming was guaranteed by laws of evolution common to nature and history alike.[3]

Such an attitude was superficially consistent with Marxism, at any rate when the doctrine was taken in the form given to it by writers like Plekhanov and Kautsky. What it left out was the *complexio oppositorum* of bourgeoisie and proletariat, which made the transition from

[3] The representative Marxist journal of the period, Kautsky's *Neue Zeit,* symbolized this confident spirit in its very title. But outside Germany too it was a commonplace among socialists that the New Age called for men and measures which no other party could supply. This argument turned the flank of bourgeois thought, which had hitherto relied upon the identification of industrial and scientific progress with "free enterprise." What it amounted to was that capitalism was *not progressive enough.*

capitalism to communism dependent upon a political upheaval. It also ignored the implication of Marx's view that communism would transcend the categories of bourgeois society, including its morality.[4] On the conventional evolutionary view, the lineaments of the future could be deduced from tendencies already inherent in the present, whereas Marx held that bourgeois society was historically unique and not necessarily a model for ages yet to come. Mankind, on this assumption, would presumably conserve certain general acquisitions of bourgeois civilization, but their nature was not clearly specified. This approach was consistent with the belief that socialism and communism would emerge from a proletarian revolution which, so far from generalizing bourgeois social relations, would stand them on their head. Although the mature Marx no longer operated with the concept of alienation, he retained the notion that bourgeois nature was in some sense a travesty of human nature. Contemporary civilization might contain the germ of further developments, but they existed in a stunted form, so that one could not simply extrapolate from them to the socialist future. That future indeed was quite likely to revive some elements of the distant past which had been sacrificed to bourgeois progress, although it did not follow that mankind could or should take Rousseau's advice and aim at the simple life.

What was immediately involved, in the opinion of both Marx and Engels, was a new understanding of the dialectic of history: a dialectic exemplified by the survival of certain antique remnants (among them tribal life) which pointed obscurely towards the classless and stateless society of the future. That society would validate the utopian longing for perfect freedom and equality, though it would do so on the basis of material and cultural traits acquired during the antecedent epochs. Meanwhile the necessary critical motivation was furnished quite simply by the class struggle. This struggle indicated the general direction which mankind had to take if it wanted to transcend the bourgeois horizon. Consequently there was no need for an Archimedean standpoint outside history (of the kind that philosophy had traditionally

[4] See his *Critique of the Gotha Program,* 1875 where this point is exemplified with reference to economic equality under full communism. For a discussion of this topic see Korsch, pp. 45 ff; also Eugene Kamenka, *The Ethical Foundations of Marxism* (London, 1963).

undertaken to supply), quite apart from the fact that belief in the possibility of such a location in extrahistorical space was an illusion. It was only necessary to generalize from the existing condition of things to arrive at the standpoint of revolutionary materialism, i.e., communism. Inversely, once it was grasped that communism implied the abolition of class rule, it was impossible to retain the reformist illusion that the proletarian movement could be contained within the existing society. The revolution and the proletariat thus stood in an organic relation to each other: the advent of communism signified the emancipation of the class whose unpaid labor sustained the edifice of bourgeois society.[5]

The restatement of this revolutionary viewpoint—after an intervening phase of quasi-pacifist positivism and evolutionism—occurred as a by-product of the Russian Revolution. In this respect 1918 was a turning point on the scale of 1848. Once the Communist movement had revived the original Marxian vision, it was no longer possible to assimilate Marxism to positivism. On the other hand, the practical application of the doctrine—under conditions unforeseen by Marx and Engels—laid bare a theoretical flaw: the revolutionary proletariat, which on Marx's assumption was the prime vehicle of the transition from capitalism to socialism, existed as a decisive factor only in retarded countries. The class struggle thus appeared in a new light. By projecting the upheavals of the nineteenth century backward upon European history, Marx had laid bare the mechanism whereby bourgeois society had come into being. His theory was superior to others in the measure in which it stressed social conflict as the central motor of the bourgeois revolution, taking this term in its widest sense to include the whole movement of European history since the crumbling of feudalism. Conversely, with the termination of the bourgeois age (which in Western Europe might be dated from the war of 1914-18) it became possible for the first time to grasp the interconnection between the whole modern development and the proletarian class movement. The latter now appeared as an aspect of the bourgeois revolution, and Marxism as the theory of that revolution.

[5] "The theoretical propositions of the Communists merely express in general terms the actual conditions of an existing class struggle, or of an historical movement going on under our very eyes." *Manifesto of the Communist Party,* Marx-Engels *Selected Works,* (Moscow, 1951), Vol. I.

The totalitarian reconstructions of the twentieth century plainly followed a different pattern. Paradoxically, political conflicts became more violent as traditional class antagonisms diminished. Movements such as communism and fascism demonstrated an unforeseen capacity for transcending class lines and grouping the most varied elements under their banners. The European civil war ceased to be a class war. It assumed the shape of a deadly struggle between rival armies equally subversive of bourgeois society. The fictitious notion of a conflict between bourgeoisie and proletariat gave way to the realization that the new totalitarian elites operated independently of their social origins. Communism ceased to represent the working class. Fascism disclosed itself as a mortal threat to the bourgeois way of life. Bourgeois society crumbled, and as its pillars gave way, economic determinism itself was buried beneath the ruins.

From Utopia to Technocracy

Saint-Simon, Proudhon, and Marx had accustomed their followers to regard the historical process as the final guarantor of those "utopian" aims which the Enlightenment had formulated in an abstract manner unrelated to the actual march of events. The ultimate goal—rationality for Saint-Simon, justice for Proudhon, freedom for Marx—was envisioned as the term of a development in the course of which men would learn to master their environment. While Marx described Saint-Simon as a utopian and Proudhon as a dilettante, he inherited their confidence in the future. Indeed he effected a synthesis linking Saint-Simon's technological enthusiasm with Proudhon's emphasis on the class struggle. The Marxian vision combined firm hope in the advent of a rational society with an equally firm condemnation of the wretched present. Yet in the conventional sense Marx was not an optimist. His gloom stemmed from an awareness of the cost to mankind of every step forward in the struggle to "humanize" its circumstances. The ascent is long and arduous. Moreover, the final outcome is bought at the price of suffering which can never be made good: there is no way of compensating the dead for the burdens they bore, no retrospective balm for the toil and agony imposed upon past generations. The frivolity of the Enlightenment finds no echo in Marx's writings.

When he voices confidence in man's future, his tone is Aeschylean, not Voltairean: there is to be an end of senseless suffering and violence (and of slavish belief in nonexisting deities), but no forgetfulness of the past. The materialist is to remember what it has cost mankind to escape from its bondage to nature: a category under which Marx subsumes "civilized" institutions such as war and the state, along with the whole legacy of bestial cruelty men have inherited from their animal past. The price will not indeed have been paid in vain, but it will have been exacted from those whose voices can no longer be heard. On these grounds Marx refuses to celebrate the onward march of civilization. Hegelian to the end, he retains the notion that history is kept going by its "negative" side: mankind is obliged to wade through mud and blood. The utopians, with their hankering for miraculous cures and rational shortcuts, were ineffective because they closed their eyes to the real cost of progress.

For all that, the Marxian view preserves the earlier faith in a rational organization of society: now (in the nineteenth century) made historically possible by the industrial revolution. To the Saint-Simonians—most of them ex-pupils of the *École Polytechnique*—this goal presented itself as a technical problem, though it was tacitly understood that the issue of political power would at some time have to be faced. In the end it mattered little to them whether the desired transformation was effected by a benevolent autocrat or by the "open conspiracy" of the enlightened. Like their Fabian successors a century later, they were quite willing to experiment with both solutions. Also like the Fabians, they treated the new discipline of sociology as a means of constructing rational utopias, which were somehow expected to transfer themselves from the drawing board to the real world, without the intervention of anything so disagreeable as the class struggle. The technocratic aspect of utopianism is present already in Saint-Simon. Almost extinguished in Marx, who characteristically refused to draw blueprints of the future, it survived in the pre-Marxist schools of Russian socialism. In the end it rose to prominence once more in the Bolshevik regime with its almost metaphysical faith in planning. When Lenin in 1920 defined communism as "the Soviets plus electrification," he was unconsciously reverting to Saint-Simon who, to be sure, would have treated the embryonic workers councils as a useless encumbrance. The Stalinist dictatorship, with its exaltation of the engineer, was Saint-Simonian to the hilt, and quite properly gained the applause of numerous technologists, some of whom in their enthusiasm even joined the Communist party. An enlightened dictatorship fulfilled the secret dreams of an intelligentsia traditionally suspicious of bourgeois democracy and impatient for a shortcut. Though rationalized in Marxist terms, the underlying attitudes were technocratic and unhistorical: utopia was to be won by a stroke of the sword.[6]

How could such notions be squared with the Marxian stress upon history and the class struggle? Marx had treated the utopians as doctrinaires in the tradition of the eighteenth century. True to their heritage, they had eliminated the time factor from their calculations. Instead of grounding their hopes in the real movement of material forces, they were forever appealing to reason. Conversely, the superiority of the new "scientific" standpoint lay in the patient analysis of the material process—ultimately, the effect of technological change upon production relations—which subtended the shadow play of ideology. Yet the Marxian doctrine could also be interpreted in rationalistic terms. The very phrase "scientific socialism" lent itself to an equivocation. Science after all had been the original inspiration of Baconian and Cartesian rationalism. If it stood for detachment and willingness to learn from the study of facts, it also reflected a growing confidence in man's ability to replace his natural environment by a rational one: in other words, to construct an artificial world. For the true utopians science was a *deus ex machina* which would permit mankind to escape from history. For Hegel, on the contrary, the logic of history was uniquely mediated by the time factor: each new phase of the process emerged from the anterior stage through a painful transition marked by the lapse of historical time. In the Marxian conception these notions were held in balance: historical logic could not

[6] For the role of the *École Polytechnique,* see F. A. Hayek, *The Counter-Revolution of Science* (Glencoe, 1955), pp. 110 ff. For the technocratic content of utopianism in general, see Georges Duveau, *Sociologie de l'Utopie et autres essais* (Paris, 1961). The filiation of ideas from Saint-Simon to Marx is discussed in Georges Gurvitch, *Les Fondateurs français de la sociologie contemporaine. I. Saint-Simon sociologue* (Paris, 1955), especially the introduction, where Proudhon appears as the link between Saint-Simon and Marx, and the latter as the inheritor of "un Saint-Simonisme Proudhonisé" (p. 8).

dispense with the time element, for "Mankind always sets itself only such tasks as it can solve."[7] On the other hand, the very notion of a task awaiting a solution opened the door, however inadvertently, to the rationalist approach, with its readiness to prescribe instant remedies for real or fancied ills. "Science" was a *Janus bifrons* which could be invoked by historians and technocrats alike. If to the former it signified the study of objective processes, the latter might derive from it the confidence necessary to decree the reshaping of the social environment.

Taken together, the utopian and the technocratic strains mingled in the positivist outlook from which Marx's French forerunners had drawn their confidence in the advent of a truly rational and scientific order. In the rudimentary doctrine embodied in the "positive system," what was later called sociology appeared as "social physics," and the latter was defined as the search for laws of progress as necessary and as unalterable as those of gravitation. Behind Comte there stood Newton and the "mechanical materialism" of the French Enlightenment. Though formally abandoned or qualified by Engels, these modes of thought reappeared in his version of Marx's doctrine, which became canonical for Communists once it had been given the Soviet *imprimatur*. In this roundabout fashion, what had originally been the inspiration of the early pre-Marxian French socialists reached France once more by way of Russia, to become the official doctrine of the French CP. The "social physics" of Comte, now renamed "scientific socialism," guaranteed the final outcome of the class struggle, much as in its bourgeois form the doctrine had underwritten the onward march of civilization.[8] The difference was less profound than might have been supposed from the change in vocabulary. Comte and Marx (as interpreted by Engels) appeared to be saying the same thing so far as "progress" was concerned, though they differed as to the outcome. Were they not both concerned with the collective development of the human race and with the "iron laws" governing this development? If Marx stressed the impact of technological change, the materialist conception of history could be said to have underpinned the faith in

[7] *A Contribution to the Critique of Political Economy,* Preface.
[8] See Comte, *Opuscules de philosophie sociale* (Paris, 1883), English tr., *Early Essays on Social Philosophy,* ed. by F. Harrison (London, 1911).

progress. Inversely, once the importance of technology had been grasped, it became possible to envisage a future state of affairs when the "administration of things" would be turned over to scientists and their helpers. Then indeed society would be truly rational, for it would now be possible to rearrange the technological base of the economic process. The infrastructure of history would cease to operate in the blind, uncontrolled fashion analyzed by Marx. On this positivist interpretation of Marxism, it was only necessary to eliminate the anarchy of production in order to make economic relations wholly comprehensible, and at the same time wholly responsive to the collective will of the producers. Utopia lay at the end of a road which history was bound to travel, for history itself was nothing but the unfolding of man's productive powers. The dialectic of the class struggle—itself built into the fabric of capitalism, a system operative only so long as the actual producers were denied control of their tools—guaranteed the ultimate instauration of a social order under which men could at last decide freely upon the kind of existence they wished to lead.[9]

So far as the contemporary world is concerned, the technocratic utopia, for practical purposes, assumes the familiar features of the planned economy, and it does so quite regardless of any philosophical notions current among the planners. The latter need not be Marxists, let alone Communists, and are probably better served by a purely technocratic ideology than by any other. An ideology of this kind is, however, unsuitable to a workers movement—a circumstance evident since the days when Proudhon subjected the Saint-Simonians to a scornful critique whose themes were taken up once more, half a century later, by Sorel. A viable socialist movement requires cooperation between the intelligentsia and the working class. If the intellectuals insist on an authoritarian or managerial interpretation of their aims, the alliance is endangered, and the same is true if syndicalist tendencies gain the upper hand among the workers. The nature of the problem becomes comprehensible only if one abandons the doctrin-

[9] Duveau, pp. 25 ff., 40 ff. See also Claude Lefort, "Marxisme et Sociologie," *Cahiers du Centre d'Études Socialistes,* Nos. 34-35 (Nov.-Dec., 1963), pp. 14 ff. There is no point in attempting to list the official Communist literature on the subject, but reference may briefly be made to one of the standard texts, Georges Politzer's *Principes élémentaires de Philosophie* (2d ed., Paris, 1963), especially part V, "Le matérialisme historique," pp. 207 ff.

aire assumption that socialism is the intellectual expression of working-class sentiment. If it were nothing more, there would be no tension and no antagonism: the intellectuals would function simply as spokesmen of the workers. Conversely, the technocratic utopia of the planners could be installed at short notice, were it not for the actual existence of the empirical labor movement. Both viewpoints are one-sided and unhistorical. Their undialectical opposition was overcome in the Marxian synthesis, which made it possible to interpret the common aim (socialism) in terms appropriate to the intelligentsia and the workers alike. All could now march together under a common banner, since it was understood that socialism signified the emancipation of the workers from exploitation. The problem had at last been solved —"at a higher level." What the solution lacked was an explicit awareness of the fact that socialism had become the bond linking two distinct strata whose alliance was tenuous and might come apart if too much pressure was applied by one side or the other. There was perhaps a limited unconscious gain from closing one's eyes to this situation. It certainly made it easier for socialists to proclaim in good faith that they were simply translating into specific terms the inherent aims of an as yet immature labor movement. Moreover, to the degree that a working-class elite gradually took over from the pioneers, some of the old tensions did actually vanish. It became possible to identify Marxism and the working-class movement without doing violence to the facts.

The consensus was endangered from two sides. First, the Soviet regime staked its existence on the success of a planned economy and thereby made evident what was inherent in socialism from the very beginning: that the organizer was due to become the key figure of the new society. Next, the collapse of liberal market economics in the 1930s and the introduction of semi-nationalized "mixed" economies in Western Europe after 1945, led to the widespread adoption of planning techniques which reinforced the role of the public authorities without altering the character of decision-making at the point of production. The upshot was a revival of syndicalism—violent in the Soviet sphere (as in the Hungarian revolt of 1956), more or less peaceful in Western Europe, where the labor movement gradually learned to support central economic planning, without quite trusting the planners. At the same time the rise of technocratic tendencies on both sides of the geographical and political divide produced a sharpened awareness of the common features underlying modern capitalism and contemporary socialism alike. It became evident that the two camps were, unsystematically and haphazardly, working towards a common goal. That goal might tentatively be described as the global spread of modern technology, or more precisely as the unification of the world under the leadership of the technically most advanced nations. It only needed the addition of interstellar space rivalry between the major powers for everyone to perceive that the effective unification of the planet had become possible. Once there was talk of flying to the moon, all sublunary problems necessarily came to be seen as forming a whole. Not that the world had been pacified—that part of the original utopian program was still far from being accomplished—but its pacification was now seen to be in the common interest of all concerned, whatever their ideological standpoint. In this perspective, the residual differences between rival economic systems and political creeds took on a different aspect. It began to look as though the world might realize utopia by subjecting itself to the control of planners and scientists, and this quite irrespective of the class struggles still raging in those parts of the globe where the industrial revolution had disrupted the ancient fabric of traditional society. Whatever the immediate outcome of these struggles, the probable end result appeared to be a technological society consciously planning its future under the direction of scientists and administrators. The dialectic of the East-West conflict was merely hastening a consummation inherent in the progressive unfolding of industrial civilization.

If this was the global setting, its general features reproduced themselves on the national scale, so far as France was concerned, under conditions where the "withering away" of the ancient political forms could be studied with almost scientific precision. France had always been Europe's political laboratory. As it had pioneered in political democracy after 1789, so now it led the movement towards economic planning, state control—and technocracy. The Gaullist revolution merely capped a development in train since 1940, when the Third Republic gave up the ghost. Parliamentary government once more went into eclipse, after a brief revival in 1946, when it became evident that its procedures were no longer adequate to the management of a modern industrial country with a semi-planned economy. What took its place was an authoritarian structure which at first seemed to be wholly dependent on the charismatic appeal of a national hero. Only gradually was it perceived that the regime held the loyalty of the new key stratum: the elite of administrators and managers (public and private) who had committed themselves, without quite realizing it, to the essentially socialist idea of a planned economy no longer subject to the vagaries of the market place.

Technocracy grew out of a political stalemate of which the decay of liberal democracy was merely one aspect. As was remarked before, the class conflicts which disrupted French society since the 1930s could find no issue because neither bourgeoisie nor proletariat held the key to the future. That key was held by the technical intelligentsia, but the new stratum lacked an adequate political consciousness. Hence its fitful attempts to assert itself[10] were marked by a groping uncertainty which its ideologists promptly elevated to the dignity of a principle by styling their outlook "pragmatic." What was really at stake was the formulation of a postliberal doctrine which would incorporate the heritage of socialism, while dispensing with the class struggle; but under French conditions this aim could not be avowed, perhaps not even perceived. The shock would have been too great, and in any case the Communists stood ready to remind left-center opponents of the Gaullist regime that the CP held the loyalty of four or five million voters without whom the democratic Left could not reach power. This in turn was just why the technical intelligentsia in the main lent its support to the regime: its mild authoritarianism (combined with preservation of constitutional government and traditional republican liberties) seemed preferable to the Fourth Republic's chaotic muddle of pressure-group politics.[11]

[10] Primarily in the form of modernizing movements patterned on the Rooseveltian New Deal. This was the real significance of the Mendès-France episode, and also the reason for that experiment's failure: in France no serious reforming movement could get along without a socialist or nationalist ideology. Mendèsism in one of its aspects was an unsuccessful precursor of Gaullism (and largely attracted the same clientele). From a different viewpoint it was an attempt to realize socialist goals while by-passing the labor movement. Its technocratic character was apparent to serious observers, and also accounted for the distrust it inspired among Communists.

[11] André Philip, *La Gauche: Mythes et réalités* (Paris, 1964); see also the account of the colloquy held at Saint Germain-en-Laye on Jan. 27-28, 1962,

What rendered the theoretical issue crucial was the decadence of liberal democracy and the stabilization of a regime which was authoritarian without being dictatorial, and economically progressive without being overtly socialist. Its "technocratic" character lay hidden at first behind the dramatic political convulsions caused by the Algerian war and the collapse of parliamentary rule. From the standpoint of the liberal-conservative bourgeoisie prominent during the later stages of the Fourth Republic, Gaullism was simply an improvisation, if not an aberration. The S.F.I.O. at first treated it as a defensive reaction against the menace of a military coup d'état, and indeed campaigned officially in favor of the Gaullist Constitution of 1958—a circumstance seldom remembered in later years, when the party of Guy Mollet had gone into opposition and even on some occasions concluded a tactical alliance with the Communists. The latter from the start opposed the Fifth Republic—and demanded a return to the Fourth! In their eyes, parliamentary democracy still had a useful role to play, provided it could be brought under the control of the CP, or of a Popular Front dominated by the CP. In Communist literature the new regime was described as "antidemocratic," the implication being that the Communists stood for democracy—an odd reversal of roles. As for the *petite gauche* assembled around Sartre and the *Temps Modernes* group, it displayed its customary clairvoyance by denouncing Gaullism as the precursor of Fascism and urging its own supporters to take to the *maquis*. In all this confusion it was left to a handful of independents, who had learned something from the history of the past decades, to suggest that Gaullism might conceivably be the traditionalist façade of an altogether novel phenomenon—as indeed it turned out to be. For their pains they were promptly denounced as crypto-Gaullists, and accused of aiming at an alliance with the ruling bureaucracy. The left-wing *Parti Socialiste Unifié* (to which most of

---

and published under the title *La Démocratie à refaire* (Paris, 1963), with contributions by René Rémond, Georges Vedel, Jacques Fauvet, Étienne Borne, Maurice Duverger and others. For the Communist viewpoint see Gilbert Mury, "Actualité de la lutte des classes," *Cahiers du Communisme* (April, 1963), pp. 42-56. Not surprisingly, Communist writers tended to fasten upon the "abstract" and seemingly nonpolitical character of the doctrine put forward by the planners in order to demonstrate once more that capitalism was built upon exploitation. What they failed to see was that their critics might concede this, without for this reason accepting their intepretation of the class struggle.

these revisionists adhered) thereby perhaps lost a chance to become the political vehicle of the technical intelligentsia.

Yet where the orthodox failed, the revisionists in the end succeeded in relating doctrine to reality. Their success, however, disclosed that the link between theory and practice could no longer take the form of a revolutionary class movement. That movement had in fact collapsed and been replaced by the totalitarian Communist apparatus, which in turn had severed its links with the working class and transformed itself into the nucleus of a new ruling bureaucracy. The fact that in France the final move was blocked, while in the USSR and in Eastern Europe the full logic of totalitarianism had been permitted to work itself out, made possible the preservation of certain illusions about the nature and function of the French CP. But from a theoretical viewpoint this difference was immaterial. Once Stalinism had shown its face, the problem was posed in identical terms for Marxists in East and West alike. And Stalinism in this context signified more than a particular terrorist phase in the history of the Soviet party, let alone the pathological behavior of the dictator. The term stood for a system which had survived its creator. Orthodoxy and revisionism defined themselves in relation to that system. Broadly speaking, three attitudes were possible so far as France was concerned: qualified acceptance of the Soviet model; return to "primitive Communism"; or an advance beyond the Leninist dogma. The first was the solution adopted by the CP leadership and its official ideologists; the second became a rallying point for "Chinese" tendencies, and for sectarian splinter groups in which youthful Trotskyists and old embittered Stalinists met on a common platform; the third and last was the work of those revisionists whom we have already encountered. Instead of trying to disentangle their fleeting personal affiliations, we may usefully try to define the substance of their political creed.

The point to note is that revisionism related both to Marxist theory and to Leninist practice, without for that reason involving a return to the Social Democratic tradition. There was no significant movement towards the S.F.I.O., though some prominent civil servants retained contact with it. If the revisionist intellectuals as a group favored a political organization, it was the PSU: a motley coalition of Mendèsists with technocratic leanings, and old-style left-wingers who had abandoned the two major parties because they were not radical enough, had dragged their feet during the Algerian war, and in general gave the impression of having accepted the status quo. From the viewpoint of these radicals, the PSU had the merit of not being tainted with either Stalinism or reformism. This was perhaps another way of saying that it possessed neither a mass following nor a political platform; but intellectuals rarely bother about such things, and in any case the PSU could be regarded as a stimulant to the two major organizations. Its theorists—from the Keynesian Mendès-France, whose conversion to socialism had come rather late in the day, to the neo-Marxist Serge Mallet, who had gone through the CP—constituted a potential brain trust at the disposal of whatever left-wing coalition might some day be returned to power. In the meantime its publications gave promise of a modest theoretical renovation in the fields of economics, sociology, and political thought properly so called. Seen in the light of the CP's continued sterility, the evident exhaustion of the S.F.I.O., and the grotesque antics of the semi-anarchist ultra-Left, with its emotional commitment to China, the eclecticism of the PSU made a sobering impression. At the very least it testified to an awareness that a new start had to be made.[12]

The topic is evidently inseparable from the larger problem of accounting for the decay of all traditional forms of political thought in France. After what has been said before, the relevant conclusions can be summarized briefly: the postwar industrial revolution had brought about a redistribution of social functions at the expense of the private entrepreneurs, while at the same time the labor movement had failed to throw up a political elite able and willing to displace the bourgeoisie as the socially dominant class. Since the evolution of industrial capitalism enforced some degree of socialization, the necessary measures had to be taken by the state: concretely by the bu-

[12] This was clearly part of an international phenomenon to which the vague term "New Left" began to be applied from about 1960 onward. See the introduction to *Cahiers du Centre d'Études Socialistes,* Nos. 42-43, (May, 1964), and Henri Lefebvre's paper "L'État et la société," *ibid.* The consistent revisionists—notably Gilles Martinet and Serge Mallet—were quite clear that the labor movement must seek an alliance with the technocratic stratum if "socialist planning" was ever to become a reality. This was rather more than the syndicalist rank-and-file were prepared to take even from professed Marxists (let alone from Mendès-France, whom the *militants* did not really trust).

reaucracy, which thus lent its decisive weight to the planners. The latter, while increasingly hostile to economic liberalism, were not enamored of Marxism, which they associated with an antiquated vision of the class struggle. They therefore tended to regard themselves as a balancing force. At the same time the growing prestige of centralized planning attracted the support of the technical intelligentsia and thus permitted a reformulation of socialism in terms which appealed to the managerial stratum and the educated class in general. The new doctrine was both anticommunist and antiliberal; it thus made contact with the authoritarian temper of bureaucrats and others disgusted with laissez-faire and vaguely sympathetic to planning as a technique for promoting economic growth. While the whole phenomenon was international, the peculiar character it assumed in France was due to the sharpness of class antagonisms and the residual strength of the Communist party. The latter was committed to attitudes which in practice ran parallel to those adopted by the more retrograde sections of the bourgeoisie and peasantry: those wedded to economic liberalism. In the three-cornered struggle between the modernizing forces, the conservative-liberal bourgeoisie, and the Communists, the pivotal position was held by elements entrenched in the bureaucracy who—after operating behind the scenes during the chaotic Fourth Republic—stepped forward prominently in the 1960s to impose a solution. Their ideology (insofar as they possessed one) was technocratic and authoritarian; in other words, it was Saint-Simonian. There was no inconsistency, for their actual role corresponded fairly closely to that envisaged by the early socialists who were also—a circumstance often forgotten—the first theorists of the industrial revolution. Utopia and technocracy went together; indeed they had done so from the start. It was only necessary to rid industrial society of its accidental bourgeois encumbrances for the pure logic of technocratic rule to make its appearance.

There was nothing in all this that need have surprised the Communists, had they taken their own theorizing more seriously. After all it was Lenin who made the first real breach in the fortress of orthodox Marxism. As against Marx, for whom socialism in the final analysis expressed the unconscious aims of the proletariat, Lenin from 1902 onward had proclaimed the decisive role of the intelligentsia in giving political direction to the working-class movement. True, Russia was a backward country and the revolution to which he then looked forward was a bourgeois one. And indeed its outcome—as his Marxist critics never failed to remind him—could not transcend the horizon of capitalism, whatever the illusions of the participants. But this same outcome was decidedly nonbourgeois, and the authoritarian system of planning to which it gave rise corresponded in some manner to the technocratic utopia of those early socialists who had not yet discovered the labor movement. From the latter's standpoint it remained to be said that the "emancipation of the working class" was a *social* aim—and not to be confused with the mere conquest of political power.[13]

Humanism and Alienation

If the role of Marxist doctrine in contemporary France can be reduced to a formula, it may be summed up by saying that from the vision of a revolutionary future it has turned into the critical contemplation of an eternal and seemingly unchangeable present.[14] Theory

[13] See François Perroux, *Industrie et création collective: Tome premier: Saint-simonisme du XXe siècle et création collective* (Paris, 1964). Duveau, "Utopie et Planification," pp. 22 ff; originally published in *Cahiers internationaux de sociologie,* XVII (1954), 75-92. André Hauriou and Pierre Naville, "Structures sociales et actions de masse," *Cahiers du Centre d'Études Socialistes,* No. 13-14 (Jan., 1962). See also the discussion, "Les Marxistes et la notion de l'État," *ibid.* (May, 1964). This was the sequel to a lengthy debate within the PSU on the significance of Gaullism: at one point it threatened to split the Socialist Left as it had already split the S.F.I.O. See Yvan Craipeau, *ibid.,* p. 3: "Le débat sur l'évolution de la société et ses conséquences a finalement eu lieu au sein même du *Parti Socialiste Unifié.* . . . Derrière le problème des rapports avec la technocratie c'est tout le problème de l'État qui se trouvait posé. Les affrontements y ont été à ce point violents que les adversaires ont finalement dû mettre sous le boisseau cette discussion qui menaçait de faire exploser le parti."

[14] For further reading on this subject see Pierre Naville, *Vers l'automatisme social? Problèmes du travail et de l'automation* (Paris, 1963). Jean-Yves Calvez, *La Pensée de Karl Marx* (Paris, 1956). Pierre Bigo, *Marxisme et Humanisme: Introduction à l'oeuvre économique de Karl Marx* (Paris, 1953, 1961). Henri Lefebvre, *Critique de la vie quotidienne* (Paris, 1947, 1958), and *Introduction à la modernité* (Paris, 1962). Kostas Axelos, *Marx Penseur de la technique* (Paris, 1961), and *Vers la pensée planétaire* (Paris, 1964). Perroux. Duveau. And the publications of the *Arguments* group (notably the journal itself until its suspension in 1962). The major platform for debates on Marxist humanism during the late fifties and early sixties was furnished by the left-wing Catholic monthly *Esprit.* By comparison, Communist writers remained almost mute on the

and practice are no longer indissolubly linked, save for a handful of dissident Communists outside the CP who cling to the traditional idea of a "total" revolution arising from the action of a class-conscious proletariat. Official Communism, while paying lip service to such notions, in fact pursues a pseudo-revolutionary strategy aimed at the conquest of power within the existing, highly stratified society. This perspective automatically reduces the genuinely radical aspect of Marxism—its critique of human alienation—to the status of a mere aspiration. The gap between utopianism and practice, which Marx had closed, has reopened within the Communist movement itself. The latter now takes its place among the other alienations imposed upon the citizens of modern society. The "critical theory" preserves the image of a better future, at the cost of making it plain that its realization is not imminent. Marxist thought becomes reflective. Communism —to paraphrase Marx—has helped to change the world; the task now is to understand it.[15]

The disenchantment underlying the new mood is rooted in the very political practice which at one time was expected to realize the aims embodied in the Marxian vision. Because Communism has not overcome the alienation of man in practice, it cannot plausibly assert it as its goal in theory. The example presented by the USSR is not conducive to optimism, whatever the attraction it may hold for "underdeveloped intellectuals" from the more backward parts of the globe. "La négation de l'État capitaliste n'a pas entraîné la mutation ou dépérissement de l'État communiste parce que la contradiction *industrielle* (*et non pas seulement capitaliste*) entre maîtres et servants des machines n'a pas été évacuée."[16]

---

subject until 1963-64, when the growing "revisionist" pressure at last obliged both the official *Cahiers du Communisme* and the *Nouvelle Critique* to enter the fray.

[15] Kostas Axelos, "Thèses sur Marx," in *Vers la pensée planétaire,* p. 177: "Les techniciens ne font que *transformer* le monde de différentes manières dans l'indifférence universalisée; il s'agit maintenant de le *penser* et d'interpréter les transformations en profondeur, en saisissant et en *expérimentant* la différence qui unit l'être au néant"—a suggestive formula which has the incidental advantage of enabling the Existentialist to make the transition from Marx to Sartre (in Axelos' case to Nietzsche and Heidegger as well).

[16] Perroux, pp. 80-81; also p. 103: "La spécificité du rapport capital-travail ainsi comprise est plus résistante et plus générale que la spécificité dans le capitalisme; *elle subsiste en quelque société industrielle que se soit.*"

What characterizes the present situation is that the consequent theoretical strains are now reflected in Communist literature itself. This is largely a consequence of gradual de-Stalinization; in part it springs from an awareness that the urgently necessary "return to the classics" cannot stop short at the point where the young Marx first developed his critique of society. The "subversive" character of his early writings—subversive in the eyes of the Soviet bureaucracy, above all—is indeed obvious, but so is their potential value to a movement anxious to claim the inheritance of humanism. In the years immediately following the 1945 upheaval, the whole topic could be dismissed as academic. By the 1960s it had become a vital matter to reintegrate the early Marx within the accepted corpus of doctrine, if the party was not to be further discredited in the eyes of the intellectuals. The operation involved some risk, but it also facilitated discussion with opponents. In the long run the CP could only gain from it, whatever the embarrassment involved in having to concede that the Leninist interpretation of Marxism was not the only possible one.[17]

In all fairness it has to be conceded that the difficulty was not merely of a political order. At bottom it stemmed from the unsolved (and perhaps insoluble) problem of eliminating the utopian element from scientific socialism. The original rediscovery of the young Marx in the 1930s had been due to writers who at that time still adhered to the Communist vision, but who interpreted it in accordance with the idealist tradition of classical German philosophy. After 1945 these revisionists were joined by the Existentialist school, and finally by the theologians.[18] At this stage the party theorists might have been for-

[17] Even this dangerous corner might be rounded without disaster, given a little ingenuity in the manipulation of the *depositum fidei*. See Roger Garaudy, "A propos des 'Manuscrits de 1844' de Marx et de quelques essais philosophiques," *Cahiers du Communisme* (March, 1963), pp. 107 ff., where it is blandly asserted that the compromising documents "peuvent être considérés comme l'acte de naissance du marxisme, car pour la première fois nous voyons converger dans ce texte les 'trois sources' du marxisme si clairement dégagées par Lenine: la philosophie classique allemande (de Kant à Hegel), l'économie politique anglaise, et le socialisme français." See also Roger Garaudy, *Karl Marx* (Paris, 1964) and the review of this work by Guy Besse in *Cahiers du Communisme* (Oct., 1964), pp. 106 ff., where *inter alia* the reader is reminded that Marx owed something to Kant and Fichte, as well as to Hegel.

[18] Pierre Bigo's preface to the third edition of *Marxisme et Humanisme*, originally published in 1953, i.e., before the Communists had caught up. Their initial reaction may be studied in a pamphlet entitled *Les marxistes répondent à*

In the claim to humanism — Lukacs —
a

given for scenting danger. After all, Marx himself in the *Manifesto* had warned against attempts to dissolve the revolutionary faith in a vague nonpolitical humanism. There was a further embarrassment: if the positivist standpoint was abandoned, it was not easy to escape the conclusion that Marxism was really a species of metaphysics, which was just what Catholic writers like Bigo and Calvez were affirming. Along this slippery road there loomed the danger of a thorough-going retreat from the materialist position.[19]

The party authorities, after a good deal of hesitation, in the end settled the matter in the time-honored fashion proper to an institution which must cater simultaneously to the intelligentsia and to the masses: the various rival interpretations were declared to be compatible with each other and with the *depositum fidei*. Marxism was a philosophy, but it was also a science. It was in the great tradition of Western metaphysical speculation, and at the same time it represented a break with that tradition. Furthermore, its scientific doctrine was fully in accordance with classical political economy, but it also constituted a critique of political economy, and a demonstration that its categories reflected the bourgeois ideology. In short, there was no problem at all. Marx had effected a synthesis of philosophical thought and revolutionary practice. The concept of "alienation" in particular was relevant to the political struggle, inasmuch as it had been elaborated by Marx under the impact of his first acquaintance with the Parisian workers. It embodied a critical awareness of the existence of man *under capitalism*. As for the relationship of Marxism to traditional philosophy, the "revolution of thought" effected by Marx in 1844-45 consisted quite simply in his passage from abstract speculation to concrete practice, and Marxism was to be defined as the theory of a practice

leurs critiques catholiques (Paris, 1957). Even then there was a perceptible difference between the more rigid adherents to the "scientist" standpoint, e.g., Henri Denis and Pierre Vilar, and those willing to treat Marxism as a philosophy. For the latter see Guy Besse, *La Pensée* (Nov., 1953), pp. 47 ff., where it is flatly asserted that "Marxism is not positivism." This, of course, was just the opposite of what *La Pensée* had been telling its readers for years.

[19] See Bigo, Preface to the 3d. ed., p. xxxv: "Si le marxisme est une métaphysique, c'est qu'il se réfère implicitement à un absolu, qu'on appelle 'la nature' ou 'l'homme.' Et la position matérialiste est à son tour menacée. On comprend que les marxistes préfèrent ne jamais discuter sérieusement une question qui les intéresse cependant au plus haut point, mais dont ils sentent confusement qu'elle les divise et peut-être les menace."

which was that of the Communist party.[20] Thus Garaudy could write in *Cahiers du Communisme* (March, 1963, p. 114): "Cette 'révolution' n'est pas le passage de la métaphysique à la dialectique. Sinon cette 'révolution' daterait d'Héraclite ou de Hegel. Cette 'révolution' n'est pas le passage de l'idéalisme au matérialisme. Sinon cette 'révolution' daterait de Démocrite ou d'Épicure, d'Helvétius ou de Feuerbach. Cette 'révolution' c'est le passage de la spéculation à la *pratique*." This formulation got rid of some of the ideological ballast imposed upon Western Marxists by their Soviet mentors, but it sidestepped the real issue: the transition from speculation to practice had been mediated for Marx by his belief in the revolutionary role of the proletariat—a class characterized by the "total loss of humanity" and destined to bring about its "total recovery."

In the light of the drastic simplifications current during the Stalinist era, the new orthodoxy represented a considerable advance. Its intellectual level was now distinctly superior to the once-admired Soviet model and more or less in tune with the cautious attempts made in Poland and elsewhere to restore a proper understanding of Marxism without abandoning the Leninist connection. For all that, the widely advertised "return to Marx" had a scholastic character, inseparable perhaps from an operation conducted under circumstances where theory and practice had fallen apart. The unabridged text of Scripture had, so to speak, been made available to the faithful at long last, but on the understanding that they were to swallow it whole and not subject it to critical reflection. Insofar as fundamentalism is always preferable to fraud, this was a gain: the party's official ideologists could now, with a good conscience, claim that they were not hiding anything. What they could not do was to make plausible the further assertion that Communist practice was the faithful mirror of Marxist theory.

Marx's critique of bourgeois society had from the start involved a reconsideration of the central tenets of political economy. These

[20] Auguste Cornu, *Karl Marx et Friedrich Engels* (Paris, 1962). Vol. III, especially p. 90, where reference is made to the "two fundamental themes" of the 1844 MSS: "description de l'homme aliéné dans la société bourgeoise et suppression de l'aliénation dans la société communiste, thèmes que Marx associait étroitement en montrant qu'aussi bien la formation de l'aliénation que sa suppression resultaient du développement du système de la propriété privée."

propositions went back to the individualist philosophy of the seventeenth century which underlay the assumptions of Smith and Ricardo. In contrast to the "Ricardian socialists" (and to Proudhon), Marx held that the new science of economics could not be given a radically different character simply by being purged of its evident class bias. In particular he rejected the notion that it was possible to derive socialist conclusions from a "law of value" based on the assumption of equal exchange among individual producers. An egalitarian doctrine formulated in terms of free and equal exchange remained bourgeois in character, even if it was used to promote cooperative ideas. If Proudhon—like the Ricardian socialists in England who preceded him—believed that he could attack the bourgeoisie on its own ground by standing political economy on its head, this to Marx was an illusion typical of a man who understood Ricardo even less than he did Hegel. Political economy was, historically speaking, the intellectual creation of the bourgeois class, and it was naive to suppose that it could be employed as the theoretical instrument of the proletarian revolution: a revolution destined to do away with the social relations that constituted the market economy. The emancipation of the working class involved *inter alia* its intellectual emancipation from the categories of bourgeois thought—the very categories which the economists treated as eternal and universal. Any movement which fell short of this goal would merely serve to perpetuate the existing order under another name, or disclose itself as a species of utopianism irrelevant to the conditions of modern society. As Marx put it, in a critical note on the Ricardian socialist J. F. Bray, "ce rapport égalitaire, cet idéal correctif qu'il voudrait appliquer au monde, n'est lui-même que le reflet du monde actuel, . . . il est par conséquent totalement impossible de reconstituer la société sur une base qui n'en est qu'une ombre embellie. À mesure que l'ombre redevient corps, on s'aperçoit que ce corps, loin d'en être la transfiguration rêvée, est le corps actuel de la société."[21]

For all that, Marx did not believe that it was possible to ignore the

[21] Marx, *Misère de la philosophie* (1847), in MEGA, I, vi, p. 157, and Engels' preface to the German edition of 1884, where the point is driven home that the attempt to derive socialist conclusions by taking literally the egalitarian professions of the bourgeois economists could only result in the construction of a reactionary utopia.

corpus of doctrine which the economists had worked out in their attempt to understand the operation of the new society. He was not an anarchist and did not, in the manner of Proudhon and Bakunin, dispense with theoretical analysis or with the troublesome burden of history. But neither was he a reformist in the manner of Rodbertus or Lassalle, who thought it possible to place the new science of economics in the service of the labor movement. His attitude was more complex and dialectical. So far as the analysis of bourgeois society went, he was quite willing to employ the technical apparatus of political economy, and indeed did so with telling effect in his polemic against Proudhon. At the same time he insisted that the concepts of economics were applicable to one system only: that of capitalism. There was no suprahistorical economic science, and no way of formulating socialist —let alone Communist—aims in terms of bourgeois economics. Yet the labor movement inevitably had to work within a historical context defined by bourgeois society, and this context included economic thought, along with the capitalist mode of production of which economics was the theoretical reflection. The proper procedure thus was to subject both the mode of production and its intellectual expression to theoretical and practical *criticism*. And this was just what Marx undertook to do.

The *Economic and Philosophic Manuscripts* of 1844[22] occupy a well-defined point in Marx's intellectual development from a quasi-Jacobin to a Communist position. They mark the conclusion of his idealist phase, before he had assimilated the new scientific standpoint. In the *Manuscripts* political economy is not so much transcended as rejected in the name of a revolutionary humanism which counterposes "man" to "economic man;" quite in the manner of Feuerbach and Hess, who had initiated Marx into the "materialist" critique of Hegel. This procedure is continued in *The Holy Family* (1845)[23] where Proudhon is criticized on the grounds that he "overcomes economic alienation only within the bounds of economic alienation,"[24] while of Hegel the reader is told that he "takes the

[22] MEGA, I, iii, pp. 33-172; cf. the English translation now available (New York, 1963), ed. by Dirk J. Struik.
[23] *Die Heilige Familie,* MEGA, I, iii, pp. 173-388.
[24] *Ibid.*, p. 213.

position of modern Political Economy."[25] The Marx of 1844-45, in short, defined his "revolutionary materialism" in terms of a humanist philosophy which undercut the concepts of economics by denouncing them as inhuman. Yet when Proudhon a year later did just that (in his *Philosophie de la misère*, 1846) Marx—who in the meantime had assimilated Ricardo and virtually adopted his terminology—rounded on his former ally and denounced him as a moralizing ignoramus. Reacting violently against his own past, he reproached Proudhon for reproducing "the illusions of speculative philosophy."

This, however, was not the end of the matter. In 1857-58 Marx was still busy introducing a philosophical critique of bourgeois society into the first draft of *Capital*[26] and as late as 1867 the first published volume of that work presented—in the well-known passage on the "fetishism of commodities"—a revival of the concept of "alienation" (though that term itself had now disappeared). These critical sallies were irrelevant to the strictly economic analysis of capitalism, but they served as a reminder that Marx had not abandoned his original position. The latter might be formulated by saying that the value-relations which appear in the exchange of commodities are not relations between material "things," but between their producers, who for their part have no means of communicating with one another save indirectly by way of the market. What happens under capitalism is that the basic economic activity—production of goods for the purpose of satisfying material needs—takes on the mysterious character of a process in which commodities appear to meet behind the backs of the human beings who have produced them, and to settle the fate of those beings: to the point of condemning them to death by starvation if for some reason the exchange mechanism has been disturbed. Bourgeois society is just that particular form of social life in which individuals are ruled by an economic activity which has escaped from their control and assumed the phantasmagoric form of an exchange between commodities. What are really social relations between men appear as economic relations between material goods. This "fetishism" is an aspect of what Marx in 1844 had defined as "human self-alienation." Man's essential activity, his daily labor, has been projected outward in

[25] *Ibid.*, p. 157.

[26] Marx, *Grundrisse der Kritik der politischen Oekonomie* (Berlin, 1953).

the form of a mechanism which confronts him as an extraneous power. The economists, with their absurd Tables of the Law, are the high priests of a secular faith that justifies this alienation in the name of science. And the proletarian revolution is the event which will overturn the altars of their gods and banish the worship of money, along with all the rest of their inhuman fetishism.[27]

At first sight it is difficult to see how this philosophical critique of bourgeois society could be worked into an empirical analysis of capitalism as a system of production, and indeed Marx had some trouble doing so. As a theoretical economist he could and did abstract from the preconceptions with which, as a youthful philosopher of the Hegelian school, he had originally approached the study of economics. Yet the link was not completely broken. Marx held that capitalism—both historically and in terms of its inherent logic—rested upon the separation of the producers from their tools. The capitalist mode of production was *defined* by the antagonism of capital and labor, the latter representing not a group of free individuals bargaining with the entrepreneurs—this was precisely the liberal illusion which he was out to destroy—but a proletariat with nothing to sell but its labor power. This separation of the real producers from the means of production was, however, only an extreme form of the alienation on which bourgeois society rested. Historically, it was the outcome of a situation in which men had lost control over their own essential activity: their labor. The restitution of this control signified at once the disappearance of the "fetishism" and the overcoming of "alienation," and since the concentration of wealth and power in the hands of a dwindling number of capitalists had now become historically outmoded, it was possible to assign a term to the whole bourgeois era, which (so far as Europe was concerned) had already lasted long enough. Socialism was both the inevitable goal of the process and the *restitutio in integrum* of a state of affairs antedating the institution of private property: the producer need not in

[27] For the "fetishism of commodities," see *Capital,* I, i, section 4. For an extensive discussion of the whole subject from an orthodox Marxist standpoint see Korsch, pp. 129 ff. See also Daniel Bell, "The Debate on Alienation," in *Revisionism,* ed. by Labedz (New York, 1962), pp. 195 ff. The question to what extent the later volumes of *Capital,* and the drafts published by Kautsky under the title *Theories of Surplus Value,* are concordant with the standpoint adopted by Marx in the passages just quoted, need not enter into consideration here.

future be separated from his tools. This reversal of roles would restore to labor the dignity it lost when it came to be treated as a commodity. Hence the "critique of political economy," by laying bare the mechanism which subtended the bourgeois mode of production, was at once truly scientific and truly revolutionary. It pierced the veil of illusion which covered the operation of the system, and thereby rendered the exploited class conscious of the situation against which it was instinctively rebelling.

Plainly a doctrine such as this, which comprehended philosophy, history, sociology, and economics within a single sweeping movement of thought, gave an enormous advantage to the Communists over their rivals. No one who had grasped the Marxian conception could ever again rest content with Proudhon's moralistic railings, or with the utopian schools of socialism, which simply generalized the typical institutions of bourgeois society into a system of centralized planning.[28] Yet it is no less evident that acceptance of the Marxian viewpoint placed a heavy mortgage upon a movement linked with the Soviet Union and its peculiar system of state-controlled production. It clearly was not possible to go on forever affirming that the mere fact of state ownership removed social relations in the USSR from the sphere of exploitation and alienation. But an admission, however qualified, that alienation remained a feature of Soviet society was tantamount to subversion. This accounts for the extreme caution with which the ideologists of the French CP (not to mention their superiors in Moscow) approached the subject. The gulf separating theory from practice was considerably wider than in the case of reformist Socialists who—if they were honest—might simply acknowledge that some social inequalities would persist. It was after all no disgrace for Socialists who believed in planning to concede that the workers would still be directed by others, if no longer "exploited" in the technical sense, since the economic surplus would cease to be monopolized by the possessing class. Communists, committed at the same time to

[28] For the Saint-Simonians this was evident: they even extolled the banking system, and indeed Saint-Simon himself looked forward to a future order ruled by a committee of bankers. From the Marxian viewpoint such an outcome would represent the very extreme of alienation, since monetary credit is totally abstract and involves not even commodities, let alone their producers, at the same time that it places the latter under the control of a handful of financial manipulators, however well-intentioned.

Marx and to Lenin, were in a more awkward position. Their case rested on the thesis that alienation and exploitation were peculiar to capitalism. If this assertion ceased to be plausible, the "union of theory and practice" fell apart. There was then a choice between trying to reconstitute it or admitting defeat altogether. The first solution could only take the form of a candid admission that the Syndicalist or Trotskyist critique of the USSR was valid: Soviet socialism was bureaucratic, not democratic, and must be democratized by a proletarian class movement against the new privileged stratum. The second entailed the tacit abandonment of true egalitarianism and the more or less explicit acceptance of the Soviet regime as the best possible. In opting for this latter solution, the French Communist party—a Stalinist apparatus with an instinctively syndicalist mass following—remained true to the historical logic which had presided over its destiny from the beginning. Unable to close the gap between its professed aims and the stubborn resistance of material facts, it divorced theory from actuality. What remained after this separation was the familiar spectacle of a pseudo-revolutionary movement whose ideologists continued to recite a litany no longer related to its practice.[29]

The same discordance manifested itself in the realm of political theory. It has already been shown how the French CP transformed the Leninist concept of proletarian dictatorship into the Stalinist doctrine of state-worship. To the extent that Stalinism was officially dethroned in the USSR from the mid-fifties onward, it became possible for Communists in France to revert to Lenin's standpoint, thereby restoring the ambiguities of a doctrine which Marx had originally

[29] Hence the tortuous character of the apologetics already cited. The topic was evidently less embarrassing for theologians, who had only to cite Marx in order to bring out the inconsistency of their Communist opponents. See Bigo, p. 40, especially his comments on the curious pronouncements of the French CP's principal expert on Soviet economics, Charles Bettelheim. For the latter, as for the official Soviet economists, the "law of value"—which for Marx characterized bourgeois production relations—remained valid under socialism as understood in the USSR. This was of course tantamount to saying that commodity production would continue. See also Ernest Mandel, *Traité D'Economie Marxiste* (Paris, 1962), II, pp. 426-30, where the author comments on the official Soviet doctrine that wage remuneration takes place under socialism "in accordance with the quantity *and quality* of work performed for society": a significant departure from the Marxian formula laid down in the *Critique of the Gotha Program.*

evolved from his reading of French history. The doctrine treated the state as a necessary evil and the dictatorship as a temporary expedient to be abandoned at the first opportunity. This was in tune with the Jacobin-Blanquist tradition, and to that extent the return to orthodoxy facilitated the CP's efforts to reintegrate itself within the national community: an effort obstinately pursued in the 1960s, after experience had demonstrated that the former approach led to complete isolation. On the other hand, the partial acceptance—however halting and qualified—of the traditional democratic standpoint made irreparable the breach with those consistently totalitarian movements abroad which for good reason remained faithful to the Stalinist dogma. In their eyes the French CP began to look almost Social Democratic, and its political creed like a revamped version of Kautsky's orthodox Marxism. As if this were not enough, the new formulation, while fairly adequate politically, was quite indefensible philosophically when judged in the light of Marx's own utterances on the subject.[30]

For Marx, and indeed for all genuine Marxists, the demolition of state worship was an aspect of that consistent demystification which formed the theme of his "materialist" critique of ideology. It did not matter to him whether the actual "withering away" of the state was conceived as a short-term or a long-range goal: what counted was that the labor movement, and in particular its vanguard, should here and now dispense with the myths which political theory had constructed around the state as an entity supposedly different from, and superior to, civil society. As a philosopher—or rather as a critic of philosophy—Marx had already rebelled against Hegel before he came to question the economics of Smith and Ricardo. So far as he was concerned, Hegel's worship of the state was an instance of that persistent idealist perversion which it was his purpose to correct. The perversion consisted in identifying the "higher" stratum (politics) with a spiritual significance absent in the "lower" region (civil society), which latter was pictured as an inferior domain given over to the passions, while the state stood for reason, order, and the moral life in general. This

[30] Henri Lefebvre, "Les Sources de la théorie marxiste-léniniste de l'état," *Cahiers du Centre d'Études Socialistes* (May, 1964), pp. 31 ff. Claude Lefort, "Marxisme et sociologie," *ibid.*, No. 34-35, pp. 14 ff. Pierre Fougeyrollas, *Le marxisme en question* (Paris, 1959), pp. 92 ff. Yvon Bourdet, *Communisme et marxisme: notes critiques de sociologie politique* (Paris, 1963), pp. 90 ff.

idealist view of the topic was just what Marx challenged when he inverted the traditional conception. On the Marxian assumption, the dependence of the higher functions on the lower is to be understood as a social relation which has come about historically and does not mirror a timeless or "natural" order of being. It is simply an aspect of that "objectivation" or "alienation" whereby every human artifact—religion, art, politics, law—takes on the phantasmagoric character of a superhuman creation inexplicable on ordinary materialist or naturalist principles. Specifically, the disjunction between state and society is destructive of any rational apprehension of reality, inasmuch as it makes a mystery of the political process. Once the latter is shown to be rooted in the "production and reproduction of material life," the notion that the state embodies a "higher principle" divorced from ordinary daily existence falls to the ground. In the same way it is impossible to take seriously the claim that the disjunction can be overcome by democratizing political life. Democracy, like every other form of government, rests on the antagonism between the concrete needs of the individual and the abstract claims of the body politic. Its superiority over other forms of rule is relative, not absolute, and its proclamation of the "Rights of Man" is vitiated from the start by the embarrassed, and embarrassing, distinction between "Man" and "Citizen." This distinction is just what, from a consistently materialist standpoint, is wrong with the whole idealist tradition of political thought: it conceives the individual as a selfish being who must be kept in order by some authority imposed from above. Hence it consecrates the state, and with it the alienation of man from his own social existence. Marx was not indifferent to democracy. On the contrary, he recommended it (as against Hegel's authoritarianism) as "the general form of the State in which the formal principle is at the same time the *material* principle"; but he added the characteristic rider that "the modern French have understood this to mean that in a true democracy the political State must disappear."[31]

This perspective may be described as utopian, and indeed the whole idea of *dépérissement* had been inherited by Marx from Saint-Simon.

[31] MEGA, I, i, p. 435. In addition see the *Economic-Philosophic Manuscripts* (1844), and Marx's *Introduction to a Critique of Hegel's Philosophy of Right* (1843-44), in MEGA, I, i, pp. 607 ff, and his antecedent critical essays of 1842-43.

Whether or not one regards it as realistic, it is crucial to the Marxian understanding of history, and to the role which Marx assigned to the proletarian revolution. Quite possibly Marxian socialism—like Rousseauist democracy before it—can retain its relevance only by shedding its claim to represent a total philosophy. On this assumption, the vision of a stateless and classless future will eventually take its place with other aims transcending the empirical understanding of the historical process (and the actual march of that process). This leaves intact the corpus of scientific insights which historians, economists, and sociologists owe to Marx. The point here is that such an outcome—for which indeed the time appears to be ripe—is destructive of the claims made on behalf of Communism, though it need not disturb those socialist schools which have somehow managed to adapt themselves to the evolution of contemporary industrial civilization. The critique of bourgeois thought-forms remains an indispensable aspect of any socialist theory which lays claim to being taken seriously, and such a critique can hardly fail to operate with the analytical concepts worked out by Marx. But this is a very different matter from possession of a "total" world view. It is only the latter which makes possible the rise of a totalitarian movement, for without an all-encompassing doctrine one cannot undertake the complete reconstruction of society.

The debate over humanism and alienation must be seen in this context. Its increasingly metaphysical character bears witness to the fact that for the Communists, as well as for their positivist critics, theory and practice no longer form a whole. This is of course just why so prominent a part could be taken in these debates by philosophers and theologians. Once it is tacitly understood that the world is not to be made new, it follows that philosophy as an "existential activity of man" has not been abolished. Its practitioners retain their separate existence in the measure in which the logic of history retains the character of an object study. Were it otherwise, history itself would perhaps already have come to an end.

Bureaucracy and Totalitarianism

"One has hardly begun to measure the complexity of the questions [illegible] by the theory of alienation." In these terms Henri Lefebvre a [illegible] situation which since then has certainly not been simplified by the progressive disintegration of the Leninist-Stalinist edifice.[32] Writing shortly after the Hungarian rising of October-November 1956 and in the midst of the confusion provoked by the first essay in "de-Stalinization," the French Communist party's one-time chief apologist—by now a heretic on the point of exclusion—sought a middle-ground between the faith he had once defended and the radical repudiation of Leninism. To a philosopher the problem naturally posed itself in doctrinal terms: "Est-ce que l'aliénation disparait dans la société socialiste? Est-ce qu'il n'y a pas, en U.R.S.S., ou dans les pays qui construisent le socialisme, des contradictions signifiant des formes nouvelles—ou renouvelées—de l'aliénation économique, idéologique, politique?"[33] To this discreetly phrased inquiry the Hungarian workers and students had replied by pitting themselves against the armed might of "their" state, while for years before this event millions of East Germans had answered it by, in the Leninist phrase of 1917, "voting with their feet." But though belated, and phrased in time-honored academic fashion, the question had the merit of centering the debate upon the terrain where it belonged: the phenomenon of class conflict under the regime of "bureaucratic collectivism." At one blow, the traditional dichotomy "bourgeoisie-proletariat" was replaced, in the thinking of critically minded Marxists, by a new and disconcerting one: the antagonism of rulers and ruled in a totally planned and bureaucratized society which was also a hierarchical one.[34]

It was not to be expected that the analysis of this situation and its historic origins would be furnished by professional philosophers, though Lefebvre's later writings (as well as those of the *Arguments* group) did break new ground in familiarizing readers with the humanist

[32] Henri Lefebvre, *Critique de la vie quotidienne. Preface to the 2d ed.* (1956-57), p. 10.

[33] *Ibid.*, p. 11.

[34] For the prewar discussion see Bruno Rizzi, *La bureaucratisation du monde* (Paris, 1939). This essay initiated the internal disintegration of the Trotskyist movement, whose founder had still clung to the notion that the USSR was in some sense a "workers state." By the 1960s this belief had been dissipated even for the majority of Trotsky's former adherents. Rizzi, *La lezione dello stalinismo* (Rome, 1962). For the gradual evolution of those among Trotsky's original French followers who after 1948 emerged from the self-styled Fourth International to adopt an independent standpoint (more or less in tune with the Sy[illegible] calist tradition) see the periodical *Socialisme ou Barbarie* [illegible] April 1949 onward.

core of Marx's doctrine. The echo of these discussions has already been noted. It is not derogatory to the authors to say that the debate was confined to readers of philosophic literature. The fact is self-evident, and it is noted here only because those concerned could not help realizing that they were divorcing theory from practice, i.e., denying the first principle of their creed. To remain consistent they had either to stop calling themselves Marxists or try to discover a different way of reconstituting the lost unity of thought and action. The first solution was adopted by the consistent revisionists of the *Arguments* group, the second by the various representatives of left-wing Communism or revolutionary Syndicalism who fell back upon the notion of a revolutionary proletariat "betrayed" by its political organizations. It was only when the depoliticization of the masses in the 1960s was seen in the context of an evolution affecting *all* industrialized societies that this escape route was barred. It was then acknowledged at long last that the phenomenon signified the disappearance of the revolutionary proletariat as a political force. Concurrently, Marxism was at last understood as *the theory of the bourgeois revolution* and the self-criticism of the society born from that revolution. With this belated illumination, the phenomenon of communism fell into place as an attempt to model the proletarian emancipation on the analogy of the earlier revolution. Once this was grasped, it became possible to see where Marx himself had unwittingly introduced bourgeois thought-forms into the workers movement. His doctrine was no longer criticized in terms of its real or alleged shortcomings as a *Weltanschauung,* but understood as the theoretical counterpart of a certain phase of the class struggle: a theory which no longer supplied the key to the understanding of what was occurring at the all-important political level.[35]

[35] On this subject see, above all, the writings published in *Socialisme ou Barbarie;* e.g., Pierre Chaulieu and Claude Montal in No. 10 (July-Aug., 1952). Chaulieu, "Sartre, le stalinisme et les ouvriers," *ibid.,* No. 12 (Aug.-Sept., 1953), and "Sur le contenu du socialisme," No. 17 (July-Sept., 1955). Claude Lefort, "Organisation et parti," *ibid.,* No. 26 (Nov.-Dec., 1958). Paul Cardan, "Prolétariat et organisation," *ibid.,* No. 27 (April-May, 1959), and No. 28 (July-Aug., 1959), also "Le mouvement révolutionnaire sous le capitalisme moderne," *ibid.,* Nos. 31, 32, 33 (Dec. 1960-Feb., 1961; April-June, 1961; Dec., 1961-Feb., 1962), and "Marxisme et théorie révolutionnaire," Nos. 36, 37 (April-June, 1964; July-

At the start of this evolution, in the years immediately following the war and the great strike movements of 1947-48, the debate among Trotsky's erstwhile followers and their sympathizers was still conducted in time-honored fashion. It was taken for granted that the Russian Revolution had originally been a proletarian one; that the working class, having seized power in October 1917, had subsequently lost control and would have to regain it; and that the revolutionary potential of Western Europe was not yet exhausted and might be actualized in a new crisis. All these certainties disappeared one by one between the late forties and the early sixties. By the mid-sixties it had become abundantly clear that revolutionary movements would henceforth be confined to the "third world" of pre-industrial countries and to the backward fringe areas of Europe. So far as France was concerned, the evidence of depoliticization was at last accepted: not as a temporary phenomenon consequent upon the unlamented disappearance of the parliamentary regime, but as a permanent feature of the new society. The latter now was described in terms derived from contemporary Western sociology, with the stress on bureaucratization and the displacement of the bourgeoisie by a new stratum in charge of the planned economy. In this perspective the East-West conflict appeared increasingly as a political clash between two blocs whose internal development tended to converge. As against the Maoist variant of Stalinism—which had its followers among the unsophisticated—the ascription of bureaucratic and state-capitalist features was impartially extended to China as well as to the Soviet Union.[36]

This analysis at first left open the question what form the class struggle might yet take in the more developed countries. Around 1949, when the radical Left—from Sartre to the Fourth International—still pursued the *ignis fatuus* of the proletarian revolution, this topic tended to be debated in traditional fashion: there would be a new cyclical crisis of capitalism, to which the working class might perhaps

[36] Cardan, *Socialisme ou Barbarie,* Nos. 36 and 37, where the author also takes issue with Marx's general theory, on the grounds that strictly speaking it applies only to a single case: the genesis of European capitalism. It does not, in his view, correspond to earlier developments "ni à la constitution de la bureaucratie comme couche dominante aujourd'hui dans les pays arriérés qui s'industrialisent." (No. 36, p. 13).

respond under the leadership of a purged and renovated vanguard. In the 1960s it was frankly acknowledged by the more alert survivors of the Trotskyist tradition that a cyclical debacle on the scale of 1930-33 was improbable, owing to the new direction taken by the bureaucratized state capitalism of Western society, and that in any case the working class and its organizations had ceased to play a revolutionary role. "La crise du capitalisme a atteint le stade où elle devient une crise de la socialisation comme telle, et elle affecte le prolétariat tout autant que les autres couches."[37]

To sum up: the traditional view—extrapolated by all the Leninist factions from their reading of Marx, and supposedly confirmed by the October Revolution—saw the proletariat as the irreconcilable antagonist of the bourgeoisie in a society doomed to perdition by insoluble internal contradictions. From the new standpoint—which was described as post-Marxist, but might equally well have been called neo-Marxist—the working class appeared as the foundation of a stable hierarchical order, and the labor movement as a subculture structured on the larger political culture of which it formed part. The remarkable thing is that the distance between these two intellectual positions was covered in less than fifteen years, and largely by the same theorists. Though the attendant splits did disclose a latent tension between old-fashioned militants and intellectual revisionists, as well as between former Leninists who continued to believe in the need for a vanguard, and latter-day anarcho-syndicalists for whom the very term *organization* had become suspect.[38]

[37] Cardan, *Socialisme ou Barbarie,* No. 33, p. 72; also p. 73: "La disparition de l'activité politique parmi les ouvriers est le résultat à la fois et la condition de l'évolution du capitalisme que nous avons décrite. Le mouvement ouvrier, en transformant le capitalisme, était en retour transformé par lui, les organisations ouvrières ont été integrées dans le système d'institutions de la société établie, en même temps qu'assimilés dans leur substance par elle; leurs objectifs, leurs modes d'action, leurs formes d'organisation, leurs rapports avec les travailleurs se sont modélés à un degré croissant sur les prototypes capitalistes."

[38] Lefort, "Organisation et parti," *Socialisme ou Barbarie,* No. 26, presents an interesting *autocritique* on the part of a former Trotskyist who until 1948 had adhered to the Fourth International—until he discovered it to be a mere caricature of the Third, with the same centralized methods and the same claim to infallibility, minus the power; for Cardan's attempt to salvage the bare notion of a political organization, while rejecting the Leninist vanguard concept, see his article "Prolétariat et organisation" in the following two numbers of *Socialisme ou Barbarie,* where Lenin's (and Kautsky's) organizational authoritarianism is

It was in fact impossible to raise the issue of bureaucracy without asking to what extent the labor movement had itself prefigured the new society which was beginning to emerge from the ruins of the Second World War. The topic was doubly disconcerting because it involved both the traditional faith in organization and the concept of planning as a rational order imposed by the public authorities (the state) upon the "anarchy of production." Under both headings, certain conventional assumptions now began to look suspiciously like an anticipation of a bureaucratic order substituting itself for a bourgeois one. So much might indeed be granted by reformist Socialists, for whom this would simply involve a subsidiary problem of making the new society as democratic as possible—no more and no less. From the neo-Trotskyist, or anarcho-syndicalist, standpoint—which was that of the radical Left in France after 1945—the matter presented itself in a different light. If the dichotomy of bourgeoisie and proletariat was giving way to a new cleavage between the planners and the planned, or between bureaucrats and workers, it was time to reassemble the revolutionary movement upon a new basis. If not the working class as a whole, then at least the minority of class-conscious militants must resume its independence vis-à-vis the Socialist or Communist bureaucrats, and the Marxist intellectuals who had worked out the strategy of the preceding period.[39]

What these writers had grasped was the link between the internal structure of the Communist party and the hierarchical character of the planned and centralized society established after the seizure of power

---

traced back to Marx's belief in a "science" of socialism (No. 27, p. 65). For Lefort's critique of Sartre's ultra-Stalinist identification of the working class with "its" party see *Les Temps Modernes* (April, 1953); also Chaulieu, "Sartre, le stalinisme et les ouvriers," *Socialisme ou Barbarie,* No. 12 (Aug.-Sept., 1953).

[39] Montal, *Socialisme ou Barbarie,* No. 10, pp. 21-23. "Le parti signifie l'effort de la classe pour penser sa lutte sous une forme universelle . . . il signifie la sélection d'une partie de l'avant-garde qui forme un corps relativement étranger à la classe, fonctionnant selon ses lois propres et se posant comme la direction de la classe." "Lorsque se révèle le charactère ouvertement contre-révolutionnaire du parti après 1917 . . . il est possible de voir que la contradiction ne réside pas dans la rigueur du centralisme mais dans le fait même du parti; que la classe ne peut s'aliéner dans aucune forme de représentation stable et structurée sans que cette représentation s'autonomise. C'est alors que la classe peut se retourner sur elle-même et concevoir sa nature qui la différencie radicalement de toute autre classe." Also Yvon Bourdet, *Communisme et marxisme,* pp. 81 ff.

by a political elite so constituted: the one necessarily prefiguring the other, though only under circumstances where political freedom had been destroyed. At this point it was clearly no longer possible for men in the syndicalist tradition to accept Trotsky's version of Leninism. After all, Trotsky no less than Lenin had demolished the autonomy of the Russian workers movement and handed it over to the tender mercies of the absolutist political organization from which in due course the new hierarchy of planners, managers, and directors had arisen. In the light of what had occurred, the very notion of a revolutionary vanguard, or political party, now became suspect. The directing function monopolized by the vanguard disclosed itself as a latent menace for the working class. The emancipation of the workers was negated by the very act that promised to guarantee it: the seizure of power. Even under democratic conditions it seemed that the class tended to remain passively subject to the control of a political elite of leaders who had constituted themselves as an autonomous force. But why was the same not true of the bourgeoisie, which, after all, had in its time also permitted itself to be led by political parties rooted in its soil? The answer appeared to be this: for the bourgeoisie, politics had always been an epiphenomenon, because the social order which it controlled was organized in such a way that the political authority had no real control over the free play of forces in the market place (including the market of ideas), whereas the new planned and centralized society invested the bureaucracy with powers which might be monopolized by a political elite that had arisen from the bureaucracy of the labor movement. Moreover, the bourgeoisie had from the start been a privileged class, directing the new instruments of production and imposing its way of life upon the rest of society, while the working class had nothing but its numbers and its organization; and this organization had now escaped from it and assumed an autonomous character *modeled upon the bureaucratic structures of late capitalist and post-capitalist society*. The Communist party—and, for that matter, the Socialist party too, given the opportunity—was able to amalgamate with the controlling groups of the new society because its internal organization prefigured the structure of command appropriate to an industrial hierarchy in which the major line of division ran between the controllers and the rest. Not only had the labor movement been bureaucratized: Its very nature—the nature of a movement passively awaiting guidance from an elite supposedly in possession of the correct insight into the process of history—positively encouraged the growth of authoritarian structures, once the passage from capitalism to socialism (or from unplanned market capitalism to planned state capitalism) had been effected.[40]

If the division between leaders and led was inherent in the concept of an organization equipped with a "scientific" doctrine, the political conclusion was evident. The formula of the coming bureaucratic age ran: "Knowledge equals power," where "knowledge" stood for "intellectual knowledge" and "power" for "control over operatives." Totalitarianism was a special variant of bureaucratic omniscience and omnicompetence. In principle every bureaucracy was totalitarian, and a labor bureaucracy most of all, since it rested upon a class condemned to passivity by the production process itself. This thesis was borne out by the historical evidence. All the organizations created by the working class—from simple trade unions to the Communist party—had in due course transformed themselves into autonomous mechanisms sustaining a system of exploitation, and they had done so in the Western democracies no less than in the USSR. For the more consistent Syndicalists the fault lay in the very notion of an organization separated from the masses. For those who refused to accept this conclusion it lay in the defeat of the proletariat consequent upon the transformation of industrial society. On either assumption the revolutionary movement no longer had a perspective pointing to victory; indeed it was questionable whether there still existed such a movement, save as a permanent protest against exploitation and alienation.[41]

[40] Cardan, "Prolétariat et organisation," No. 27, p. 73. "La prétention du parti qu'en possédant la théorie il possède la vérité et doit tout diriger n'aurait aucune portée réelle si elle ne recoupait pas chez le prolétariat la conviction—chaque jour reproduite par la vie sous le capitalisme—que les questions générales sont l'appanage des spécialistes et que sa propre expérience de la production et de la société n'est pas 'importante.' Les deux tendances traduisent le même échec, trouvent leur origine dans la même réalité et la même idée, sont impossibles et inconcevables l'une sans l'autre." This, in his view, was the link between Marxism and Lenin's authoritarian doctrine of the vanguard: the very notion of "scientific" socialism tended to encourage passivity on the part of the masses, doctrinaire certainty on the part of their leaders.

[41] Cardan, *Socialisme ou Barbarie* No. 27, p. 72: "La dégénérescence signifie que l'organisation tend à se séparer de la classe ouvrière, qu'elle devient un

In their own manner these suggestions reinforced the revisionist thesis introduced by those former Communists who during the same period had gravitated towards the technocratic wing of the PSU and the other neo-Socialist formations. Both groups expressed, though in different language, the belief that the labor movement, along with the rest of society, was undergoing a structural transformation. The difference was one of tone rather than of substance. To the revisionists the change was on the whole a welcome one, since it went with a rapid rise in living standards and the modernization of the economy under planned direction. Their opponents took a more somber view of the decay of revolutionary sentiment and the integration of the working class within a social order no longer subject to the cyclical crises of the market economy. They challenged the revisionist assumption that the development of the productive forces was to be welcomed under any circumstances, and that the labor movement had an interest in furthering the aims of the new technocracy. There was more than a hint in these polemics that revisionism in the eyes of its critics had begun to represent a new class interest—one divorced from the continued existence of the industrial proletariat. On grounds of principle it was asserted that exploitation and alienation had merely changed their form. This was not in fact denied by the revisionists; they argued, however, that the bureaucracy and the workers were in some sense partners in a common enterprise, though the partnership was heavily weighted in favor of the privileged class.[42]

What neither side disputed was that the bureaucracy had become the central problem of the new society, and of the labor movement itself. That society had remained capitalist while ceasing to be bourgeois. It was no longer dominated by market relations, and to that extent the Marxian critique no longer applied. For Marx, the

---

organisme à part. . . . Mais cela ne se produit pas *à cause* des défauts de la structure des organisations, de leurs conceptions erronées, ou d'un maléfice lié à l'organisation comme telle. Ces traits négatifs expriment l'échec des organisations qui à son tour n'est qu'un aspect de l'échec du prolétariat lui-même."

[42] P. Canjuers, "Sociologie-fiction pour gauche-fiction (à propos de Serge Mallet)" *Socialisme ou Barbarie,* No. 27 (April-May 1959). Jean Delvaux, "Les classes sociales et M. Touraine," *ibid.* For the revisionist position see in particular S. Mallet, *Temps Modernes,* No. 150-51 (Aug.-Sept., 1958) and No. 153-4 (Nov.-Dec., 1958). For the Marxist (but non-Communist) critique of reformism see André Gorz, *Stratégie ouvrière et néo-capitalisme.*

split had run between the possessing class and the proletariat. For the neo-Marxists it ran between the bureaucracy and the toilers under its control. That control had assumed a hierarchical form, not because anyone had willed it, but because the character of the production process had given rise to a new privileged stratum which was now busy fortifying its position with the aid of quasi-socialist ideologies. The old society had been dominated by the anonymous power of capital. The new society was subjected to the conscious will of the bureaucracy. For classical Marxism, exploitation arose from the transformation of human labor into a commodity. For the neo-Marxists it was rooted in the division of labor between controllers and controlled. This division was characteristic of all modern bureaucratic regimes, including those that styled themselves socialist. In that sense the class struggle remained international, though revisionists and radicals parted company over the question whether the movement still had a revolutionary perspective.[43]

The Communists had believed in the existence of inexorable laws of history which guaranteed the final triumph of the proletarian cause. The revisionists, whatever their political coloration, rejected the belief in a predetermined outcome of the struggle, along with the idea of history as a process whose logic could be grasped by the intellect. For them, the only historical logic available to the thinker was that which explained the past by treating as rational the determined result of former struggles. The future might be conjectured, not extrapolated with "scientific" precision: it remained open and undetermined. In this regard any revolutionary *praxis* could only start from the Marx of the *Theses on Feuerbach,* not from the author of *Capital* who had come to believe that social history unfolded with the consistency of a natural law. Marxist orthodoxy had been "scientific" and had ended by adapting itself to a process quite different from that which it had originally predicted. In casting determinism overboard, the revisionists freed themselves from the heritage of positivist scientism which in the second half of the nineteenth century had transformed Marx's original

[43] Cardan, *Socialisme ou Barbarie* No. 35, p. 9: "Le mouvement traditionnel a toujours été dominé par les deux conceptions du déterminisme économique et du role dominant du parti. Pour nous, au centre de tout se place l'autonomie des travailleurs, la capacité des masses de se diriger elles-mêmes, sans laquelle toute idée de socialisme devient immédiatement une mystification."

vision into the ideology of the labor movement, now itself reduced to subordinate status within a society whose basic characteristics had not altered. The "union of theory and practice" remained an aspiration. It could no longer be proclaimed as a fact. Different conclusions were possible: depending on whether or not they accepted the logic of political pluralism in a modern democracy, post-Marxian socialists might try to make the best of the situation, or revert to the syndicalist tradition. From the fact that the proletarian class movement had proved incapable of transforming society it was possible to conclude that its historic role was exhausted and that socialists must try to work with the technical intelligentsia rather than with the masses following in its wake. Alternatively, those left-wing radicals whose primary loyalty was to the proletariat might entrench themselves in an attitude of inflexible opposition to the technocracy and its political allies: if the working class could not actually come to power, if indeed the "conquest of political power" was a fatal illusion, then at least the labor movement should retain its autonomy and fight for its interests within the new social order. Revisionist socialism and radical syndicalism both represented possible options. In their different ways, their spokesmen saw the situation as it really was. The same could not be said of the Communist party, a pseudo-revolutionary mass movement which increasingly tended to become a subculture within a society it could neither conquer nor transform. Orthodox Marxism offered no way out of the impasse. Its very character as an orthodoxy testified to its defensive role.

Conclusion

A historical study is not the proper place for the consideration of those larger issues which are inevitably bound up with the intellectual core of Marxism. It has not been possible in the preceding pages to tackle philosophical subjects properly so called. The aim has been more modest: to give a brief account of the part Marxism has played over a century in equipping the French labor movement for the tasks confronting it. The actual interplay of theory and practice within the movement has furnished the theme. Such generalizations as have emerged draw their relevance—so at least it is hoped—from the topical importance of the subject, not from the personal preferences of the author. These would have pointed in a different direction: towards a critical dissection of the work of those French thinkers who have undertaken to acclimatize Hegel and Marx in France. Such an analysis remains to be done. It may derive some advantage from the historical sketch offered in the foregoing pages, but to be at all commensurate with its own subject matter it would thereafter have to proceed along different lines. Above all it would present itself as a study of contemporary French philosophy in its various manifestations: Thomist, Cartesian, Positivist, Existentialist, neo-Hegelian, Phenomenological, and finally Marxist. The names of Jacques Maritain, Alexandre Kojève, Jean Hyppolite, Jean-Paul Sartre, Maurice Merleau-Ponty, Emmanuel Mounier, and Henri Lefebvre, among others, would occur more frequently (as would those of younger scholars), and the emphasis would rest upon the continuity of a philosophical tradition within which Hegelianism has now come to take its place. However subversive from the standpoint of orthodox Marxism, such an investigation would unquestionably correspond to the current state of affairs, so far as the academic world is concerned. But it lies outside the purview of the present study, whose immediate aim is satisfied if it has succeeded in clarifying the *practical* relevance of Marxist *theory*.

Yet there is a point where the two planes intersect. The very circumstance that it has become possible to treat Marxism as a philosophic system reveals something about its destiny. A system of this kind may continue to be enormously influential, as a codification of past intellectual upheavals, but its function is quite different from that of a revolutionary doctrine unifying theory and practice. It was only in the latter guise that Marxism possessed a uniqueness denied to other philosophies. Indeed the very term "philosophy" is not applicable to it insofar as it is (or was) the theory of a revolutionary movement supposedly able to close the gap between speculative contemplation and empirical practice. It is just because there is now a Marxist school of thought among others (and a Communist party alongside other parties) that the whole enterprise appears to have fallen short of its original purpose. That purpose from the start transcended the traditional categories of political thought, but it also transcended the traditional notion of philosophy as a self-contained activity. There was to be an end to speculative contemplation of a world order regarded as immutable. Philosophy was to become *real:* its principles—liberty and rationality—were no longer to figure as ideals unrelated to human practice. They were to take on flesh, come down from the speculative heavens, and assert themselves as the actual practice of a humanity no longer suspended between blind empiricism and the passive contemplation of transcendental aims not realized in actuality.[1]

Now it is evident that from the traditional metaphysical viewpoint

[1] For a scholarly and dispassionate discussion of this theme, see F. Chatelet, *Logos et Praxis. Recherches sur la signification théorique du marxisme* (Paris, 1962), especially Ch. III, pp. 89 ff. See also Georges Gurvitch, "La dialectique chez Marx," in *Dialectique et sociologie* (Paris, 1962), pp. 118 ff.; and Henri Lefebvre's review of Sartre's *Critique de la Raison dialectique, Nouvelle Revue Marxiste* (July, 1961); as well as Kostas Axelos, "Y a-t-il une philosophie marxiste?," in *Vers la pensée planétaire,* pp. 178 ff.

—but also from the Hegelian standpoint, which in this respect is thoroughly traditional—a Promethean revolt of this kind was bound to fail. This, however, is merely to say that metaphysical contemplation belongs to a different order of thought. There is no common ground, unless Marxism too is understood as a total philosophy. In the latter case it may survive the shipwreck of the movement with which it has been associated: no longer the theory of a revolutionary practice, but a "vision of the world" like the systems of Descartes, Hobbes, Spinoza, or Hegel. When they are political, such visions retain their significance in the degree to which they embody anticipations of the future. They are in this sense utopian and practical at the same time, for while they record a world-historical defeat, they also signalize an intellectual breakthrough into a new dimension of history. If Spinoza or Rousseau anticipated religious tolerance, or democracy, before either could be realized in actuality, why should not Marx have anticipated the classless society of communism? This is a possible way out of the difficulty, but in salvaging the system such an attitude discards its immediate practical relevance, separates theory from practice, thought from action, and thus in the end reverts to that contemplative disposition which Marx believed he had left behind.

The impossibility of a "Marxist philosophy," in the proper meaning of the term, arises not from the inadequacy of the theoretical concepts proposed by Marx or Engels, but from the character of philosophy as a speculative discipline constrained to resolve *in theory* those existential conflicts and antagonisms which subsist *in practice.* Insofar as it anticipates a distant future when social life will have become harmonious, historical combat will have ceased, and all men will be free to turn their minds from *praxis* to *teoria,* philosophy is utopian by its very nature: its peculiar mode of discourse abstracts from the actual condition of things, which is one of political strife, economic scarcity, mutual antagonism between individuals, classes, and nations. It resolves these conflicts by transcending them—in thought, thereby making more difficult their actual solution in practice, since speculative thinking becomes a means of harmonizing not merely all "legitimate interests," but the illegitimate ones as well: chief among them the interest of the ruling class in making its subjects believe that the existing world is the best of all possible ones. On these grounds, the youthful Marx had rejected not only the Hegelian system, but the entire mode of thought grounded in discursive reasoning about the nature of things, as distinct from their mundane appearance. It was left to Engels and the later Marxists to treat this rebellion against idealist speculation as an invitation to construct a rival "materialist" ontology as comprehensive as Hegel's own system. On the original Marxian assumption—as distinct from the Hegelian heritage which Marx indeed never quite repudiated—such a procedure was unjustifiable. More than that: it signified the failure of the attempt to "overcome" philosophy by "realizing" its aims in practice. Whether the project was not from the start flawed by a kind of romantic impatience to have done with theorizing and get down to work, is another question which need not concern us here.[2]

What is of importance for our theme is rather the relation of the Marxian project to the positivist mode of thought which—along with the pseudo-ontological system of "dialectical materialism," and in tacit rivalry with it—represents the contemporary form of Marxism in modern France. One may say that while the Communist party, being a mass movement, has transformed dialectical materialism into a substitute for revealed religion, the intelligentsia has come to see in Marx a precursor of its own rationalist way of thinking. In this as in other respects the current situation reflects both the national tradition and the growing influence of modes of thought common to East and West. In an age of technological acceleration and spectacular scientific achievements, it is tempting to suppose that the Marxian notion of *praxis* can be applied to practical enterprises such as "space projects" and trips to the moon. The Soviet intelligentsia indeed has no choice in the matter: Marxism-Leninism being the official philosophy, even a venture into space must be rationalized in terms of Marx's or Lenin's reflections on the role of science. French intellectuals are under no such compulsion, yet they too experience a desire to bring philosophy into line with tech-

[2] Chatelet, pp. 97 ff., 103 ff. In technical terms one may perhaps say that the replacement of speculative thinking by a "theory of action" represented a return to the pre-Hegelian conception of the world. If the real has to be made rational through applying in practice the concepts worked out by philosophy, then clearly these concepts do not mirror the totality of the world, but merely one aspect of it: the rational one, which thus becomes the rival of other aspects no less real and perhaps equally powerful in the long run. However abstract this may sound, it had political implications—as the rise of fascism was to demonstrate.

nology. In this context, the Marxian notion that *praxis* is destined to replace speculation has the proper positivist ring, though Marx intended something rather less banal than did Comte. In any case it is possible to counterpose this approach to that of Engels, for whom the "dialectic of nature" rendered comprehensible the logic of history. Marx entertained no such illusion, nor would he have wasted his time on an attempt to construct an all-embracing system to take the place of Hegel's. This having once been grasped, it becomes possible for Socialist intellectuals to style themselves Marxists, without participating in the ritual cant of Soviet Communism and its French simulacrum.

What this approach leaves out of account is the *practical* failure of that part of the *theory* which pointed beyond the alienation of speculative thought from empirical existence. Marx had seen well enough that philosophy can be displaced by science only if human relations are de-mystified and rendered transparent; and that the fulfilment of this task requires more than just a further exercise in thought. The human collectivity can dispense with metaphysics only if and when the totality of the natural and social world has become comprehensible: not only for a few privileged individuals, but for all. It is this aim which has disclosed itself as utopian. The Communist claim that it has been realized in the USSR is so plainly discredited that Soviet "philosophers" themselves have fallen silent about it. In relation to France the problem presents itself differently, since the Communist party is not in power and hence unable to silence its opponents. Yet had it been able to do so, the suppressed antagonisms would unfailingly have asserted themselves in the form of orthodox and revisionist interpretations of the doctrine. As matters stand today, the revisionists are outside the party, and in some cases have moved from revision to rejection: the latter being motivated not—as with Catholic, Liberal, or Existentialist critics of Marxism—by a different philosophical approach, but rather by a growing conviction that Marxism has come to an end together with the bourgeois epoch of which it was the critical self-consciousness.

This reading of the situation removes the ground from under the central assumption of Communism: the belief that the proletarian revolution will inaugurate the classless society, and with it the emergence of a human type in whom the antinomies of the bourgeois epoch—including the split between theory and practice—have been overcome. What remains after the shipwreck of this faith is a practice divorced from its own theory, and a doctrine which increasingly reverts to critique or contemplation. This outcome leaves unchallenged the relevance of an evolutionary socialism tacitly attuned to the technocratic necessities of the new industrial and postbourgeois age. The counterpart of this socialism is the instinctive syndicalism of the working class: now at last face to face with the controllers of the new order. It was only because Communism promised to overcome this split that Marxism could temporarily function as a theory of action. For the brief span of a generation—between 1917 and 1947, when the tide began to turn—it looked as though France might make more than a marginal contribution to the global experiment in totalitarianism. In the end, the chance was narrowly missed: 1789 turned out to be the alternative to 1917, rather than its precursor.

Yet the enduring strength of the revolutionary tradition, if it has helped to transform the French Communist party, has also enabled it to implant its roots deeply in the national soil. France now possesses what it never had in the past: a disciplined working-class movement solidly organized under the control of a party whose practical reformism is buttressed, concealed, and rationalized by a revolutionary ideology derived from the Marxist critique of bourgeois society. Since that society no longer exists, the movement once intended to subvert it has become anachronistic. Yet the survival of Communism as a permanent protest seems assured by the hierarchical structure of the new industrial order and the corresponding alienation of the working class from the actual controllers. The latter, whatever their public pronouncements, can hardly fail to see the labor bureaucracy as the mirror image of their own system of rule. Because the greater part of the French labor movement is still controlled by the Communist party, and because the CP's pseudo-revolutionary rhetoric forms part of its very being, the illusion persists that the class struggle is still going on, when in fact it has been decided in favor of a new stratum independent of bourgeoisie and proletariat alike. It is only insofar as Marxism still permits this kind of insight that its critical function may be said to have survived the catastrophe of the movement with which its name continues to be linked.

Selected Bibliography

With few exceptions, the titles listed are those cited in the notes to the text. Some standard sources and a few works of general interest have also been included.

Althusser, Louis. *Pour Marx*. Paris, Maspéro, 1966.

Andler, Charles. *La Vie de Lucien Herr*. Paris, Rieder, 1932.

Andrieux, Andrée, and Jean Lignon. *L'Ouvrier d'aujourd'hui*. Preface by Pierre Naville. Paris, Rivière, 1960.

Aragon, Louis. *L'Homme Communiste*. 2 vols. Paris, Gallimard, 1946, 1953.

Aron, Raymond. *Les grandes doctrines de sociologie historique*. Paris, Centre de documentation universitaire, n.d.

Aron, Robert, ed. *De Marx au Marxisme (1848–1948)*. Paris, Éditions de Flore, 1948.

Audry, Colette. *Léon Blum ou la politique du Juste*. Paris, Juillard, 1955.

Axelos, Kostas. *Marx: Penseur de la technique*. Paris, Éditions de Minuit, 1961.

——— *Vers la pensée planétaire*. Paris, Éditions de Minuit, 1964.

Bauchet, Pierre. *La Planification française*. Paris, Éditions du Seuil, 1962.

Belleville, Pierre. *Une Nouvelle classe ouvrière*. Paris, Collection Les Temps Modernes, Juillard, 1963.

Benda, Julien. *La Trahison des clercs*. Paris, Grasset, 1927, 1946.

Bettelheim, Charles. *Problèmes du développement économique*. Paris, Centre de documentation universitaire, 1957.

——— *Les problèmes théoriques et pratiques de la planification*. Paris, Presses Universitaires de France, 1946.

Bigo, Pierre. *Marxisme et Humanisme: Introduction à l'oeuvre économique de Karl Marx*. Preface by Jean Marchal. Paris, Presses Universitaires de France, 1953, 1961.

Bloch-Lainé, François. *Pour une réforme de l'entreprise*. Paris, Éditions du Seuil, 1963.

Blum, Léon. *L'Oeuvre de Léon Blum 1945-1947*. Paris, A. Michel, 1954, 1958.

Boisdé, Raymond. *Technocratie et démocratie*. Paris, Plon, 1964.

Borkenau, Franz. *The Communist International*. London, Faber and Faber, 1938.

Bottigelli, Émile, ed. *Friedrich Engels—Paul et Laura Lafargue: Correspondance 1868-1895*. 3 vols. Paris, Éditions Sociales, 1956-1959.

Bourdet, Yvon. *Communisme et marxisme: notes critiques de sociologie politique*. Paris, Michel Brient, 1963.

Calvez, Jean-Yves. *La Pensée de Karl Marx*. Paris, Éditions du Seuil, 1956.

Carr, E. H. *Socialism in One Country 1924-1926*. 3 vols. Vol. III, Part One. London, Macmillan, 1964.

Casanova, Laurent. *Le Parti communiste, les intellectuels et la nation*. Paris, Éditions Sociales, 1951.

Caute, David. *Communism and the French Intellectuals 1914-1960*. London, André Deutsch, 1964.

Chambre, Henri. *Le marxisme en Union Soviétique. Idéologie et institutions*. Paris, Éditions du Seuil, 1955.

Chatelet, F. *Logos et Praxis. Recherches sur la signification théorique du marxisme*. Paris, S.E.D.E.S., 1962.

Club, Jean Moulin. *L'État et le citoyen*. Paris, Éditions du Seuil, 1961.

——— *Pour une démocratie économique*. Paris, Éditions du Seuil, 1964.

——— *Un Parti pour la Gauche*. Paris, Éditions du Seuil, 1965.

Collinet, Michel. *La tragédie du Marxisme*. Paris, *Calmann*-Lévy, 1948.

——— *Du Bolchévisme: Évolution et variations du Marxisme-Léninisme*. Paris, Amiot-Dumont, 1957.

Colloque "France-Forum" de Saint-Germain-en-Laye. *La Démocratie à refaire*. Paris, Les Éditions Ouvrières, 1963.

Cornu, Auguste. *Karl Marx et Friedrich Engels*. 3 vols. Paris, Presses Universitaires de France, 1955, 1958, 1962.

Cottier, Georges M.-M. *L'Athéisme du jeune Marx: ses origines hégéliennes*. Paris, Librairie philosophique J. Vrin, 1959.

——— *Du romantisme au marxisme*. Paris, Alsatia, 1961.

Crozier, Michel. *Le Phénomène bureaucratique*. Paris, Éditions du Seuil, 1964.

Dansette, Adrien. *Histoire de la libération de Paris*. Paris, Fayard, 1946, 1958.

——— *Destin du Catholicisme français 1926-1956*. Paris, Flammarion, 1957.

Denis, Henri. *Valeur et capitalisme*. Paris, Éditions Sociales, 1957.

Desanti, Jean. *Introduction à l'histoire de la philosophie*. Paris, La Nouvelle Critique, 1956. Collection Les Essais de la Nouvelle Critique.

Desroche, Henri. *Signification du Marxisme.* Paris, Éditions Ouvrières, 1949.

——— *Marxisme et religions.* Paris, Presses Universitaires de France, 1962.

Dolléans, Édouard. *Histoire du mouvement ouvrier 1871-1936.* Paris, A. Colin, 1946.

Dommanget, M. *Édouard Vaillant.* Paris, La Table ronde, 1956.

Durkheim, Émile. *Sociologie et philosophie.* Preface by Célestin Bouglé. Paris, Presses Universitaires de France, 1951.

——— *Le socialisme: Sa définition, ses débuts, la doctrine Saint-Simonienne.* Ed. and with a Preface by Marcel Mauss. Paris, Félix Alcan, 1928.

Duveau, Georges. *Sociologie de l'utopie.* Paris, Presses Universitaires de France, 1961.

Duverger, Maurice. *Les partis politiques.* 4th ed. Paris, A. Colin, 1961.

Ehrmann, Henry W. *French Labor from Popular Front to Liberation.* New York, Oxford University Press, 1947.

Fauvet, Jacques. *Histoire du parti communiste français. I: De la guerre à la guerre 1917-1939.* Paris, Fayard, 1964.

Fougeyrollas, Pierre. *Le marxisme en question.* Paris, Éditions du Seuil, 1959.

——— *La conscience politique dans la France contemporaine.* Paris, Denoël, 1963.

Friedmann, Georges. *De la Sainte Russie à l'U.R.S.S.* Paris, Gallimard, 1938.

——— *Machine et humanisme.* Paris, Gallimard, 1946, 1954.

——— *Où va le travail humain?* Paris, Gallimard, 1950, 1963.

Frossard, L. O. *De Jaurès à Lénine.* Paris, Bibliothèque de documentation sociale, 1930.

Garaudy, Roger. *Le communisme et la renaissance de la culture française.* Paris, Éditions Sociales, 1945.

——— *Le communisme et la morale.* Paris, Éditions Sociales, 1945.

——— *Une littérature de fossoyeurs.* Paris, Éditions Sociales, 1948.

——— *L'Église, le communisme et les chrétiens.* Paris, Éditions Sociales, 1949.

——— *Perspectives de l'homme: Existentialisme, Pensée Catholique, Marxisme.* Paris, Presses Universitaires de France, 1961.

——— *Dieu est mort: Étude sur Hegel.* Paris, Presses Universitaires de France, 1962.

——— *Qu'est ce que la morale marxiste?* Paris, Éditions Sociales, 1963.

——— *Karl Marx.* Paris, Éditions Seghers, 1964.

Goldmann, Lucien. *Recherches dialectiques.* Paris, Gallimard, 1959.

Gorz, André. *Stratégie ouvrière et néo-capitalisme.* Paris, Éditions du Seuil, 1964.

Graham, B. D. *The French Socialists and Tripartisme, 1944-1947.* Canberra, The Australian National University; London, Weidenfeld and Nicolson, 1965.

Guérin, Daniel. *La lutte de classes sous la première république.* Paris, Gallimard, 1946.

——— *Jeunesse du socialisme libertaire.* Paris, Rivière, 1959.

Gurvitch, Georges. *Les Fondateurs français de la sociologie contemporaine. I. Saint-Simon sociologue.* Paris, Centre de documentation universitaire, 1955.

——— *Le Concept des classes sociales.* Paris, Centre de documentation universitaire, 1954.

——— *Pour le centenaire de la mort de Pierre-Joseph Proudhon.* (Cours public 1963-64). Paris, Centre de documentation universitaire, 1964.

——— *Dialectique et sociologie.* Paris, Flammarion, 1962.

——— *La Vocation actuelle de la sociologie.* Paris, Presses Universitaires de France, 1963.

Hamon, Léo, ed. *Les nouveaux comportements politiques de la classe ouvrière.* Paris, Presses Universitaires de France, 1962.

Hainchelin, C. *Les origines de la religion.* Paris, Éditions Sociales, 1955.

Histoire du Parti communiste français (manuel). Elaboré par la Commission d'Histoire auprès du Comité central du PCF. Paris, Éditions Sociales, 1964.

Histoire du parti communiste français. 3 vols. Anon. Paris, Éditions Unir, 1962-65.

Hobsbawm, E. J. *Labouring Men: Studies in the History of Labour.* London, Weidenfeld and Nicolson, 1964.

Humbert-Droz, Jules. *L'Oeuil de Moscou à Paris.* Paris, Juillard, 1964.

Hyppolite, Jean. *Études sur Marx et Hegel.* Paris, Rivière, 1955.

——— *Introduction à la philosophie de l'histoire de Hegel.* Paris, Rivière, 1948.

Jaurès, Jean. *L'Armée nouvelle.* Paris, Rouff, 1910; 2d ed., 1915.

——— *Anthologie de Jean Jaurès.* Ed. by Louis Lévy. Paris, Calmann-Lévy, 1946.

——— *Les origines du socialisme allemand.* New edition. Preface by L. Goldmann. Paris, Maspéro, 1959.

Jordan, Z. A. *Philosophy and Ideology: The development of philosophy and Marxism-Leninism in Poland since the Second World War.* Dordrecht, Reidel, 1963.

Jouhaux, Léon. *Le Syndicalisme et la C.G.T.* Paris, Éditions de la Sirène, 1920.

Kamenka, Eugene. *The Ethical Foundations of Marxism.* London, Routledge and Kegan Paul, 1963.

Kojève, Alexandre. *Introduction à la lecture de Hegel.* Paris, Gallimard, 1947.

Korsch, Karl. *Karl Marx.* London, Chapman and Hall, 1963; New York, Russell and Russell, 1963.

Kriegel, Annie. *Aux origines du communisme français 1914-1920*. 2 vols. Paris, Mouton, 1964.

——— *Le Congrès de Tours. Naissance du parti communiste français*. Paris, Éditions Juillard, collection "Archives," 1964.

——— *Les Internationales ouvrières*. Paris, Juillard, 1964.

Lacroix, Jean. *Marxisme, existentialisme, personnalisme*. Paris, Presses Universitaires de France, 1962.

Lafargue, Paul. *Le déterminisme économique de Marx*. Paris, Giard, 1909.

——— *Théoricien du Marxisme*. Texts selected by J. Varlet. Paris, Éditions sociales internationales, 1933.

Laurat, Lucien. *Staline, la linguistique, et l'impérialisme russe*. Paris, Les îles d'or, 1951.

——— *L'Économie soviétique*. Paris, Librairie Valois, 1931.

——— *L'Accumulation du capital d'après Rosa Luxembourg*. Paris, Rivière, 1930.

Le Brun, Pierre. *Questions actuelles du syndicalisme*. Paris, Éditions du Seuil, 1965.

Lecoeur, Auguste. *Le Partisan*. Paris, Flammarion, 1963.

——— *L'Autocritique attendue*. St. Cloud, Éditions Girault, 1955.

Lefebvre, Henri. *Le Matérialisme dialectique*. Paris, Félix Alcan, 1939; PUF 1949, 1957, 1962.

——— *L'Existentialisme*. Paris, Éditions du Sagittaire, 1946.

——— *Critique de la vie quotidienne*. First ed., Paris, Grasset, 1947; 2d ed., Paris, L'Arche, 1958.

——— *Problèmes actuels du marxisme*. Paris, PUF, 1960.

——— *Pour connaître la pensée de Karl Marx*. 3d ed. Paris, Bordas, 1956.

——— *Pour connaître la pensée de Lénine*. Paris, Bordas, 1957.

——— *La Somme et le reste*. Paris, La Nef, 1959.

——— *Introduction à la modernité*. Paris, Éditions de Minuit, 1962.

Lefebvre, Henri, and Norbert Guterman. *Introduction aux morceaux choisis de Karl Marx*. Paris, Gallimard, 1934.

——— *La Conscience mystifiée*. Paris, Gallimard, 1936.

——— *Morceaux choisis de Hegel*. Paris, Gallimard, 1938.

——— *Cahiers de Lénine sur la dialectique de Hegel*. Paris, Gallimard, 1938.

Lefranc, Georges. *Le mouvement socialiste sous la Troisième République*. Paris, Payot, 1963.

——— *Histoire des doctrines sociales dans l'Europe contemporaine*. Paris, Aubier, 1960.

——— *Histoire du front populaire 1934-1938*. Paris, Payot, 1965.

Leroy, Maxime. *Histoire des idées sociales en France*. 3 vols. Paris, Gallimard, 1946-54.

Lévi-Strauss, Claude. *Anthropologie structurale*. Paris, Plon, 1958.

Lhomme, Jean. *La grande bourgeoisie au pouvoir 1830-1880*. Paris, Presses Universitaires de France, 1960.

Ligou, Daniel. *Histoire du Socialisme en France 1871-1961*. Paris, Presses Universitaires de France, 1962.

Louis, Paul. *Histoire du socialisme en France*. Paris, Rivière, 1950.

Lukács, Georges. *Existentialisme ou Marxisme?* Paris, Éditions Nagel, 1961.

——— *Histoire et conscience de classe. Essais de dialectique marxiste.* (1923) Tr. by K. Axelos and J. Bois. Paris, Éditions de Minuit, collection "Arguments," No. 1, 1960.

Maitron, Jean. *Histoire du mouvement anarchiste en France 1880-1914.* Paris, Société universitaire d'éditions et de librairie, 1955.

Mallet, Serge. *La nouvelle classe ouvrière*. Paris, Éditions du Seuil, 1963.

——— *Les paysans contre le passé*. Paris, Éditions du Seuil, 1962.

Man, Henri de. *Au-delà du marxisme*. Paris, Félix Alcan, 1927.

Mandel, Ernest. *Traité d'Économie marxiste*. 2 vols. Paris, Juillard, 1962.

Marcel, Gabriel. *Existentialisme chrétien*. Paris, Plon, 1947.

Marchal, Jean. *Deux essais sur le marxisme*. Paris, Librairie de Médicis, 1955.

Maritain, Jacques. *La Philosophie morale*. Paris, Gallimard, 1960.

Martinet, Gilles. *Le marxisme de notre temps*. Paris, Juillard, 1962.

Marx, Karl. *Misère de la philosophie. Réponse à la philosophie de la misère de M. Proudhon*. Paris, Éditions Sociales, 1961.

Marx, Karl. *Early Writings*. Tr. and ed. by T. B. Bottomore. New York, McGraw-Hill, 1964.

——— *Economic and Philosophic Manuscripts of 1844*. Ed. by Dirk J. Struik. New York, International Publishers, 1964.

——— *Selected Writings in Sociology and Social Philosophy*. Ed. by T. B. Bottomore and M. Rubel. London, Watts and Co., 1956; New York, McGraw-Hill, 1964.

Marx, Karl and Friedrich Engels. *Études philosophiques*. Paris, Éditions Sociales, 1947.

Mascolo, Dionys. *Le communisme: dialectique des besoins et des valeurs*. Paris, Gallimard, 1953.

Mendès-France, Pierre. *La République moderne*. Paris, Gallimard, 1962.

Merleau-Ponty, Maurice. *Humanisme et terreur. Essai sur le problème communiste*. Paris, Gallimard, 1947.

——— *Sens et non-sens*. Paris, Éditions Nagel, 1948.

——— *Les Aventures de la dialectique*. Paris, Gallimard, 1955.

——— *Signes*. Paris, Gallimard, 1960.

Moch, Jules. *Confrontations*. Paris, Gallimard, 1952.

Mollet, Guy. *Bilans et Perspectives socialistes*. Paris, Plon, 1958.

Monatte, Pierre. *Trois scissions syndicales*. Paris, Éditions Ouvrières, 1958.

Monnerot, Jules. *Sociologie du communisme*. Paris, Gallimard, 1949.

Morin, Edgar. *Autocritique*. Paris, Juillard, 1959.

Mounier, Emmanuel. *Le Personnalisme*. Paris, Presses Universitaires de France, 1959.

Mury, Gilbert. *Essor ou déclin du catholicisme français?* Paris, Éditions Sociales, 1960.

Naville, Pierre. *Psychologie, marxisme, matérialisme.* Paris, Rivière, 1946, 1948.

——— *La vie de travail et ses problèmes.* Paris, A. Colin, 1954.

——— *L'Intellectuel communiste.* Paris, Rivière, 1956.

——— *Le Nouveau Léviathan. I: De l'aliénation à la jouissance.* Paris, Rivière, 1957.

——— *L'Automation et le travail humain.* Paris, Centre National de la Recherche Scientifique, 1961.

——— *Vers l'automatisme social? Problèmes du travail et de l'automation.* Paris, Gallimard, 1963.

——— *La classe ouvrière et le régime gaulliste.* Paris, Rivière, 1964.

Naville, Pierre with G. Friedmann. *Traité de sociologie du travail.* Paris, A. Colin, 1961, 1962.

Nizan, Paul. *Les Chiens de garde.* Paris, Maspéro, 1960.

Paillet, Marc. *Gauche année zéro.* Paris, Gallimard, 1964.

Perroux, François. *L'Europe sans rivages.* Paris, PUF, 1954.

——— *L'Économie du XXe siècle.* Paris, PUF, 1961.

——— *Le IVe Plan français (1962-1965).* 2d ed. Paris, PUF, 1963.

——— *Industrie et création collective. I: Saint-simonisme du XXe siècle et création collective.* Paris, PUF, 1964.

Philip, André. *Henri de Man et la crise doctrinale du socialisme.* Paris, Gamber, 1933.

——— *Le socialisme trahi.* Paris, Plon, 1957.

——— *Pour un socialisme humaniste.* Paris, Plon, 1960.

——— *La Gauche: mythes et réalités.* Paris, Aubier, 1964.

Politzer, Georges. *Principes élémentaires de Philosophie.* Paris, Éditions Sociales, 1963.

Réflexions pour 1985. Paris, La Documentation française, 1964.

Rizzi, Bruno. *La bureaucratisation du monde.* Paris, 1939.

——— *La lezione dello stalinismo.* Rome, Opere Nuove, 1962.

Rosmer, Alfred. *Le mouvement ouvrier pendant la guerre.* Paris, Mouton, 1936-59.

Rossi, A. *Physiologie du parti communiste français.* Paris, Société d'éditions littéraires françaises, 1948.

——— *Les Communistes français pendant la drôle de guerre.* Paris, Plon, 1951.

——— *Le Pacte Germano-Soviétique. L'histoire et le mythe.* Paris, Preuves, 1954.

Rubel, Maximilien. *Bibliographie des oeuvres de Karl Marx.* Paris, Rivière, 1956. Supplement, Rivière, 1960.

——— *Karl Marx. Essai de biographie intellectuelle.* Paris, Rivière,1957.

——— *Karl Marx devant le Bonapartisme,* Paris–The Hague, Mouton, 1960.

St. Antony's Papers No. IX: International Communism. Ed. by David Footman. London, Chatto and Windus, 1961.

Sartre, Jean-Paul. *L'Existentialisme est un humanisme.* Paris, Éditions Nagel, 1946.

——— *Matérialisme et révolution. Situations III.* Paris, Gallimard, 1949.

——— *Réponse à Albert Camus. Situations IV.* Paris, Gallimard, 1964.

——— *Albert Camus. Situations IV.* Paris, Gallimard, 1964.

——— *Paul Nizan. Situations IV.* Paris, Gallimard, 1964.

——— *Merleau-Ponty. Situations IV.* Paris, Gallimard, 1964.

——— *Colonialisme et néo-colonialisme. Situations V.* Paris, Gallimard, 1964.

——— *Problèmes du marxisme, 1. Situations VI.* Paris, Gallimard, 1964.

——— *Critique de la raison dialectique.* Paris, Gallimard, 1960.

Sartre, Jean-Paul, David Rousset, Gérard Rosenthal. *Entretiens sur la politique.* Paris, Gallimard, 1949.

Sauvy, Alfred. *La prévision économique.* Paris, Presses Universitaires de France, 1954.

Schram, Stuart R. *Protestantism and Politics in France.* Alençon, Corbière et Jugain, 1954.

Sebag, Lucien. *Marxisme et structuralisme.* Paris, Payot, 1964.

Semaines Sociales de France. 47e Session-Grenoble 1960. *Socialisation et personne humaine.* Lyon, Chronique Sociale de France, 1961.

Serge, Victor. *Mémoires d'un révolutionnaire.* Paris, Éditions du Seuil, 1951.

Sorel, Georges, *La décomposition du marxisme.* Paris, Bibliothèque du mouvement socialiste, 1907.

——— *Réflexions sur la violence.* Paris, Éditions du mouvement socialiste, 1908.

——— *Matériaux d'une théorie du prolétariat.* Paris, Rivière, 1919.

Spitzer, A. B. *The Revolutionary Theories of Louis Auguste Blanqui.* New York, Columbia University Press, 1957.

Suffert, Georges. *Les Catholiques et la Gauche.* Paris, Maspéro, 1960.

Thorez, Maurice. *Fils du peuple.* Paris, Éditions Sociales, 1937 and successive editions.

Trotsky, Léon. *La révolution trahie.* Paris, Grasset, 1937.

Vandervelde, Émile. *Le socialisme contre l'État.* Brussels, Éditions de l'Institute Émile Vandervelde, 1949.

Verret, M. *Les marxistes et la religion.* Paris, Éditions Sociales, 1961.

Walter, Gérard. *Histoire du parti communiste français.* Paris, Somogy, 1948.

Willard, Claude. *Les Guesdistes. Le Mouvement Socialiste en France (1893-1905).* Paris, Éditions Sociales, 1965.

Williams, Philip M. *Crisis and Compromise: Politics in the Fourth Re-*

public. 2d ed. London, New York, Toronto, Longmans Green and Co., 1964.

Wright, Gordon. *Rural Revolution in France: the Peasantry in the 20th Century*. Stanford, Stanford University Press, 1964.

Zevaès, A. *De l'introduction du marxisme en France*. Paris, Rivière, 1947.

PERIODICALS

Arguments
Cahiers de l'Institut de Science Économique Appliquée
Cahiers du Communisme
Cahiers Internationaux de Sociologie
Cahiers du Centre d'Études Socialistes
Clarté
Contrat Social
Économie et Politique
Est et Ouest
Esprit
France-Observateur (Le Nouvel Observateur)
La Nouvelle Critique
La Nouvelle Revue Marxiste
La Pensée
Revue Française de Sociologie
Revue Socialiste
Socialisme ou Barbarie
Les Temps Modernes
La Tribune Socialiste
La Voie Communiste

Index